Discord®

for dummies®

A Wiley Brand

Discord®

by Tee Morris

Discord® For Dummies®

Published by: **John Wiley & Sons, Inc.,** 111 River Street, Hoboken, NJ 07030-5774, www.wiley.com

Copyright © 2020 by John Wiley & Sons, Inc., Hoboken, New Jersey

Published simultaneously in Canada

No part of this publication may be reproduced, stored in a retrieval system or transmitted in any form or by any means, electronic, mechanical, photocopying, recording, scanning or otherwise, except as permitted under Sections 107 or 108 of the 1976 United States Copyright Act, without the prior written permission of the Publisher. Requests to the Publisher for permission should be addressed to the Permissions Department, John Wiley & Sons, Inc., 111 River Street, Hoboken, NJ 07030, (201) 748-6011, fax (201) 748-6008, or online at www.wiley.com/go/permissions.

Trademarks: Wiley, For Dummies, the Dummies Man logo, Dummies.com, Making Everything Easier, and related trade dress are trademarks or registered trademarks of John Wiley & Sons, Inc. and may not be used without written permission. Discord is a trademark of Discord, Inc. All other trademarks are the property of their respective owners. John Wiley & Sons, Inc. is not associated with any product or vendor mentioned in this book.

LIMIT OF LIABILITY/DISCLAIMER OF WARRANTY: THE PUBLISHER AND THE AUTHOR MAKE NO REPRESENTATIONS OR WARRANTIES WITH RESPECT TO THE ACCURACY OR COMPLETENESS OF THE CONTENTS OF THIS WORK AND SPECIFICALLY DISCLAIM ALL WARRANTIES, INCLUDING WITHOUT LIMITATION WARRANTIES OF FITNESS FOR A PARTICULAR PURPOSE. NO WARRANTY MAY BE CREATED OR EXTENDED BY SALES OR PROMOTIONAL MATERIALS. THE ADVICE AND STRATEGIES CONTAINED HEREIN MAY NOT BE SUITABLE FOR EVERY SITUATION. THIS WORK IS SOLD WITH THE UNDERSTANDING THAT THE PUBLISHER IS NOT ENGAGED IN RENDERING LEGAL, ACCOUNTING, OR OTHER PROFESSIONAL SERVICES. IF PROFESSIONAL ASSISTANCE IS REQUIRED, THE SERVICES OF A COMPETENT PROFESSIONAL PERSON SHOULD BE SOUGHT. NEITHER THE PUBLISHER NOR THE AUTHOR SHALL BE LIABLE FOR DAMAGES ARISING HEREFROM. THE FACT THAT AN ORGANIZATION OR WEBSITE IS REFERRED TO IN THIS WORK AS A CITATION AND/OR A POTENTIAL SOURCE OF FURTHER INFORMATION DOES NOT MEAN THAT THE AUTHOR OR THE PUBLISHER ENDORSES THE INFORMATION THE ORGANIZATION OR WEBSITE MAY PROVIDE OR RECOMMENDATIONS IT MAY MAKE. FURTHER, READERS SHOULD BE AWARE THAT INTERNET WEBSITES LISTED IN THIS WORK MAY HAVE CHANGED OR DISAPPEARED BETWEEN WHEN THIS WORK WAS WRITTEN AND WHEN IT IS READ.

For general information on our other products and services, please contact our Customer Care Department within the U.S. at 877-762-2974, outside the U.S. at 317-572-3993, or fax 317-572-4002. For technical support, please visit https://hub.wiley.com/community/support/dummies.

Wiley publishes in a variety of print and electronic formats and by print-on-demand. Some material included with standard print versions of this book may not be included in e-books or in print-on-demand. If this book refers to media such as a CD or DVD that is not included in the version you purchased, you may download this material at http://booksupport.wiley.com. For more information about Wiley products, visit www.wiley.com.

Library of Congress Control Number: 2020934813

ISBN 978-1-119-68803-7 (pbk); ISBN 978-1-119-68801-3 (ebk); ISBN 978-1-119-68809-9 (ebk)

Manufactured in the United States of America

10 9 8 7 6 5 4 3 2 1

Contents at a Glance

Table of Contents

Introduction

'm just going to come out and address the massive gorilla in the room: naming a communications platform Discord is just plain weird.

And naming a platform as powerful, as efficient, and as awesome as the one I'm about to introduce you to Discord makes no sense to me.

Yet here we are. *Discord For Dummies.*

Maybe you've already heard of this platform and are looking to broaden your skill set on it. Maybe you are, like me, on a streaming platform — Twitch (`https://twitch.tv`) being my preferred place for streaming shenanigans — and people on your chat are asking about your Discord. Maybe you are looking to find something to replace your Facebook seeing as Discord hasn't been called before Congress concerning privacy issues. Maybe you are just plain curious about this platform. (Or maybe you are one of those folks who has mastered Discord, is making a nice chunk of change from it, wanted to see who the heck I was in writing this book, and intend to poke fun at it next time you're online, to which, all I can say is *"Yooooo, thanks for the shout-out!"*) Whatever the reason, you're here, and I appreciate it. I'm here to talk to you about Discord. It's a chat engine. It's an audio app. It's a video chat app. A lot is happening here, and I'm your guide in this beginner's approach to this communications platform.

Discord For Dummies offers you a deep dive and a step-by-step approach to an exciting platform that, while designed for gamers, offers so much more in the ways of communication. Beginning with the question at the forefront of your mind — what is Discord? — this book takes you through an up-and-coming platform that serves as primary game comms for fireteams worldwide and virtual meeting spaces for event organizers. By the time you reach the end of this book, you should know where to go in Discord to get things done, how to build a community, how to connect with people through audio and video, and even have some fun on this journey with me.

About This Book

Discord For Dummies should be these things to all who pick up and read it (whether straight through or by jumping around in the chapters):

>> A user-friendly guide in how to establish a server, work with audio, work with video, and build a community

>> A terrific reference for choosing the right hardware and software to improve on your Internet communications, whether it is for gaming or otherwise

>> The starting point for the person who knows nothing about audio, video, VoIP, chat, community building, community management, or how to turn a computer into a communications bank

>> A handy go-to think tank for any beginning server manager who's hungry for new ideas on what goes into a good stream and fresh points of view

>> A really fun read

There will be plenty of answers in these pages, and if you find the answers too elementary, I will provide you plenty of points of reference to research. I don't claim to have all the solutions, quick fixes, and resolutions to all possible Discord queries, but I will present to you the basic building blocks and first steps for building a community around your favorite game(s), charity, non-profit, podcast, or stream. As with any *For Dummies* book, my responsibility is to offer you a foundation on which to build your Channel and grow. You may not hear me talk about your favorite Discord server. In fact, you may think "Why didn't you talk to [insert favorite Discord server admin here]? They would have been a great feature." My mission is to teach you the basics, and in covering the basics, I might have missed some details. However, this book should provide you with a solid foundation.

This book was written as a linear path from setting up a profile for yourself to strategies in community engagement and management. However, not everyone will read this book from page one to the end. If you've already gotten your feet wet with the various aspects of Discord, feel free to jump around from section to section and read the parts that you need. I provide plenty of guides back to other relevant chapters for when the going gets murky.

Foolish Assumptions

It doesn't matter what platform you're on. If you have a browser, Discord can work for you. If you have a computer, a solid connection to the Internet, and a lot of curiosity, you are ready to go. Just remember, the operating system just makes the computer go. It's the browser that offers you a first look at the platform. I'm here to provide you tools not only for making Discord work, but also for making all aspects of it work — text, audio, and video.

What you have in your hands here is a detailed look at Discord, a mix of how-to exercises for a variety of the platform's features, and offered strategies on how to build, engage, and manage a community. I go into communication via text, via audio, and via video. There's a look in here at working on Discord through your browser, on your desktop, on your smartphone, and on your tablet. So if you know nothing about Discord, "You have chosen wisely," as we heard in *Indiana Jones and the Last Crusade*. If you know something about Discord, you might gain some insight into community management strategy, in working with bots, or upgrading your Discord rig. So, yes, *Discord For Dummies* offers something for everyone.

However, as I've seen after *For Dummies* books hit the shelves, there are going to be assumptions made about this title. So let's cover the short list on what this book is not, and never will be:

>> This book offers suggestions and strategies on creating a community around your Discord. This platform is not a turnkey solution. Your community just won't "appear" nor does this book make the claim "If you build it, they will come." Building a community takes time and effort, and *Discord For Dummies* won't build a community for you.

>> There is a revenue-generating option in Discord, and although I cover it, I do not encourage you to quit your day job. This is not a "Make Money with Discord" book.

>> This book will have some answers for you, but when changes happen, this book will not instantly update. (Not until a 2nd Edition, at least.) I will, however, try to address any major changes on my stream. See "Beyond the Book" for details.

If you are looking for a solid start to Discord, this is the book for you. I'm thrilled you're here.

Icons Used in This Book

You might be working through an exercise or reading a chapter, making some real progress with understanding Discord, when suddenly these little icons leap out, grab you by the throat, and wrestle you to the ground. (Who would have thought Discord was so action-packed. Like an episode of *Altered Carbon*, huh?) What do all these icons mean? Let's take a look.

TIP

When I'm in the middle of a discussion and suddenly I have one of those "Say, that reminds me . . ." moments, I give you one of these tips. There are those handy little extras that are good to know and might even make your background in Discord a little better than average.

REMEMBER

So you're working hard on one of these exercises, and you come across this icon. Skip this at your own peril. This is one of those "Seriously, you can't forget this part! Otherwise the bus drops under 55 mph and explodes!" Okay, maybe you don't have to worry about the bus, but the Remember icon is one you want to pay close attention to.

WARNING

Sometimes I interrupt my train of thought with a "Taihoa, Bro." (That's Māori for "Pump the brakes, man.") moment — and this is where I ask for your completely undivided attention. The Warnings are exactly that: flashing lights, ah-ooga horns, dire portents. They're reminders not to try this at home because you'll definitely regret it.

Beyond the Book

You can find a little more helpful Discord-related information on https://www.dummies.com, where you can peruse this book's Cheat Sheet. To get this handy resource, go to the website and type *Discord For Dummies Cheat Sheet* in the Search box.

In addition to the website, this book comes with a companion stream on Twitch, airing on Sunday afternoons. From your browser of choice, visit https://www.twitch.tv/theteemonster, and follow (or subscribe) to receive notifications when I go live to take your questions on Discord, Twitch, podcasting, and content creation. And maybe, on occasion, I may be joined online or in-studio by special guests. Your questions are encouraged, as I'll try and cover concepts in this book explored in greater detail, and maybe touch base on topics too advanced for this title but more than suitable for the stream.

Where to Go from Here

At this point, many *For Dummies* authors say something snappy, clever, or even a bit snarky. Chuck and I did so often throughout editions of *Podcasting For Dummies* and *Twitch for Dummies*. My best tongue-in-cheek material is saved for the pages inside, so here's a more serious approach.

If you want to hop around the book, that's your decision, but I suggest planting yourself in front of a computer, pointing a browser to https://discordapp.com, and starting with Chapter 1. Together, we check out a few links, put together a profile (and eventually a server), and then we start working on that streaming persona. Along the way, I'm going to suggest ideas, concepts, and strategies that will educate, inspire, and enlighten you. And through it all, we are going to work together to create a community that will rally around you for whatever cause you believe in, be it a favorite game or worthwhile charity.

Limber up, folks. This is going to be a fun ride. Don't forget your towel.

1

Getting Started with Discord

Chapter **1**

The Lowdown on Discord

When social media offers up a new platform, it fills me both with excitement and dread. I love learning something new. Any opportunity to teach myself something to add to my arsenal of life hacks, daily routines, and day-to-day productivity, I look at as a good thing, in social media especially. I've always been a believer that social media is a fantastic tool of communication. With so many ways to get your message out, its possibilities are endless. A new platform means new options other platforms may not offer or possible replacements for routines that once worked wonders for you but seem to be losing their efficiency. Additionally, if the platform becomes a sensation, you become something of a founder in its community, a trustworthy voice on how the new communications avenue works. Awesome!

But here is where the dread settles in with me. When I hear about something new, whether new to social media or new to me, my first thought is always the same: *Great. One more platform to add to the stockpile.* See, the downside of learning something new is that you won't necessarily become an expert within the first day or two of picking it up unless you spend uninterrupted hours diving into every aspect of it. Then, once you have a grasp of it, you have to fit it into the rotation of all the *other* social media platforms you have tied to your name. This also means setting aside time, or pockets of time, to manage this new platform with all the other platforms you have active. There is only so much time in the day, and if your full-time job is social media, you know how tough it can be creating content for audiences across platforms. If your full-time job isn't social media, then content creation across platforms just got a *lot* tougher. And now you have a new platform to contend with. And that's if the platform takes off, lest it become like other social media hot flashes in the pan that everyone joins only to abandon a week or two later. Awesome.

Welcome to a look inside my brain when I first started *streaming* — creating content live online through a service like Twitch (https://www.twitch.tv), Mixer (http://www.mixer.com), or YouTube (https://www.youtube.com) — and I was asked, "So what's your Discord server?"

Are you kidding? I have to know this thing called Discord (see Figure 1-1) if I want to know Twitch?

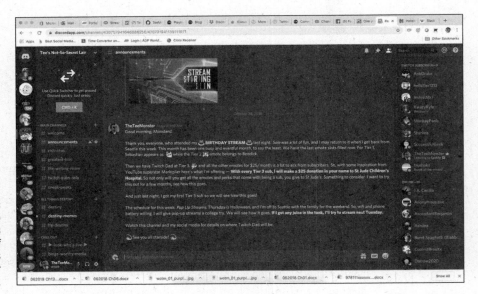

FIGURE 1-1:
Welcome to Discord, a Swiss Army knife of communications for you and your team.

No, Discord is not necessarily a necessity for streaming, but if you want to build a community, if you want to extend your reach as a content creator, and if you want to level up your online communications game, yes, you will need Discord.

Awesome.

So What Exactly Is VoIP?

All right, maybe learning something new won't be so bad if you have a good reason for picking up yet another platform. That is a sound reason to get behind taking time to traverse the learning curve, so where do you begin with Discord? Or where do you begin your serious look at why you need yet one more platform added to your growing palette of applications?

So let's step back a bit and talk about what is at the heart of Discord: audio chat. Discord is one of many apps taking advantage of *Voice over Internet Protocol (VoIP)*, a method commonly used for the delivery of media communications (audio, video, and data files) through online connections using audio and video *codecs* (formats used for compressing a lot of data into order to make it manageable for exchange). Think of how the JPEG format takes a huge image file and makes it only a few megabytes. Codecs are similar to that. Instead of data being transmitted over a circuit-switched network, digital data is transmitted over a packet-switched network: the Internet.

Perhaps the biggest name of early VoIP that changed the way the world communicated was *Skype* (see Figure 1-2; `https://www.skype.com`), offering free calls anywhere internationally by using closed networks for private user bases. The Danish software first reached the public in the summer of 2003. Provided you have broadband Internet, Skype offers up audio and video calls of better quality than standard telephone connections. Along with VoIP, a handy chat function is included for the exchange of data files.

FIGURE 1-2:
Skype brought free international communications to everyone around the world with a broadband Internet connection.

Here's where things start to get a little dicey with VoIP. While the audio and video quality of these calls was unparalleled, a lot of factors would come into play, beginning with the quality of the broadband Internet. Not all broadband is created equal, and in rural areas and developing nations, dial-up was still the way to connect in 2003 and later. Even if broadband is up and running on both the sending and receiving ends of a VoIP call, sending files during a call could disrupt or outright end a call on account of the size of the files being exchanged, the upload/download limitations of the broadband connection, and the amount of traffic on both parties' end.

Then there's security. Each point of a VoIP connection creates a potential vulnerability, as firewalls, if not configured properly, can block incoming and outgoing calls. Additionally, distributed denial-of-service attacks can easily take down VoIP systems, rendering them busy. And these are just two of many vulnerabilities that VoIP can bring to a professional or home network. Free global communication is a very cool thing, but it also comes with a lot of compromising possibilities. So while an improvement over your usual hard-wired telephone calls, VoIP is hardly perfect.

So What Exactly Is In-Game Chat?

Now as VoIP has its checkered reputation, it did introduce the idea of open communications within online games. The concept of built-in chat options, a feature that is usually expected in team-oriented games, be they MMOs (massively multiplayer online games), FPS (first person shooters), RPGs (role playing games), or some other flavor of video game with communications between team members, completely changed how we play on our chosen platforms. *In-game chat* was introduced in 2006 with Nintendo's *Metroid Prime Hunters,* offering gamers real-time audio through the Nintendo DS's built-in microphone. In-game chat was also offered that year with Nintendo's *Pokémon: Diamond and Pearl.*

Today, in-game chat is everywhere. Bungie's *Destiny* offers Fireteam Chat to keep Guardians connected when you lead a raid team into the Garden of Salvation. Epic Games' juggernaut *Fortnite* also comes with native chat, allowing you to tell that 10-year-old who just fragged you the best place to store his or her Legendary pump shotgun. Even cutthroat pirates can make new friends through in-game chat in Rare Studios' *Sea of Thieves,* pictured in Figure 1-3.

FIGURE 1-3:
Thanks to in-game chat, streamer BBXH (https:// twitch.tv/ bbxh) can give the order to raise the main sail, drop anchor, and give a sloop to starboard a broadside in *Sea of Thieves.*

Then you have Xbox Live and PlayStation Network. Consoles are offering their own audio channels to give their gamers a more social experience. Can't game with your friends in *Call of Duty: Modern Warfare*, as you are enjoying an adrenaline rush from *Dead by Daylight?* No worries. Sign on to Xbox LIVE or PSN and enjoy some casual hangout time with your crew. So long as you are logged into your console's respective network, you can chat with your friends, build your network to include others, and swap media ranging from screen captures to game play. And don't worry about not having the right gear straightaway. Consoles will offer you the basics (such as an earbud with a mic and an audio jack in your controller) so you can start chatting straight out of the box.

In-game chat has become so prevalent, it is now a feature expected by gamers. It's the ability to connect that appeals to players, as the gaming experience becomes something more social and more inclusive. From my own experience with in-game chat, it's always fun to be able to work with fellow gamers in a tight scenario (be it PvP or PvE) and execute audibles. Feels good, man. However, the quality of the chat varies from game to game. *Destiny's* native Fireteam Chat, for example, is barely better than the audio quality of a hard-wired telephone call. Another limitation of native in-game chat is that it is native to that game, so if you want to just hang out with your mates while gaming, you have to be in that particular game.

Console chat tends to have better audio quality as opposed to native in-game chat, provided that the network you're on is having a good hair day. If someone in your party is suffering from connection issues, their audio will be spotty at best, popping and locking harder than a Cirque du Soleil performer. Sometimes, incompatibility in gaming gear (microphones, headsets, and so on) may also complicate things. A common audio issue on PSN, for example, is a Network Address Translation (NAT) error, which can occur when network settings on an individual's console are not set properly or a firewall is active. Troubleshooting can be something of a challenge and may not always be a one-solution-fits-all kind of thing. And if Xbox LIVE or PSN is offline? No soup for you.

VoIP is free and able to connect you with friends everywhere in the world, but not without a fair share of problems ranging from spotty reception to security vulnerabilities. Meanwhile, game and console developers offer their own brands of in-game communications, but if the audio quality doesn't make you suffer, connection issues will.

And that is what brings us to the subject of this book.

So What Exactly Is Discord?

Perhaps the trickiest thing to do right off the bat is define *Discord* (`https://discordapp.com`). On the surface, it looks and sounds like Skype on steroids, but it's a robust, stable communications platform available as a browser application, a stand-alone desktop application, and a mobile app for both smartphones and tablets. Discord offers the following features:

» Text chat

» Audio and video chat (group and private)

» Private text messaging

» News feeds

» Link and media sharing

» Streaming and screen sharing

Discord provides gamers, streamers, and many other creative individuals and organizations an all-encompassing platform for topic-specific chat streams, private audio channels and open public chats, interviews for podcasts and streams, and much more.

One of many reasons this platform is so closely associated with gaming is due in part to its founder, Jason Citron. Citron was the founder of OpenFeint, a social gaming platform for mobile games, and Hammer & Chisel, a game development studio. Being a gamer himself, Citron noted problems with available options providing real-time game comms. His development team introduced Discord in May 2015 to Reddit communities, where it gained popularity with eSports gamers and Twitch.tv hosts and took off from there. Within its first year, Discord was hailed by *PC Gamer* as the best VoIP service available, praising its ease of use and its stability.

Oh, and Discord costs now what it did when it was introduced: *free*.

Discord stands apart from other game comms solutions — and for many professionals reliant on using the Internet for communications — for its stability, audio quality, video quality, and ease of use. It may seem a little intimidating when you first launch it, but setup and use are incredibly easy.

CUT ME SOME SLACK, WHY DON'TCHA?

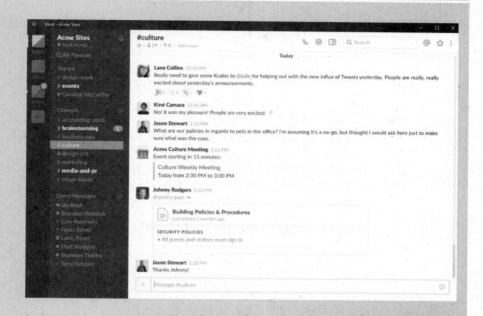

If Discord is sounding familiar to you, you might be using Slack. For myself, that confirmation came when I was introduced to it.

Program manager: So this is Slack. It's a platform for topic-specific chat streams, private audio channels and open public chats, and videoconferencing.

Me: Like Discord?
PM: *blinks* Well, I wouldn't know. I'm not a gamer.

Trust me, dude. You know.

Slack (`https://slack.com`), which stands for Searchable Log of All Conversation and Knowledge, found its roots in gaming, used as an internal communication tool for development of the online game Glitch. Slack, the cornerstone of Slack Technologies and launched in 2013, is a freemium product (the basic app is free, but additional services expanding its capabilities are unlocked at a fee) based on Internet Relay Chat (IRC) technology. While predating Discord, Slack experienced some growing pains on account of the same problems that inspired Discord. Today, Slack is considered to be one of the tech-industry standards for communications. There are a lot of similarities between Slack and Discord, and if you know Slack, you have something of a head start with Discord. If you know Discord, Slack shouldn't be too much of a challenge.

Setting Up Your Discord Account

There are a lot of flavors of Discord. You can use the communications app:

>> Through a browser

>> As a stand-alone desktop application

>> On your smartphone or tablet

You have an entire book to explore what you can do with Discord, so you're going to spend some quality time using Discord through your browser. You'll get comfortable with things and then gradually stretch your reach to other ways to enjoy connecting with old and new friends.

Setting up your server

Your first to-do item with this new platform is to set yourself up on Discord first. Again, it does not cost a thing for you to do this, apart from time. And remember that part I was telling you about how easy it is to set yourself up on Discord?

This investment of time you're about to make will amount to pocket change, believe me.

1. **Launch your browser of choice, and go to** https:// discordapp.com.

Discord offers you two options: Download for Your OS or Open Discord in Your Browser.

2. **Select the Open Discord in Your Browser option.**

As I mention earlier, we will jump into the stand-alone Discord app later on. For now, we will focus on the browser application.

3. **Enter a username for yourself (see Figure 1-4).**

Create a name for yourself that people in Discord will know you by.

TIP

If you are a content creator or a gamer, or if you're developing an online persona, it is best to think ahead of how you want to be known. For example, on PSN, Instagram, and Twitch, I use the moniker TheTeeMonster. So when I set up my Discord, I entered TheTeeMonster as my username. Consistency is key, so aim for the same username from platform to platform.

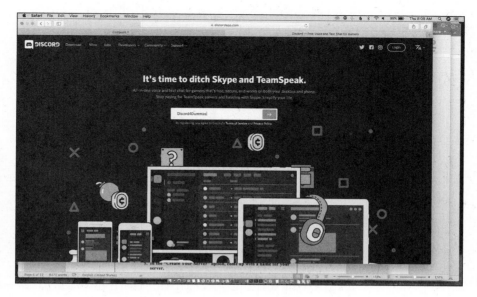

4. **Click the arrow button to the right, and verify that you're not an automated program or bot.**

5. **Verify your account by email or by phone.**

   Choose your preferred method of verification and follow the steps to assure Discord that yes, you are in fact a real person.

6. **When you're asked to set up your server or jump into Discord, click the Get Started option.**

   When you join Discord, you create what is called a *server*. This is your own private corner of Discord, and you decide how public your chat will be.

7. **In the Create Your Server dialog box, come up with a name for your server and a server name, and select the server region closest to your location (see Figure 1-5).**

   This is where you give your server a name people can remember it by. The content creator IAmTeeBot called his server The System. Aura's Discord server is called The Pit, named after his love for his pitbull Layla. Then you have James Werk's Discord, named aptly enough The Werkshop. If you don't like what you initially name your server, don't worry. You can always change it later in the Settings section of your server.

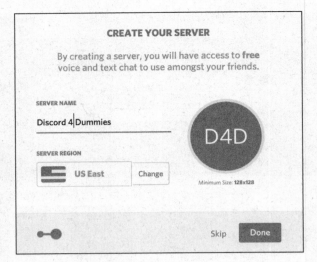

FIGURE 1-5:
When you create a server on Discord, you christen it with a name and establish a region where your server operates.

8. **Claim the server as your own with a valid email and password.**

   You will be sent an email asking you to claim the server, making you its *moderator* — the one in charge of the whole operation.

WARNING

   You are given the option of downloading the desktop app. As I mentioned before, I will go into more depth with the desktop app later on, but if you want to download it now and walk through the steps of setting things up there, feel free to jump ahead to Chapter 4. You will always have the option of downloading the app later, but let's stick together through the browser app, shall we?

   When you claim your server via email confirmation, you are live on Discord!

9. **Return to the Discord browser window, go to the top left of the app, where you see your server name, click the arrow to get the drop-down menu, and select the Server Settings option.**

   A few options are listed here, and I will cover them all eventually. Right now, I'm focusing on just the Server Settings option.

10. **In the Server Overview section, you can upload an icon for your server. (See Figure 1-6.) To do so, click the default icon (the initials of your server name in a blue circle) or click the Upload Image button, and find on your computer an image or logo representative of you or your organization. Select it and then click the Open button to upload it.**

    The server's unique icon or *avatar* allows users to recognize your server at a glance. You will want to have an avatar for your server as well as one for yourself. Discord recommends an image at least 512 x 512 pixels for an avatar.

FIGURE 1-6:
An avatar is a
representative
image of you and
your Discord
server. It's a good
idea to have a
unique avatar
for both.

11. **Change server regions or rename your server if you find yourself in need of a rebrand.**

Scroll to the bottom of Server Settings, click the Save Changes button, and then press the Esc key to return to Discord.

On starting off your server, Discord is very much the blankest of canvases. I mean, it is quiet. Very quiet. Like when you're wandering through the *Nostromo* in the opening shots of *Alien* — that kind of quiet!

Discord gets that and doesn't want you to feel put off, so when you first arrive, it automatically highlights things to do, such as *Set a Status*. You might also see an exclamation point floating around the user interface. On clicking the exclamation point, tips are revealed on neat stuff you can do straight out of the box. These tips also appear whenever Discord changes features and functions, so keep an eye out for those.

Just above your server icon, you should see the Discord icon (if it reminds you of a gaming console controller, you would be correct), your shortcut to the Home section. Clicking that icon immediately takes you to the Activity section, the area of Home always featured on your arrival to Discord. The Home feature offers four options:

» Activity

» Library

» Nitro

» Friends

CHOOSING AN AVATAR

Choose a good avatar in much the same way you would select a user image or user icon for any social media platform. You want something that represents you at a glance, but not an image with a lot of detail or one so small you don't recognize it at a glance. The avatars pictured here are all designed to make the most of the limited space given for them. Note there are no fine details or mid-to-wide shots of people, just simple icons, logos, or headshots. Consider this when creating or selecting images for your avatar.

I'm going to do a deep dive into all of these options, but not straightaway. Let's find a pace crawling before we challenge gravity and start walking. What you need to do first is fill in blanks in your profile and explore some of the control functions that Discord offers you as the moderator of your server.

Setting up your profile and parameters

Discord respects how important identity is. When communicating online, you want to make a good first impression, and you want your Discord to feel warm, inviting, and (more important) lived in. But when sharing information and data, you want to know exactly what you're sharing and how you're sharing it. It's as if in the age being social with our social media, we are grappling with this weird sense of paranoia. (Thanks, Facebook and Cambridge Analytica!)

Discord gets this, which is why Discord has its User Settings set up the way it does.

1. **Go to the bottom-left corner of Discord, and click the gear wheel.**

2. **Click the Edit button in the My Account section.**

3. **Move your cursor to the default Discord icon, located on the left side of the window, and click the words "Change Avatar," when they appear (see Figure 1-7).**

   User Settings is your comprehensive panel for everything pertaining to your personal account. Here, you are changing your avatar to give you a specific look. You can change your avatar for yourself at any time.

FIGURE 1-7:
My Account offers you options to change your user name, avatar, verified email, and password, building a persona for you to take through Discord.

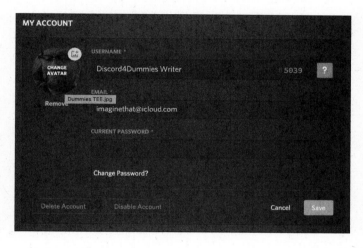

4. **Find an image that's appropriate for yourself, and click the Choose button.**

   Formats you can use for avatars include JPG, PNG, and GIF. The minimum size for an avatar is 128 by 128 pixels.

TIP

   Although you are able to change your username, there is a four-digit identifying number off to the right that is *not* an editable option. (See Figure 1-7.) This *unique ID number* is part of your Discord identification. You see it pop up with your own and other Discord users when tagging them in posts. That is perfectly normal.

5. **When you have made all the changes you wish to make, click the Save button to return to the User Settings section.**

6. **Click the Privacy and Safety option to review the default settings, and make adjustments where you want.**

   The Privacy and Settings option is one way Discord works to keep you and your server safe and secure. Safe Direct Messaging gives you the ability to disable any virus scans on attachments and URLs sent to you confidentially, or grants Discord the right to scan anything coming to you from an individual. Server Privacy Defaults allows you to accept or deny private messages, and Who Can Add You as a Friend puts limitations on who can add you as a friend. (You can be a member of a server and not necessarily be someone's friend on Discord.) Finally, there is How We Use Your Data, offering transparency for all the data exchanged here. All this is Discord working with you to make sure you know how much you are sharing and with whom you are sharing.

7. **Single-click the Connections option. The various apps that seamlessly integrate with Discord include:**

   - Twitch
   - YouTube
   - Blizzard.net
   - Steam
   - Reddit
   - Facebook
   - Twitter
   - Spotify
   - Xbox LIVE

   If you have any live accounts with these services, connect them here with your Discord. (See Figure 1-8.)

8. **Click the Billing option to manage credit cards authorized for in-app purchases, such as Discord Nitro and exclusive games. Click Add Payment Method and then authorize a debit or credit card (if so desired) for your Discord account.**

   This is not necessary for hosting a server. Discord is still free, but for games and Nitro features, charges will apply. For more about Discord Nitro, take a look at Chapter 4 for details.

9. **Click the X at the top right or press the Esc key to return to Discord.**

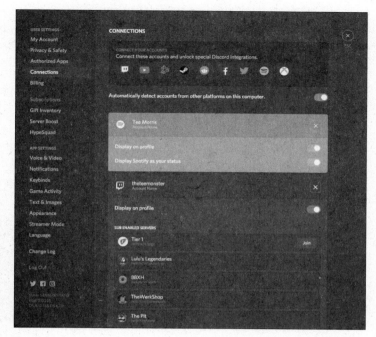

FIGURE 1-8:
Discord
integrates with
Twitch, Spotify,
YouTube, and
other popular
apps through
Connections,
found in your
User Settings.

In this introduction, I skipped Authorized Apps because this section will get more attention after you finish Chapter 7. Authorized Apps pertains to integrated software that automates specific functions in your server. This software, commonly known as *bots,* can be managed from here. Once you have some bots working hard in your server, you will revisit this feature.

Discord's User Settings are all about being social while staying secure. You can still purchase services, introduce yourself to new people from various parts of the world, and still keep an eye on the data you share. It's okay to open up when online, but it's a good thing to remain safe.

TIP

Another way Discord works to keep you safe is with Two-Factor Authentication, an option offered under My Account. While not mandatory, Two-Factor Authentication asks the user for a second passcode when logging into Discord, adding to your account a second layer of protection from any malicious hackers.

Setting up your Discord application

Let's make Discord truly ours now, shall we? Under the App Settings section of our User Account settings, we get into the nuts and bolts of how everything works here. What are we using for audio and video inputs? How do we want Discord to look for us? How do we want to be notified on new interactions and when? We set up all this here. There is a lot to customize in Discord, and this is all part of the experience in making this platform feel like a place you want to spend a lot of time on with friends. So why not make it your own?

1. **Go to the bottom-left corner of Discord, click the User Settings gear wheel, and click to Voice & Video in the App Settings section (see Figure 1-9).**

   At the top of the window are the input and output settings for your audio.

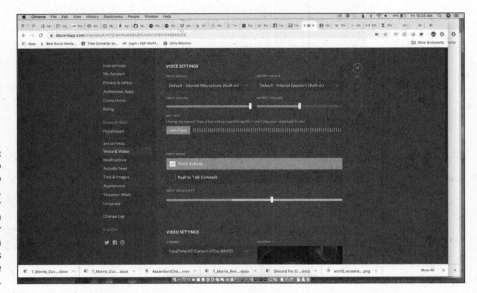

FIGURE 1-9: Voice & Video grants you audio and video chat, using either the built-in options of your laptop or plug-in accessories you have incorporated.

2. **Check the quality of your incoming signal by clicking the Let's Check button.**

   When looking for the best audio signal, you want to make sure your signal is bouncing within the green of the readout, or the Volume Unit (VU) meter. If you are too loud, the signal will be loud and distorted, or *overmodulated*. Consult Chapter 5 for more tips on how to set good, balanced audio.

3. **Just underneath the VU meter, you should notice that Voice Activity is selected, meaning that audio communications is enabled. Leave Push to Talk unselected.**

   Push to Talk is where you have to use a keyboard shortcut to communicate with others in your chat, like a traditional Citizens Band (CB) radio. Push to Talk is handy if you are hosting interviews or roundtable discussions, but your location is seeing a lot of traffic. Another use is if you are recording an interview or panel discussion, but only in an engineer capacity. Push to Talk silences your audio but allows you to interject if you need to inform the party of any technical issues.

4. **Video Settings allows you to choose what your video input device will be. Select a camera from the Camera drop-down menu.**

   The Preview window gives you a quick look to assure the signal is good. Underneath Video Settings, Advanced options will help you troubleshoot any problems your audio may encounter.

5. **Click the Notifications options on the left side of your screen to specify how you want to be notified when new messages arrive.**

   If you prefer not to receive notifications on your desktop, make sure the Enable Desktop Notifications option is turned off.

REMEMBER

These preferences pertain to your Discord app on a global level. You have the ability to control notifications for specific servers and specific channels. Refer to Chapter 7 for more.

6. **Choose an approximate time from the drop-down menu for when you will be away.**

   AFK stands for *away from keyboard* and is commonly used when users are no longer at their desk or laptops but still online.

   Text-to-Speech Notifications, when enabled, will read out all or specific notifications.

7. **If necessary, enable Text-to-Speech for Notifications.**

8. **Scroll down to Sounds to see all the alerts currently enabled.**

   They include

   - Message
   - Deafen
   - Undeafen
   - Mute
   - Unmute
   - Voice Disconnected
   - PPT Activate
   - PPT Deactivate
   - User Join
   - User Leave

- User Moved
- Outgoing Ring
- Incoming Ring
- Stream Started
- Stream Stopped
- Viewer Join
- Viewer Leave

You can enable notifications and then use these options to decide which notifications for which you will hear an audible alert. You can control which activity will notify you with an audible alert. Go on and take a look at the various Notifications options in detail in Chapter 7.

9. **Click the Activity Feed and search for games that you play in the Search for Games bar.**

The latest news and links for games you follow appear in your Activity Feed, accessed from the Home option.

10. **Click Text and Images to review how you want media to appear in Discord posts, and make adjustments if desired.**

How media is displayed can be customized from channel to channel on your server. Chapter 3 offers a detailed look at how to incorporate media and decide if some channels will allow it or not.

11. **Click Appearance (see Figure 1-10) to customize the look and feel of your Discord.**

Appearance not only allows you to adjust Discord on an aesthetic level, but also grants accessibility for any users needing assistance on visuals. Play around with the options here to see what works best for you.

TIP

For my developers reading Discord, this is where you — yes, *you* — can really customize the platform. Under Appearance's Advanced section, you'll find Developer Mode, which will help in integration of bots and custom commands with Discord's application programming interface (API). For more about these functions, take a look at Chapter 7.

Discord's last two User Settings, Streamer Mode and Language, are quickly covered here. If you want to work in a different language, select your preferred language under the Language option. Streamer Mode is covered in Chapter 6 when I talk about integration with your streaming account and routines.

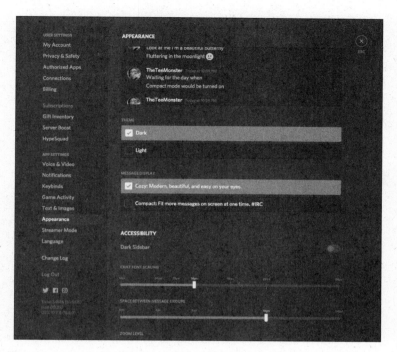

FIGURE 1-10:
If you prefer your Discord UI to be light or dark, or if you need to change font sizes, Appearance gives you the tools to make your UI perform to your own accessibility needs.

Then, at the bottom of the list of options for User Account options, there is the Change Log option. This option is occasionally offered to you upon launching the Discord app, but it's easily accessed here. The Change Log is a list of updates and quick fixes to the platform, as well as a look at the continuing efforts from the Discord development team to improve the platform, be it through a new feature, a chance for you to volunteer for a Beta group to test something new, or an opportunity to catch the Discord team at a live appearance. If change is coming to your server, the Change Log where you can read up on it.

And that wraps up your Discord preferences. Your server is all set up, and you are ready to go! Okay, it is a little quiet at present. I would enjoy the quiet, because I'm about to bring the boom!

Joining a Discord Server

Along with this book, the best way to learn is to watch others do what you want to do. While we have set up a server for ourselves, we are in something of a holding pattern, as we need to understand how all these connections work. Presently, we are speaking in a bubble, and we need to take a look at other communities to see how they run things. No two Discord servers are alike, and you will want to learn from others so that you know how this platform works.

So how do you join servers?

No cover at the door: Joining open servers

Underneath your Server's avatar are two icons: Add a Server and Server Discovery. We will use both to help you out in your first steps in building a community.

1. Click the magnifying glass below the plus sign in the top-left corner of the Discord app.

This icon is your Server Discovery tool.

A directory of servers appears below a search bar, prompting you to search various topics. The Server Discovery Directory, shown in Figure 1-11, is your guide to open communities that welcome new users to their servers.

2. Scroll down to review the featured communities, or click the Next button at the bottom of the directory to review another offering of Discord servers.

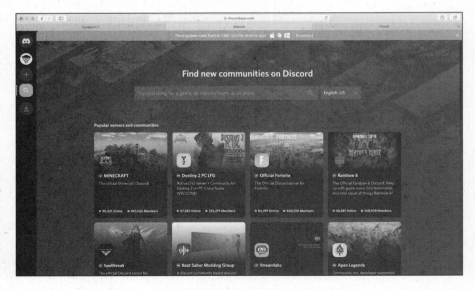

FIGURE 1-11: Server Discovery is one way of finding new communities with other users who have something in common with you.

3. **When you have found a community you want to join, click that server.**

Whether you click the server or the View button, you will be ushered to a holding area that usually features the rules of a server. It will be in your best interest to read this page *carefully* before clicking the Join Server button located at the bottom right of Discord.

4. **When you're ready, click the Join Server button.**

When a server is joined, an avatar for that server appears on the left side of your Discord. You can begin chatting, provided that the room allows chatting (see Chapter 2).

5. **Return to the Server Discovery tool, and this time, enter a favorite video game in the Search bar, located above the featured servers.**

At present, Discord's search directory is limited to gaming topics. In the case of nongaming interests, you will find discussions on individual servers.

WARNING

6. **Repeat Steps 2 and 4 to join a server that interests you.**

Now that you have joined servers, you should notice those servers in your left sidebar. To visit the servers, simply click the server's avatar, and you find yourself there, ready to chat. The various topics with the hashtag symbol are called *channels*, where engagement happens. Here, you discuss whatever the channel's topic features. I go deeper into channels in Chapter 2.

By invitation only: Joining private servers

This is how you can jump into popular, public servers, but there are plenty other servers — like your own — you can enjoy, provided that you have an *invitation*. For the purposes of this book, I am going to use my server (TheTeeMonster's Not-So-Secret-Lair) as the example of what to do when you get an invite to a server.

When you receive an invite, a URL will be provided. The link can be sent via email, text, or chat.

1. **When you receive the link, click the link to launch Discord and join the new server, or copy the link to your Clipboard by pressing Ctrl+C (Windows) or ⌘+C (macOS).**

The invitation URL for my server is https://discord.gg/62dvzyk.

2. **If you copied the URL, click the Add Server button, located above the Server Discovery button.**

3. **Select the Join a Server option.**

4. **Enter the URL in the provided field (see Figure 1-12) and then click the Join button.**

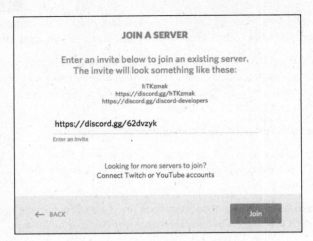

JOIN A SERVER

Enter an invite below to join an existing server.
The invite will look something like these:

hTKzmak
https://discord.gg/hTKzmak
https://discord.gg/discord-developers

https://discord.gg/62dvzyk

Enter an Invite

Looking for more servers to join?
Connect Twitch or YouTube accounts

← BACK   Join

FIGURE 1-12:
By clicking on the Add a Server icon (the green "+" sign), you have received a URL to another server. This is where you use the invite to gain access.

You have joined a server via invitation. Simple as that.

But if you spend some time at this server and find the discussions are not to your liking, follow these steps:

1. **Find the server you want to leave in the left-hand sidebar of your Discord. Right-click it to access the Options menu.**

2. **Choose the Leave Server option from the drop-down menu.**

3. **Confirm this decision by clicking the Leave Server button.**

TIP

Let's be honest — https://discord.gg/62dvzyk is not the easiest URL to remember. Not by a long shot. This is why, when I publicize my website, I use https://bitly.com to create an easier URL to use. That way, when people use the bit.ly link — http://bit.ly/discord4tee — it can be easily recalled and entered into a browser of choice and an invite offered. For ideas on publicizing your Discord, check out Chapter 2.

Now that you have set up your own server, refined your profile, and joined servers, it's time to make connections and begin tapping into what Discord can do. There are discussions happening right now, and it's time to make your voice heard. You might make a few new friends as you continue this adventure in Discord.

Chapter **2**

Hailing Frequencies Open

The setup for Discord may feel a bit intense. There's a lot to the application, but when you consider Discord's aim to truly make this application your own, it makes sense. The developers set out to create a place that you could truly call your own and customize it as much as possible. And if you've got dev skills, the sky's the limit. So yes, we have successfully worked through a lot of behind-the-scenes details.

But let's get to what Discord was made for: communication.

Instead of giving you a hard shove into the deep end of the pool, you are going to want to master the most basic form of comms in Discord. I'm speaking of the *text features*, which, a bit like the preferences of the application, are vast and detailed. They are also easy to pick up and "git gud" at, as gamers would say.

Before we get to talking, we really should get people in our network to talk with. (Stands to reason, doesn't it?) So let's start building that community we will be cultivating here.

Connecting with Friends

The Beatles were right when it comes to the importance of friends. They do help you get by, but you have to connect with them first in Discord. *Friends* are people on Discord who directly connect with you. They do not necessarily have to be on your server. Making that connection usually happens through an invitation.

So if people can connect with your server and communicate freely with you on the various topics (which I cover later in this chapter), why would you even need to have friends distinguished in Discord?

Friends in Discord (see Figure 2-1) can be regarded as something like "Gold" or "Tier 2" status on your server. Friends can be given special privileges ranging from open direct messaging to being able to see what servers you have in common. It may seem that the distinctions may be insignificant at first, but there is something to having an inner circle of contacts, especially when your community starts to grow.

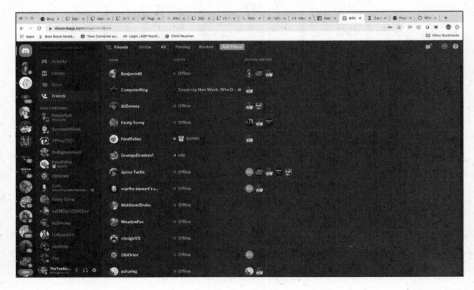

FIGURE 2-1:
The Friends list in Discord offers you the ability to see who is on when you are on, as well as what other servers you have in common.

Finding friends online can be a pretty easy process once you know where to look and *how* to look.

1. **In the Discord browser window, click Home and select the Friends option.**

2. **Select the Add Friend option on the far right and click it.**

   For new users, the Add Friend option is highlighted. Experienced users also have this option highlighted, in green, but it will not be as prominent as for those brand-new to Discord.

You can send a friend request to anyone on Discord, provided you have the user's name and unique four-digit ID number.

When adding friends, remembering the number can be something of a hassle. However, you can easily send a friend request to people by clicking their username or avatar to pull up their Profile. By clicking the Send Friend Request button (see Figure 2-2), you can easily reach out to make a connection with someone.

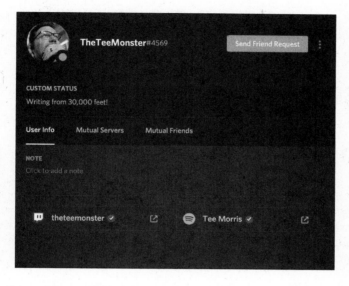

FIGURE 2-2:
Making friends on Discord is easy once you know how. Click a username; then click the user's avatar to quickly find out more about them.

3. **To copy your own username and four-digit ID number, move your cursor to the lower left of Discord and click your username at the bottom of the app.**

   By clicking your own username, both your name and your Discord ID number are copied so you can use it in other locations, like Facebook, Twitter, Instagram, and other social media platforms.

   When a friend request arrives, the Home icon at the top left of Discord alerts you.

4. **Click it, go to the Friends option, and then click the Pending option.**

   Any friend requests waiting for your approval appear here. They will remain pending until you accept or reject the request.

5. **Select the check sign to accept the friend request or the X icon to ignore it.**

And just like that, you are making friends on Discord. Now, remember, these are members of the inner circle of your server. It is a good idea to make sure those you are bringing on to your Friends list are people you know and people you *trust*. When you get to know folks in your community, it's not a bad idea to grow your Friends list and bring more people into that inner circle. It's good to have folks in your corner that you can count on and keep close when managing a community becomes tough to handle.

Thing is, be it your inner circle or your (growing) community, you will want to give people topics to talk about. These topics are called *channels* in Discord, and right now we only have the basics. And I mean *the basics* — a text and video channel, both labeled as general. As Eleanor and Chidi would say on *The Good Place*: "Ya BAY-sic!"

Let's build on this.

Something to Talk About: Channels

We have set up how to reach out and invite people to our server. These are all the steps we need to take in building a community. Before we really start to build this new corner of the Internet, we need to offer people channels to visit. What games are you currently playing? Where are your favorite places to eat? Did you binge-watch anything good on Netflix?

All these questions have the potential of becoming channels on your Discord. To add a channel, follow these steps:

1. **On the left side of Discord, find your text and voice channels in the sidebar.**

2. **To the right of the Text Channels category, click the Add Channel option (a large "+" icon) to create a new channel.**

   Channels are dedicated topics that you want to share with your followers and subscribers. Here are a few ideas for what your server can feature:

   - Food
   - Travel
   - Movies
   - Sports
   - Books

This is one of the best attributes of Discord. It offers you the ability to sort and organize your interests.

3. **In the Create Text Channel window, as seen in Figure 2-3, label your new channel a topic relevant to your interests; make sure Text Channel is the Channel Type selected, and leave the Private Channel option turned off.**

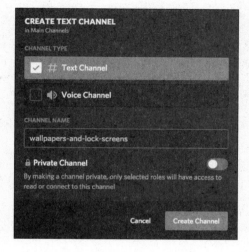

FIGURE 2-3: When creating a channel, spaces are rendered as hyphens and the title is lowercase. Make sure the channel name doubles as a brief description.

4. **Click the Create Channel button.**

5. **Repeat Steps 2–4 to create other channels of interest.**

   Channels are places for your community, but the ideas for channel come from you and your interests. (See Figure 2-4.) If you need to brainstorm for ideas on what kind of channels to create, jump ahead to Chapter 12.

6. **Right-click the Text Channel header, and select the Edit Category option.**

7. **Give the Text Channels category the new title of** Main Channels **in the Category Name field, and click the green Save button.**

   Although channels are dedicated topics of conversation, *categories* are sections of your sidebar where you can group various channels together. Categories can be expanded or collapsed, depending on your preferences.

TIP

   A channel with any new messages appears highlighted even if you have the channel collapsed. As seen here, Main Channels is collapsed but there are unread messages in the #twitch-subs-only channel.

8. **Click and drag the channels of your Discord server into their appropriate categories.**

FIGURE 2-4:
Channels help
organize your
Discord server in
providing topics
visitors and
community
members want to
talk about.

Your Discord is now live with channels available to everyone, a hub where followers, subscribers, and people who are completely new to you and your stream can take part of the conversation.

So now that you have topics of discussion, how do you create content for these topics?

Sharing Is Caring: Putting a Post Together

Let's say there is a movie trailer just released on YouTube that you want to share on a #movies channel. How would you go about doing this?

1. **Go to** www.youtube.com **and look for media (in this case, the movie trailer) you want to share.**

2. **Click the Share option.**

3. **From the window, click the Copy option, and look for a notification at the bottom-left of the browser window from which you copied the URL.**

4. **Return to your Discord server, and find the channel where you want to post the URL.**

TIP

Take a closer look at Figures 2-4 and 2-5. You see small alerts by the servers' icons. Those are the number of *tagged messages* waiting for you to review in those servers. Tagged messages are posts that are intended for everyone on the server, everyone in the channel, or you specifically.

5. **Click the channel you want to post in, and in the Message [#name-of-channel] field, type the following:**

This went live today and I am now counting down to this release. What do you think? Does this not look amazing?

[paste YouTube Link here]

6. **Press the Enter key.**

Pictured in Figure 2-5 are a message and accompanying URL posted in the channel. A preview is rendered of the link, and you can either watch the clip in Discord or click a provided link to go to YouTube.

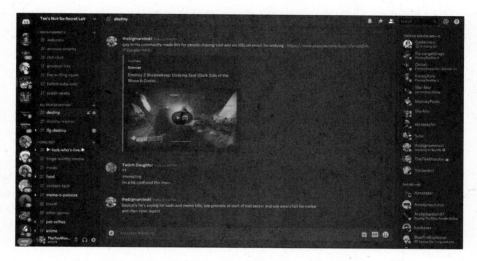

FIGURE 2-5: In Discord, it is easy to share links, images, and YouTube clips in channels.

Discord supports several kinds of media:

» URLs

» JPG and PNG images

» Animated GIFs

» MP3 files

» M4V and MP4 files

» Emojis and emotes

WARNING

The standard Discord will not upload any media files larger than 8MB.

This is how you create content in your server, and content — as you might imagine — is what keeps people coming back to your various channels. Before inviting people into your server, it would not be a bad idea to prep your channels with bits of starter content.

And here we arrive at the hardest part of starting off a server. How do we get people there? What is the trick in making friends and attracting fans? And more to the point of building a community — how do you keep people coming back for more?

Straight off the bat, folks have to know you are on Discord. So let's start telling people about your server.

Wanna Come on by for a Chat?

You have a server set up on solid foundation right now, but things are quiet because no one on Discord, or anywhere else for that matter, knows your server is live. This is where you start sending out invitations and begin to build your online community.

WARNING

Although it is great to open your world to everyone, and big communities always offer up a lot of fun for you and your fellow chatters, opening your server up to everyone and anyone can sometimes attract *trolls*. Trolls are those who join servers for the single purpose to be jerks. Oh, sure, you have people who love to get snarky on a server (right, |Drafty|?), but trolls are people that go for the jugular, mock others maliciously, and spam channels with off-topic links, images, and media. Keep in mind that the more places you put out your server's URL, the greater the chances you will attract the wrong kind of community members. I talk more about community management in Chapter 8.

Your community growth begins with an *invitation*, the proverbial key to your online kingdom. After you create your invitation, you will go into the best places to share your invitation with the world.

1. **At the top-left of the Discord browser window, find your server name, click open the drop-down menu, and select the Invite People option.**

Remember, this is the drop-down menu pertaining to your *server*. If you need to adjust something specific to your server or any server you belong to, it will be here.

In the Invite Friends to [Your Server's Name] window, you will see a URL generated pertaining to your server. To the right, you will see a Copy button.

Just underneath the generated URL for your server will be the disclaimer Your Link Expires in 1 Day. By default, any URLs currently generated have a life span of 24 hours.

2. **In Figure 2-6, at the bottom-right corner of the Invite Friends to [Your Server's Name] window, is a gear wheel. Click the gear wheel to review the Server Invite Link Settings available.**

These options offer expiration times and membership limitations for any invites you generate. This is to have control over how much new traffic your server sees.

FIGURE 2-6: To build your community in Discord, invitations should be circulated online in order to bring people to you.

INVITE FRIENDS TO DISCORD 4 DUMMIES

Share this link with others to grant access to your server!

https://discord.gg/Z8tjfK   Copy

Your invite link expires in 1 day.

☐ Set this link to never expire

3. **Click the Expire After drop-down menu, and select the Never option.**

4. **Click the Max Number of Uses drop-down menu, and select the No Limit option. (See Figure 2-7.)**

The URL you are creating that grants access to your server now has no expiration date.

5. **Click the Generate a New Link button.**

You now have a *permalink*, a static URL with no termination date, offering anyone who has it access to your server.

6. **Click the Copy button and start sharing you server's invitation.**

But now you're looking at this permalink, and maybe a thought flashes across your brain: *Okay, now what?* Well, this where the building of your community all begins. Pretty exciting! Suddenly the Internet feels a bit bigger. You have to let people know where your server is, but where is your audience? How different are the audiences from social media platform to social media platform? Where is the best place to showcase your invite on the platform of choice?

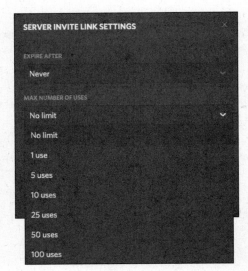

FIGURE 2-7:
By adjusting the
expiration period
and number of
users, you can
easily create a
permalink for
your Discord
server to
distribute across
social media.

SERVER INVITE LINK SETTINGS

EXPIRE AFTER

Never

MAX NUMBER OF USES

No limit

No limit

1 use

5 uses

10 uses

25 uses

50 uses

100 uses

Streaming platforms

Twitch (`https://twitch.tv`) is where I first heard of Discord. If you are unfamil-
iar with Twitch, this is a platform that offers *streaming* as a way to connect with
the world. Streaming is sharing in real-time content that a host or a group of
hosts are creating, many times on the fly and completely off the top of their heads.
Originally, Twitch — the first of many streaming platforms — was a way for
channel hosts to share their gaming experience with viewers. From its humble
beginnings, streaming now covers a variety of topics. There are many new platforms offering audio and video streaming, but four remain the popular, go-to
providers:

>> Twitch

>> YouTube

>> Mixer

>> Facebook

Discord is where you continue your stream after the stream is over and done with.
Your audience can swing by, suggest a new game, or just hang out to get to know
you behind-the-scenes and between-the-streams.

So how does streaming help get the word out on your Discord?

Content creators have a lot of helpers to get them through a stream. One such
helper is *Nightbot* (`https://nightbot.tv`), a virtual assistant that helps your

stream run smoothly and efficiently. Nightbot helps show hosts create unique *commands* or messages that you will want to post repeatedly.

1. **Go to** `https://nightbot.tv`, **and authenticate your streaming account with Nightbot.**

2. **Once you have authenticated Nightbot, go to the menu on the left side of your browser window, and click the Commands option and then the Custom option.**

   At the time of this writing, Nightbot does not support Facebook. YouTube is supported, but Nightbot only becomes active when the stream is live.

WARNING

3. **Click the blue Add Command button to create your first command for your stream.**

   For your first command, you will create a Discord invite post. This is where you will paste your server's permalink and make it easy for you to let people know you have a digital hangout for your stream.

4. **In the Add Command window, starting with the Command option, type** `!discord` **in the field.**

   Many commands in Twitch begin with an exclamation point immediately followed by a keyword. No spaces. No numbers. Keep keywords for commands simple.

REMEMBER

5. **Within the Message window, compose the following (see Figure 2-8):**

   Feel free to come in for the fun — [paste your permalink here]

6. **Select all of the message you just created, and copy (Copy+C for Windows, ⌘+C for Mac) it to your clipboard.**

7. **In the Userlevel drop-down menu, make sure Everyone is selected.**

   If you want to create commands available to everyone in Chat, available to Subscribers only, or available only to you, set permissions here for commands.

8. **Set Cooldown to 5 seconds by moving the slider all the way to the left.**

   Cooldown is where you set a clock for when the command can be used again.

9. **Make your Alias the same name as the command, or leave this blank.**

   Alias is used when embedding this command in another command.

10. **Click the blue Submit button to add this command to your list of custom commands.**

11. **Return to Nightbot's left menu and choose Timers from the options listed.**

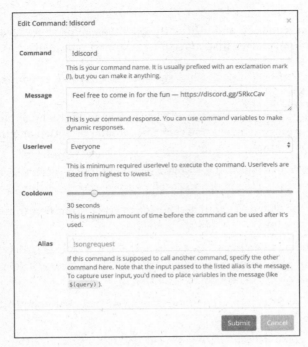

Edit Command: !discord

Command !discord

This is your command name. It is usually prefixed with an exclamation mark (!), but you can make it anything.

Message Feel free to come in for the fun — https://discord.gg/5RkcCav

This is your command response. You can use command variables to make dynamic responses.

Userlevel Everyone

This is minimum required userlevel to execute the command. Userlevels are listed from highest to lowest.

Cooldown 30 seconds

This is minimum amount of time before the command can be used after it's used.

Alias !songrequest

If this command is supposed to call another command, specify the other command here. Note that the input passed to the listed alias is the message. To capture user input, you'd need to place variables in the message (like $(query)).

Submit   Cancel

FIGURE 2-8:
Nightbot's Custom Command feature triggers frequent messages in your Chat with an easy-to-remember keyword.

12. **In the Add Command window, starting with the Command option, type** !discord **in the field.**

It is okay for you to use the same command keyword for timed commands as well as for manual commands.

13. **Within the Message window, paste the message you composed for the** !discord **command or simply reconstruct the message from Step 5.**

14. **Set the Timer slider to 20 minutes.**

15. **Click the blue Submit button to add this command to your list of custom commands.**

With this custom command, you can now type !discord into your Chat window and drop the permalink to your server to everyone watching. As the command is open for anyone to use, you can then say to your Chat Can I get someone to drop the link to our Discord in Chat? to cue those watching to drop your command in Chat.

You also have set up a *timed command* where every 20 minutes, the Discord link will appear in Chat. This is a handy method of publicity that takes some pressure off you to remember to throw that command in Chat or ask your mods to do so. Before making any of the commands live, be they manual or timed, double-check the permalink to make sure it works and takes you to your server. Never hurts to confirm that your URL is working properly.

When setting the timer on the automated commands, make sure you have time between each posting. With multiple timed messages scheduled close to one another, you run the risk of spamming your own channel. Remain aware of what you are saying and when you are saying it. Take advantage of enabling and disabling timers.

With Nightbot, inviting people to your Discord server becomes pretty easy. So easy, in fact, it is something you don't have to worry about. Your *moderators* (those individuals who are watching over your Chat while you focus on creating content) and regulars to your stream will drop a manual command for the open invite while Nightbot will, based on your set parameters, remind those watching you have a Discord.

LET ME HELP YOU WITH THAT: A WORD ABOUT BOTS

The term *bots* tends to carry a negative connotation with it as we immediately think about those automated messages that fill our Twitter streams and DMs with robo-replies encouraging you to "Follow me on Facebook . . . and Instagram . . . and Pinterest . . . and —" because that's an awesome way to build your social media presence.

Said no one legit in social media. *Ever.*

In streaming, bots also have a bad reputation as viewbots and chatbots spam channels with misleading statistics, getting streamers' hopes up only to let them down from a great height. I mean, automated programs acting like real people? Seriously, that's such a Philip K. Dick move.

Truth be told, bots are actually the best thing to add to your stream, to your social platforms, or to your Discord server, *provided you bot responsibly.* In the case of Nightbot, your keyword-enabled messages — so long as they are text-based only — can inform people where to find your latest highlight video, post frequently asked-for URLs, and quickly share other tidbits of information. Then you have bots that can add to the performance of your server, offering even more integration of your favorite social media apps. Some bots can also assist in helping you welcome new people to the server, inform you of special events happening online, and even provide a level of security for you and your community.

Don't be turned off by the term *bots* because you return to these virtual assistants in Chapter 7.

They're bots. And they're here to help.

For more on streaming, specifically streaming on Twitch, feel free to take a look at *Twitch For Dummies*, written by me. I go deep into the details of the platform, from soup to nuts.

Twitter

Another popular social media platform for gamers, content creators, and community managers is one of the original three: *Twitter* (https://twitter.com). Maybe you already have a presence on Twitter, or maybe you have a Twitter account and have stepped away from it for whatever reason. If you are on Discord, it is a good idea to be up on your tweeting skills.

There are plenty of automated services that allow you to schedule tweets, even Twitter itself provided you sign up for a business account. Free applications like Hootsuite (https://hootsuite.com) and TweetDeck (https://tweetdeck.twitter.com) offer you the ability to manage one or multiple Twitter accounts. Part of that management includes scheduling tweets.

Let's schedule a tweet using TweetDeck, so you can see how easy this is:

1. **Go to** https://tweetdeck.twitter.com **to see your default account.**

   If you are not already logged into Twitter, you will need to log in. If you are already logged in, you will automatically be taken to it.

2. **Select the New Tweet option located at the top of the menu located on the far left of the browser window, and click it to see the Compose New Tweet window (see Figure 2-9).**

3. **In the Tweet field, compose the following:**

   Wanna chat beyond 280 characters? Join me on Discord at [paste your permalink here] where tangents are welcome!

   Graphics tend to help a tweet's visibility, so when putting together your tweet, consider adding in an appropriate image or animated GIF, just to catch a little extra attention.

TIP

4. **Click the Schedule Tweet button, located just under the Add an Image option.**

   You see a calendar appear.

5. **Set the day and time you want the tweet to go live.**

   To remove the scheduled time for a tweet, you can click the *Remove* button just underneath the calendar. That only removes scheduling options, not the tweet itself.

FIGURE 2-9:
TweetDeck is a fully integrated Twitter account management tool, offering users the ability to tweet in real time or schedule tweets for later posting.

6. Click the Tweet at [Scheduled Date] button to schedule the tweet.

7. Repeat Steps 1–6 to schedule multiple tweets.

This is one way of letting people on Twitter know how to find your Discord. It's pretty easy and only takes a few minutes to schedule a tweet to appear daily. A legitimate concern with scheduling tweets though, especially multiple tweets that are all talking about the same thing, makes your Twitter account appear insincere. Automation in Twitter is nothing new, but it does come across cold and disconnected.

So let's look at some other options.

1. Go to https://twitter.com to see your account.

   If you are not already logged into Twitter, you will need to log in. If you are already logged in, you will automatically taken to it.

2. Click the New Tweet field located at the top left of the browser, and compose the following:

   Wanna chat beyond 280 characters? Join me on Discord at [paste your permalink here] where tangents are welcome!

3. Click the Tweet button, posting your tweet.

4. **Click the Profile in the menu along the left side of the browser window, and find your recent tweet at the top of your tweet stream.**

   At the Profile option, you will find all your recent tweets, along with details about your account.

5. **At the top-right corner of your tweet, click the arrow to see options for the tweet.**

6. **Select the Pin to Your Profile option.**

The Pin to Profile option takes one selected tweet and anchors it to the top of your Twitter account. Anyone visiting your profile will see the invite to Discord as the first tweet. Pinning a tweet concerning something important to you, like where people can join your Discord, is another terrific option in getting the word out about your server.

The limitation of pinning a tweet is that you can only pin one tweet at a time. If you have a special event coming up or a personal victory you want to highlight, that invitation will be returned to the chronological stream of your Twitter feed. It's no big deal to re-create a tweet, so long as you get the Discord link right. When using a pinned tweet as your open invitation to the world, just know how pinned tweets work.

Remember that Profile option you were using to look at your Twitter feed? You can also try something there.

1. **Go to** https://twitter.com **to see your account.**

2. **Click the Profile option.**

   You are given various options to edit your Profile, visible to anyone visiting Twitter (see Figure 2-10).

3. **Scroll down to the Website option and enter your Discord server's URL.**

4. **Click the Save button in the top-right corner of the Edit Profile window.**

   Your Discord server is now accessible through your profile.

TIP

If you want to feature your Discord server, but you have a website (a blog, your Twitch stream, a shortened link to a product you're promoting, and so on) you want to feature, as well, look into *your Twitter bio*. If there is room for a link, you can always put your server link in there, leaving the website option free for any other URL you want to promote.

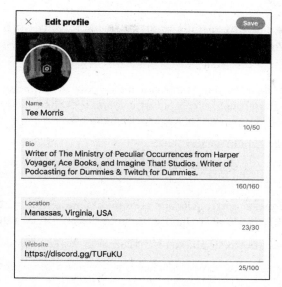

The Twitter Profile is a terrific option for publicizing your Discord server as it is always prominently featured whenever people see your profile. If there is disadvantage to using your Twitter Profile to promote your server, it may be that people can follow you on Twitter without ever checking it. However, personal experience and case studies show that profiles do matter as they serve as your first impression. This is why it is important to have a good Profile picture, a solid Cover Photo (the image that appears at the very top of your Twitter feed), and a few of the details Twitter asks for covered. If you want to go a bit deeper into Twitter, check out *Twitter For Dummies*, 3rd Edition, written by Laura Fitton, Anum Hussain, and Brittany Leaning.

Twitter offers a lot of options, but other platforms also offer potential for you to share your server. Our next platform offers you a creative way to get the word out across several platforms with a single post.

Instagram

Once upon a time, this platform was considered something of an underdog as it was something only for the visual medium, but Instagram (`https://www.instagram.com`) has evolved into one of the most powerful marketing tools in social media circles because of its ability to capture attention through photographs and video. With a clever approach to the platform, Discord and Instagram can work together to help you promote your community.

Similar to using a Twitter Profile to invite people to your server, the *Instagram profile* also offers up an option to grant visitors to your account access to your Discord.

1. **Launch and log in to your Instagram app on your smartphone, or log into your account at** https://instagram.com **and click the small Profile icon located in the upper right of the browser window.**

2. **Click the Edit Profile button.**

   Both the website and mobile app have similar interfaces, even down to the Edit Profile button, offering you details to your profile.

3. **Both the browser and mobile app versions of your profile are featured in Figure 2-11. In the Website field, enter your Discord server's URL.**

4. **Click the Save button in the top-right corner of the Edit Profile window.**

   Your Discord server is now accessible through your Instagram profile.

FIGURE 2-11: The Edit Profile window in the browser (left) and mobile app (right) offer you a place to promote your Discord server.

WARNING

You may notice that on the browser interface only, *hashtags* — quick keyword links that offer you a variety of accounts that share in common this particular tag — are active. It would be a safe assumption that, much like with Twitter, you could throw in a URL here and leave the Website option for another location online. Unfortunately, Instagram does not work that way. In User Profiles, again only those accessed through desktop browsers, only hashtags are active.

This is one way to bring attention to your Discord using Instagram. An open invite to your server is awesome for the Instagram audience. If they are enjoying the media you're sharing, it's a safe guess that they will want to know more about you, and what better way (apart from following you in Instagram, of course) than to offer them a link to your Discord server?

But what about using Instagram itself? Can you use the platform to let people know of your online community? Sure, you can. And if you're crafty about it, you can boost the word across multiple platforms with one image.

1. **Go into your Instagram app and tap the "+" symbol, located at the center of the app's toolbar running at the bottom of the screen.**

2. **Either capture an image or find a photo in your smartphone's camera roll, something you think personifies your Discord server.**

   A picture representing your Discord could really cover anything from the avatar representing your server to popular channels there.

3. **Tap the Next option in the upper-right corner of the app, and apply one of Instagram's filters or edit the photo's appearance.**

4. **Tap the Next option and then write a suitable caption for the photo.**

   Make sure to include the invitation to your server in the post.

   For the example shown in Figure 2-12, my caption reads:

   Heading somewhere special? Want to share your photos of places you've visited? In my Discord at [insert Discord server URL here] I feature a #travel channel where members are invited to post photos and video of their travels across the country and around the world. Pay us a visit and join me in TheTeeMonster's Not-So-Secret-Lair today! #discord #chat #community

FIGURE 2-12: Share an aspect of your Discord on Instagram and cover several platforms with a single post.

Under the Add Location section of the post are other platforms you can choose to post to at the same time as Instagram:

- Facebook
- Twitter
- Tumblr
- Mixi

5. **Choose which additional platforms you want to post (following the steps to link the platform to your Instagram account) and then select the Share option.**

URLs posted in Instagram posts are not active. You may notice, though, that other IG users will include links in their posts regardless. This is because when you cross-post, the URLs featured in your post will be active in their external destinations.

There is an ongoing debate between social media professionals on *cross-posting*, when one platform posts simultaneously on other platforms. Whether you perceive the approach as being lazy or efficient, cross-posting is a common practice. The ability to cross-post is offered across many apps, so take advantage of this if you want to want to boost the signal and extend the reach of your Discord server.

Take caution that any platform you utilize to promote your Discord server (or anything you want to promote, for that matter) suffers from a possibility of *overpromotion*. Although putting your Discord server in a profile is *passive* and is perfectly acceptable because it is always available without being overbearing, promoting your server in new posts and content can be seen as *aggressive* marketing. If all your posts become a link for your Discord or Nightbot is constantly spamming your Chat with a Discord link, your promotion could work against you. Just remain aware of it.

Blog and website menus

Circulating an invitation to your Discord server can occur on any platform that allows you a URL in a profile. This is how promotion of your server should go: If there is a place where you can offer people access without having to push your Discord too hard on them, take advantage of that.

One subtle way of promoting and offering access to your Discord is to offer this permanent invitation as a remote destination link on your website or blog. For example, Open Broadcasting Software (`https://obsproject.com`) offers a link to its own Discord as part of its website menu. Other developers, corporations, and other organizations will put in a Discord invitation at the bottom menu of their websites, found either under Community or Contact Us sections.

If you have a web designer working on your site or if you are using a WordPress template (and each template handles menus differently), think about where your invitation would fit.

Let's dive into a specific template in WordPress and see how it offers a way to publicize a Discord server.

1. **Log into your WordPress Dashboard by entering** `http://[yourwebsite]/wp-admin` **into your browser (if you are hosting your website/blog independently), or use WordPress.com to access your Administrator's panel for your blog.**

   The template you will be working with is the Author Pro theme. You can download this (and other free and professional themes) at `https://www.studiopress.com`, which offers technical support for its themes and frameworks.

2. **Look for the Appearance option in the left menu, and select Customize from that drop-down menu.**

   As stated before, each template can offer a different user interface, so the steps featured here may vary.

3. **Click the Menus option, and select your menu where social media links are featured.**

   The template in Figure 2-13 has a menu labeled Follow Me, which is a sub-menu featuring my social links.

4. **From the Menu interface, click the + Add Items button and add to your menu a Custom Link option.**

5. **In the Custom Link option offered, enter your server invitation in the URL field, and Discord in the Navigation Label field.**

6. **Click the small triangle next to the Custom Link label to collapse the item's options, then place your cursor on the Discord option you just created and click and drag the Discord option to where you would like it to appear.**

   The preview on the right side will update whenever changes occur.

7. **Click the Publish button, located near the top left, to accept the changes and make them live.**

FIGURE 2-13:
In the Author Pro theme from StudioPress.com, a social media menu can be edited on the left-hand side of the browser window while a preview is rendered on the right.

Now with the basics of how to make a simple post and how to let people know you have a server, you begin the process on developing a community. You might think this is a piece of cake, right? Just go on, invite people to the server, and start talking.

In a perfect world, yes, this would be everything you would need to know on how to make a Discord happen; but it's not that simple. This is the Internet, after all, which means you have to deal with the bad and the ugly along with the good. Let's take a deeper look in how you're talking on Discord, what you are sharing, and how to take steps in protecting your growing community.

Chapter **3**

Straight Talk

W e're starting to put together a place for your community. We have our Discord all set up, channels established for discussions, and avenues where the invitation is accessible to all. These are the first steps in putting together a server.

The tricky thing about the Internet, though, is *how* we talk to one another; and the Internet does not make that easy. When you are online, be it with email or with social media, it is tricky to get intention and inflection right. For some platforms, you have a choice of either upper-and-lowercase and ALL CAPS which really doesn't go far because AFTER ONLY A FEW ALL CAPS YOU HAVE TO WONDER WHY WE ARE YELLLNG??? LIKE WE'RE AT THAT PARTY IN COLLEGE WHERE THE DJ IS DROPPING A BEAT THAT YOU CAN FEEL IN YOUR SHOES AND YOU'RE LEANING INTO A FRIEND'S EAR AND SHOUTING, HOPING THEY HEAR YOU! GOOD TIMES, AM I RIGHT???

Discord offers a lot of different ways to communicate with one another, ranging from simple formatting tricks for your messages to the wide variety of media sharing available. As members of Discord, we should take advantage of this formatting in order to make sure the intent of our message is clear. There are a lot of features built into Discord to help us along, and they are there for a reason: to make us better communicators.

Formatting Text

It may not seem like a big deal having the ability to format text, but there are some real advantages to taking those extra seconds to drop in a few characters and add emphasis to your text messages. This extra touch from Discord, for me, is one way that the platform wants to help you get your message across as best as you can in a non-verbal, non-visual medium.

1. **Go to your #general channel and select the Edit Channel icon (the gear wheel) to access the Overview option.**

2. **Rename your channel here from General to Welcome, and click the green Save Changes button at the bottom of your screen.**

3. **Select the Permissions option and select the green check mark for the following:**

   - Create Invite
   - Read Messages
   - Use External Emojis
   - Add Reactions

4. **For the remaining settings in Permissions, select the red X and click the green Save Changes button at the bottom of your screen.**

   These settings, just to remind you, grant specific permissions to this channel. You are setting up the Welcome channel to be read-only and editable by you and you alone.

5. **Return to your Discord.**

6. **Still in the Welcome channel, enter the following text into the message field (see Figure 3-1):**

   A little law here on my server: If someone has a different opinion from yours, honor it. This is an issue I've seen *repeatedly* happen in Discord. There is a good chance some of you know *way more* about other things in the world than I do, and I learn a lot from all of you. However, if someone has a different opinion than yours, let it go. You don't have to agree with said opinion, but needling someone really isn't cool. If they get a fact wrong, then try to kindly offer a course correction. On the other hand, if what they get "wrong" is just an opinion (example: "I hated Season of the Drifter because I hate Gambit."), just let it go. Discord is a text-driven comm device and (like in an email) text is too easy to misconstrue.

My house. My rules. *Be excellent to each other.*

If you can't, then we have a problem and I will remedy it.

Thank you for respecting my Discord server, and each other.

To get a hard return/line break in a Discord message, use Shift+Enter on a desktop keyboard.

TIP

FIGURE 3-1:
The Welcome channel is a read-only channel on your server that offers newcomers to the server a rundown of the rules for discussion.

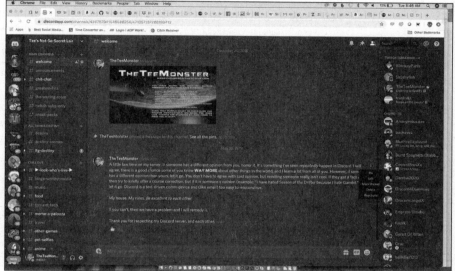

7. **Once you have the welcome message typed out, hit the Enter key or the Send icon to post your message.**

8. **Click the three vertical dots to the right of the welcome post you just created.**

9. **From the drop-down menu, select Pin to keep this post at the top of your Welcome channel.**

When you *pin* a message in Discord, this message is always found at the top of a channel. Pinning a message makes it easy to find in a channel.

Similar to pinning a message on Twitter (or any other social media platform), only one message can be pinned at the top of a channel.

WARNING

This is a #welcome message crafted for your server. You are more than welcome to rewrite this in your own voice, as this draft comes from my Discord; a #welcome should come from your voice, not mine. It should set the groundwork for your community so if any post needs to be crystal clear in its intent, it's this one. I return to the importance of the #welcome channel in Chapter 7 but I'm breaking this one down purely from a formatting perspective.

You should notice in the post different kinds of text formatting. Discord offers you the following attributes for text:

>> **_italics_:** Placing text between a pair of underscores will italicize text. You can also italicize text by using a single asterisk on either side of your text.

>> ****bold**:** When you use double asterisks, any text appearing between the two pair will be bolded.

>> *****bold and italics***:** For additional emphasis, you can simultaneously bold and italicize text by using a set of three asterisks on either side of the text you wish to format.

>> **~strikethrough~:** Strikethrough can always be fun when you want to show a sudden change of thought or illustrate how a change in one draft can differ from another. To do this, you surround the stricken text with a *tilde*, created by using the Shift key and the key to the left of your 1 key.

>> **__underlining__:** Similar to italics, you can underline text by using a pair of underscores on either side of a body of text.

WARNING

Old habits die hard. When people see underlined text, it is perceived that whatever is underlined is a link. Even though links are not underlined in Discord, it is something that happens often. Underlined text might earn you a few postings of "Hey, do you know this link is broken?" from visitors. Also, underlined text can sometimes be hard to read. Use the underline markup sparingly, and at your own risk.

It may seem to be a small thing but formatting can make a huge difference in your posting's intent. Take, for example, if you were to reply to someone's post:

You can't be serious right now? Do you hear the words coming out of your head?

There could be a thousand ways to take the tone and intent of this particular thought, but you can clarify with the right amount of formatting:

You *can't* be serious right now? Do you *hear* the words coming out of your head?

Just in applying italics, the tone changes. And then there are emojis available to you just by clicking on the smiley face off to the right. Drop a laughing face, and people know you are kidding. Drop an angry face, and your intent is made clear. Yeah, this may come across as a weird detail to point out, but there is a good reason why you have so many emojis to choose from. It's a final touch to help you fine-tune your tone, so consider using them.

PLEASE TAKE THAT TONE WITH ME

When you want to make sure your i's are dotted and your t's are crossed, it is a good idea to have a friend keeping your grammar and spelling in check, especially in today's day and age of self-appointed Grammar Police patrols waiting and watching for a chance to pounce. This is why Grammarly (https://www.grammarly.com) is available on a variety of platforms from an app on your phone to an extension for the browser of your choice. Grammarly is best known for checking spelling and grammar usage in real time when in use on your smart device or in Chrome, Safari, Firefox, or whatever you use to go from one site to another. If you are working online, though, be it on a social media platform, Gmail, or the like, you might have noticed a Tone Detector suddenly appearing at the end of your message. Currently in beta at the time of this writing, Grammarly's Tone Detector is part of your browser extension, working with you to make sure that you are striking the right note with your thoughts.

As mentioned before, it is too easy to misconstrue what is being said online; so Grammarly is not only wanting to help you make sure the spelling and grammar are on the level, the app is also working on making sure the right message is getting across.

With the ability to make sure a message is clear in its intent with just a bit of formatting, the next thing to do is to strike up a conversation. Whether it is your own Discord server or someone else's, you want to make your connections here personal.

Talk to Me: Making a Discord Post Personal

The etiquette of an online discussion is neither written down nor stringently practiced. Even with this book. It's pretty casual on Discord, and probably always will be. For a server starting off, some channels can afford to be. It would not be uncommon to see a conversation run like this:

Allora: Do you have a ship for Bakugou?

Sonny: Yes.

Allora: Who with?

Sonny: Kirishima.

Allora: XD same as everyone.

Sonny: Only logical ship.

Yeah, these kids and their anime.

This is how a conversation would go on a server's channel that tends to be quiet or has intimate (a nicer way of saying *slow*) traffic. As I have said before, all servers start somewhere; and in these early days, you might see a few chit-chats sound like this.

When your popularity, and in turn your server's traffic, picks up, you might find conversations like the above may look and feel entirely different:

Allora: Do you have a ship for Bakugou?

Sonny: Yes.

Allora: Who with?

Sonny: Kirishima.

SunSun: Hey, Tee — how's it going?

Sonny: Only logical ship.

TheTeeMonster: Not a lot. Trying to stay out of trouble. Are you headed to MAGFest this year?

Sonny: Yes.

Allora: Who with?

SunSun: I think Mer Mer and TheBigMarvinski are rooming with me.

Allora: XD same as everyone.

TheTeeMonster: Cool!

Sonny: Only logical ship.

As you incorporate a new conversation, the lines between who is talking to whom become blurred. It can be a difficult to keep track of what comment pertains to which subject.

No, there are no concrete rules on how to talk to one another on Discord, but Discord wants to help you make sure your shout-outs are heard by the right people. There's a simple way of making sure your posts and replies are reaching the intended party — *tagging*. When you want to make sure a specific person or a group of people will see a message, use their username to tag them.

1. When you visit a server's channel or see a comment on one of your channels you want to specifically reply to, or if you see a familiar name pop up somewhere in Discord that you want to say hello to specifically, type the @ symbol into the Message field.

2. In the drop-down menu that appears (see Figure 3-2), find the name that you want to direct your comment to and select it.

   If you do not see the name you want to reply to directly, begin to type out the person's screen name. When you see it, select it.

   Discord will automatically include the four-digit unique ID associated with the username.

REMEMBER

Screen names can sometimes differ from your username. If you notice in Figure 3-2, some of the names on the left differ from the names on the right. Under *Server Settings > Members,* users and moderators can change screen names to either their actual names or a different title altogether by selecting the *Change Nickname* options from the drop-down menu on the right. The ability to who can change nicknames can be found in the server's *Permissions* options.

FIGURE 3-2:
When you want to make sure a posting reaches a specific person, select that person's username from a drop-down menu offered once an @ symbol appears in the message field.

3. **After the username appears in the field, compose your message.**

4. **Click the emoji icon at the far right of the Message field to add in an emoji with your message.**

5. **Press the Return key to post your message.**

Whenever you are directly replied to on Discord, the message is highlighted in order to grab your attention from the many other messages appearing on the thread. Although your reply may not be highlighted, any tagged with your username should be difficult to miss.

Tagging members in Discord posts assures you control in your conversations, making sure you know who is seeing your message and what you're responding to, provided the origin of the conversation (also called the *thread*) is referenced. Discord takes steps to help all its members communicate clearly. Discord also wants you to be able to communicate *efficiently.* What if you have news you want to get out to a lot of people? And depending on the popularity of your server, you might need to tag a *lot* of people. Or what about tagging a specific group of people in your community?

TIP

GETTING NOTIFICATIONS

You can always have Discord notify you when replies are sent to you specifically in a server by going into the Settings of a Discord server you have joined. Go to the drop-down menu associated with a server, and select the Notifications Settings option. Selecting the Only @mentions option from the server Notifications Settings sends notifications to either your desktop or mobile device when you are tagged in a discussion. I go more into working with Discord on mobile devices in Chapter 4, and setting up when and how you receive notifications from Discord in Chapter 7.

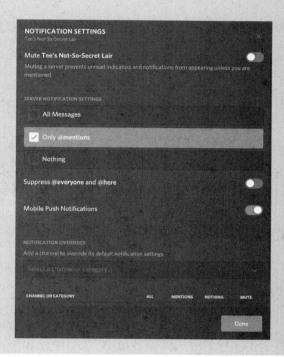

Role-in', Role-in', Role-in': Roles in Your Community

With any kind of community you build, there are going to be facets that will form. If you set up a Discord that is dedicated to gamers, you may have gamers that are on specific platforms like PS4, Xbox, Stadia, or PC. If you are a member of Kappa Kappa Psi *(Kay-PSSSIIIII!!!)* and organizing your chapter, you'll have officers, points-of-contact for various projects, and pledges. If your community is growing and you need to add a little bit of organization, then you need to assign to your server members *roles*.

Roles are titles that comes with specific permissions for what you can do in a specific server. By default, you have one role all set and ready to go in Discord: @ *everyone*. This is your default role, applied to everyone (including you) in this server. What you presently need is a Moderator role, an entry level role assignment for people in your community, and finally role assignments in order to quickly reach out to groups in your server with a single tag.

The Big Kahunas: Moderators

Moderators (or *Mods*, as they are sometimes referred to) are those who lay down the law and make sure everyone gets along in the community. If someone is getting out of line in one of your channels and you, the founder of the community, cannot or don't want to deal with it, a mod can step in and take control of the situation before it gets any worse.

1. **Go to your server in Discord, select the drop-down menu to the right of your server's name, and from the menu, select the Server Settings option.**

2. **Click Roles, select the @everyone option, and scroll down to the Text Permission section to review your current settings.**

    The permissions you should note that are active by default:

    General Permissions:

    - Create Invite

    - Change nickname

    - Read Text and See Voice Channels

    Text Permissions:

    - Send Messages

    - Send TTS Messages

    - Manage Messages

    - Embed Links

    - Attach Files

    - Read Message History

    - Mention @everyone, @here, and All Roles

- Use External Emojis
- Add Reactions
- Send Messages

Voice Permissions:

- Connect
- Speak
- Mute Members
- Deafen Members
- Move Members
- Use Voice Activity
- Priority Speaker
- Go Live

Along with @everyone being your default role, this is the template from which all other roles are built from.

3. **Turn off the following permissions:**

- Create Invite
- Change nickname
- Send Messages
- Send TTS Messages
- Manage Messages
- Embed Links
- Attach Files
- All voice permissions

This is the going to be the base from which you build your roles.

4. **Click the green Save Changes button at the bottom of your browser window.**

5. **Click the + sign to the right of Roles, and scroll to the top of the "new role" you just created. In the Role Name field, call this** Moderator.

6. **Select a color to designate your moderators at a glance.**

7. **Activate all options under Role Settings, General Permissions, Text Permissions, and Voice Permissions (see Figure 3-3).**

With all the various permissions active, the Moderator (you) and anyone else you assign this role has full control of the server and its membership. Mods can now manage membership, messages, and medi on your server.

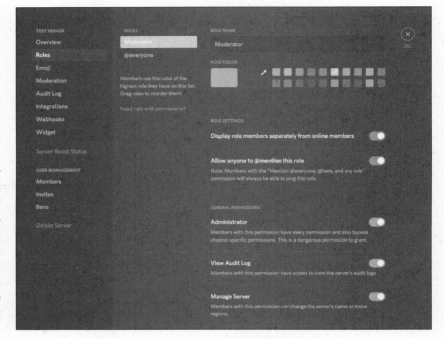

8. **Click the green Save Changes button at the bottom of your browser window.**

9. **Create a new role and call this one** Member. **Leave the color on its default white.**

10. **Activate the following options:**

- Create Invite

- Change nickname

- Read Text and See Voice Channels

- Send Messages

- Send TTS Messages

- Embed Links

- Attach Files

- Read Message History

- Mention @everyone, @here, and All Roles

- Send Messages

- Connect

- Speak

- Mute Members

- Deafen Members

- Use Voice Activity

11. Single-click the green Save Changes button at the bottom of your browser window.

12. Repeat Steps 9-11 and call this role USA. Assign it a color.

13. Repeat Steps 9-11 and call this role Overseas. Assign it a color.

You have now created four roles for your community. Your default role — @everyone — does not have a lot in the ways of privileges, but you will go on and remedy this as you assign roles to those in your server. Even yourself.

Your mission, should you choose to accept it: Assigning roles

Roles can be easily assigned to members of your community by you or by your mods. In the early stages of your server's development, you will probably want to keep an eye out for newcomers to your server. You can manually grant them the ability to post and interact fully with your community once you assign them the Member role.

And to assign roles, here's how you make that happen.

1. Go to your server name, and select from its drop-down menu the Server Settings feature.

2. In the User Management section, select Members to view all the current members of your server.

3. Click on the + to add the Member role to all your server members.

4. Go back through your server membership and assign the USA role to those members based in the United States.

5. Repeat Step 4, assign the Overseas role to those members based in countries outside the United States.

6. Once everyone in your server is assigned roles, assign yourself (and anyone you trust with your server) the role of Moderator.

7. Your Members page, when done, should resemble Figure 3-4 where everyone in your community has a role.

FIGURE 3-4:
Once roles are assigned — as seen here in my own server — you now have quick and easy ways and means of contacting groups within your community.

From here, you can see how roles could be assigned throughout your community. If you are using Discord as a way of planning a fund-raiser, you can assign roles like:

» Vendors

» POCs (Points of Contact)

» GOH (Gusts of Honor)

Then, with roles assigned, you can send out quick bulletins to those individuals with a @GOH or @Vendors tag. With the example provided for you above, if you are hosting a special giveaway, but only for those in the United States, you can send out a message to the @USA roles only, as the terms for your contest only apply to those on the United States mainland, Hawaii, and Alaska. However you organize them, roles allow you to communicate with groups formed within your community. (See Figure 3-5.)

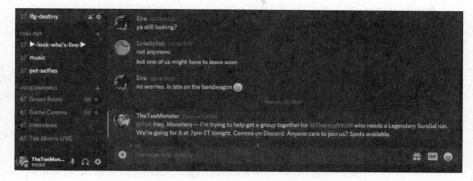

FIGURE 3-5:
By creating roles in a server, you can now send out concentrated "blasts" but only to specific factions of your communities.

TIP

Before assigning roles that change the access to a server, consider creating a role that duplicates another role, then on assigning the new role, change the older role for newer members to your server. This way, service is not disrupted to pre-existing server members.

Now hear this: Blasts with the @here and @everyone tags

While roles are convenient for factions within your community, there are certain situations that calls for you to grab everybody's attention. If you find yourself in one of those situations where you want to get the word out about something to a lot of people all at once, Discord offers two ways to talk to your community on a whole:

@here: Beginning a message with @here highlights your message and sends a notification to everyone currently online with Discord. So if you've got Discord running on a device of any kind, you will have a notification waiting for you that there is a post needing your attention.

@everyone: This is something like the Emergency Broadcast System for your server, and *should be used sparingly.* The @everyone tag highlights your post, just like the @here tag, but then sends notifications to all members of your server, including ones offline.

These two message blasters have their uses, and you should come up with a solid strategy of when and how to apply these options. If you're running a contest, but only want to reach those members who are currently online, then the @here tag will work best. If you know of an event you will be attending and want to put a call out like *Let's get together and have an unexpected meetup at this coffee shop!* to your server, then @everyone is a good idea for you to employ.

Regard the @everyone tag as something akin to the nuclear option of Discord. You should only use the tag when you deem it absolutely and completely necessary. It is also a good idea to make sure that permission to use the @everyone tag is reserved only for *moderators* and special roles designated by you.

1. **Go to your server in Discord, select the drop-down menu to the right of your server's name, and from the drop-down menu, select the Server Settings option.**

2. **Click Roles, select the @Members option, and scroll down to the Text Permission section.**

3. **Find the Mention @everyone, @here, and All Roles setting, and make sure it is turned off (see Figure 3-6).**

4. **If you have changed this setting, make sure you select the green Save Changes button at the bottom of your browser window.**

5. **Go back to the USA and Overseas Roles and repeat Steps 3-4.**

FIGURE 3-6:
By turning off the Mention @ everyone, @here, and All Roles (highlighted here) in specific roles, "message blasts" are contained to only the active channel, not the entire server.

Now, with these settings, only your mods are able to use the @everywhere and @ here tags. This means those you deem responsible enough to maintain your server and the community you're trying to cultivate will have the ability to use either tag, thus avoiding anyone wanting to aggravate your server with constant HEY! LOOK AT ME!!! posts which, yes, people will try to do because of the Internet.

REMEMBER

You can assign various roles to people, but bots can also automatically assign roles you create, and can assign these roles through reactions to certain posts or by other creative means. You do this later on in Chapter 7.

On Discord, you will find so many amazing ways and opportunities to connect and chat with one another. That is all fine and good, and this platform offers a lot of fun ways to share with each other, too. However, you might need to take a discussion out of the main threads and clock a little one-on-one time with someone. Some conversations are best kept private. Discord can make more sensitive, intimate conversations happen just as easily as the public ones.

Just Between Us: Direct Messaging

The importance of *direct messaging* you can see across all social media platforms. You have off-stream communications on Facebook, Twitter, and Instagram. Even in Twitch. There are times you want to share with the class, but there are those times you want to take a friend aside and say, *"Let's talk."*

1. **Go to any Discord server, be it your own or one where you are a member, and find the username of someone you want to message.**

Whenever you privately message someone, it is a good idea to have a rapport with them. If it is a friend you're reaching out to, you should be fine. If you only know this person you're messaging from Discord, keep things formal and polite.

2. **Click the person's name, bringing up the Profile window (see Figure 3-7).**

The Profile window offers several options for the username you just clicked. You can assign a role to this individual or make notes specific to this user. If you right-click a username, you have many more options to choose from.

3. **Located between the Note and ProTip options is a field offering you a place to write up a message to this user. Go on and type in a quick message here.**

TIP

If you don't know the person you are messaging well, a simple *Hi there!* or *Do you have a moment?* serves as a good icebreaker.

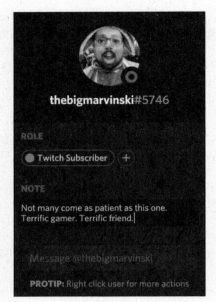

FIGURE 3-7:
The Profile
window grants
you the ability to
make personal
notes on the user
themselves
(where you met,
how you know
them, and so on)
as well as allow
you to send direct
messages.

4. **Press the Enter key to send your message.**

   Once you send your message, you should note a change in your browser
   window and UI. You have left the server and gone into the Home section.
   This is where you will manage all of your current and previous private conversations in a Direct Messages section located underneath your four main Home
   options.

5. **When a reply appears, you can go on and continue the conversation by
   typing in your response in the Message field.**

REMEMBER

   As this is a private conversation, you do not need to tag anyone else in this
   conversation. Simply type in your replies.

You still have the ability to do everything you can do in a normal conversation
thread — share links, images, media — but the chat remains out of the server and
only between you and your invited party. Some direct messages can include more
than two people. Clicking the + icon to the right of Direct Messages allows you to
create a Group DM for a party larger than two, if desired.

BEFORE YOU PRESS THAT ENTER KEY

Throughout this chapter, I have been discussing all the ways to get the tone and the intent of your messages just right. If you are wondering why I'm making such an issue of this, it is because while it can happen on any social media platform, miscommunication can happen on Discord without even trying. This trend of miscommunication can be easily traced back to email (which did lead to the mainstream popularity of emojis) where people would send a quick and simple reply, but depending on the mood you are in and how you are reading it, an innocuous reply can light a passionate argument online. It never hurts to reread your message to see if it could be mistaken in its tone.

Another problem with chat applications like Discord is stopping to ask yourself "Would I feel comfortable saying this in a room full of strangers?" before pressing the Enter key. Whether it is a joke between friends, a statement typed out in the heat of the moment, or speaking your mind on a subject that ignites your passion, you can post. The problem is how this bold statement you are about to make will reflect on you. And while you could always delete a statement that could be getting the wrong kind of attention, people have the ability to take screen captures.

It's just a good idea to have your internal editor always on high alert. The last thing you want to do is have something go viral for all the wrong reasons.

Security Clearance: Roles and Permissions Revisited

If you recall in Chapter 1, I covered a lot of ground on the settings in Discord. While I didn't dwell too much on the details of what these settings actually *do*, I did cover where all these nuances of a server could be found. Knowing where stuff is in Discord is half the battle in really unlocking the platform's potential, and assuring the server you run does not fall into complete disarray. I have covered a few of those settings in earlier exercises, and pointed out the subtle differences between a server's settings and your own account's settings. It wouldn't be a bad thing to get down and dirty in their details.

I know, I know. The last time anyone dealt with this many settings, it involved a lady with three dragons, a bunch of cranky zombies that brought the winter weather with them wherever they went, and a family that couldn't help but be a magnet for trouble. Seriously.

But you can manage this.

Let's first start by reviewing some of the permissions that you roles have. This is usually where ongoing security will be happening.

Runes of power: General permissions

The *moderator* (often times referred to as a *mod*) is you by default. When a server is set up, one of its default roles is moderator, assigned to the founder of the server. (Stands to reason, right?) So let's get a better understanding of what a mod does and what permissions he/she/they have over your server.

1. **In the Discord browser window, find your server name, click the drop-down menu, and select the Server Settings option.**

2. **Click Roles to return to the Roles section of your server.**

You may notice a difference in my server compared to your own. Along with roles like Moderators and Explorers (my own "Members" role), I have roles created by *bots* and *integrations*. Whenever you expand the capabilities of Discord, roles are automatically created to accommodate the new functionality.

3. **Click the Moderator role located under the Roles section and scroll down to the General Permissions section.**

Okay, there is a lot to unpack here. Strap in, everybody.

General Permissions is where you grant (or revoke) specific administrative responsibilities and privileges you deem certain roles should have. (See Figure 3-8.) There are quite a few just in this section, but it is important to identify each of them and briefly touch on what they do:

- *Administrator:* This one option basically grants any role in your server the same privileges as an administrator. You're basically copying the keys to your online kingdom and handing them to someone in your community. This is a big responsibility. (Even Discord points it out.)

- *View Audit Log:* This is an administrative role best suited for a developer who wants to know more about the API and how your server is running on Discord. This is a permission that is less about you having access to it and more about who in your community has access to it.

- *Manage Server:* This grants permission to change the server's name and the server's host. Again, this is a permission best left to either a moderator or higher in your community.

- *Manage Roles:* This allows users to assign, edit, and delete the various roles you have established in your community.

- *Manage Channels:* This allows anyone with this permission the ability to create, edit, and delete channels for your server. While this particular permission may seem trivial, it could get somewhat clumsy if people start creating multiple channels. This should be managed closely.

- *Kick Members:* This should be a permission granted only to moderators and administrators. If a member of your server is not acting in a manner conducive to the community, kicking a user removes them from the server. A kicked member can, however, rejoin a server with an invite.

- *Ban Members:* This is similar to Kick Members with one exception — banning members is permanent. Even with invites, a banned user cannot return to that server.

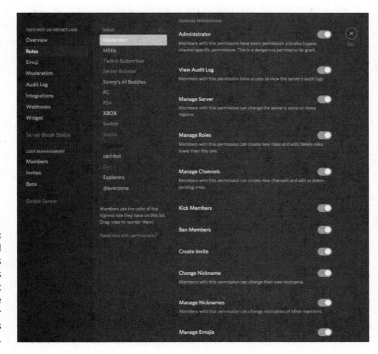

FIGURE 3-8: General Permissions grants roles different administrative rights over your server and its various members.

- *Create Invite:* If you prefer to keep invitations only as a perk of membership, and you are not promoting an open invite to your Discord, then you can offer your community the ability to generate invites, just as I discuss in Chapter 2.

- *Change Nicknames and Manage Nicknames*: Got any good inside jokes in your servers? (Mine is being called Twitch Dad by a portion of my server members.) You can grant yourself and others in the server a new nickname with these permissions active.

- *Manage Emojis:* This may sound like a trivial permission, but any role with this active offers up some creativity for the server. Anyone with this permission can create custom emojis for servers they have joined. With Discord Nitro (discussed in Chapter 4), you can even animate your custom emojis.

- *Manage Webhooks:* You may see the term *webhooks* used throughout your Settings, so you may be wondering what they are. Webhooks work with another website to generate URL messages from the second website that will automatically pop up on your Discord server, similar to how you see custom pop-up messages when new members join. A good example of this is how pull requests from GitHub (`https://github.com`) can appear automatically on your server, provided webhooks are in place. For developers, webhooks are fun to play with in Discord.

- *Read Text Channels & See Voice Channels:* While you would expect this permission to be active for your mods, Read Text Channels & See Voice Channels does what it advertises. Instead of showing the server as locked (until you join), channels are invisible so you know what people are talking about (but you cannot see the conversations).

Take a deep breath. You made it through defining General Permissions. Don't worry — the other sections are not as robust as this one. Understanding what all these permissions allow is where you start working out the minutiae of your roles. What exactly are you going to allow for your server members? Are certain roles created coming with different privileges?

And there are still more permissions I haven't covered.

Thing is, I have to cover these permissions as they serve as major tripping points for those new to Discord. Yeah, I am diving deep into the details, and I'm doing this so you can be sure the server is under control. A successful server means a lot of voices are speaking up to be heard. You want to make certain, though, at the end of the day, the server is still *your* server.

Smart talk: Text permissions

We have already covered the General Permissions for our server, and we have Text Permissions and Voice Permissions. We will be covering audio and video features in Chapters 5 and 6, respectively, but Text Permissions as we are still in our Role permissions is up next.

Text Permissions are similar to the General Permissions in that roles are granted to members of your server. However, as General Permissions cover your server and how members communicate on your server, Text Permissions are focused on how much you can share and exactly what you can share. There are a good amount of them, but easy to figure out.

>> *Send Messages:* Truth in advertising. Without this permission, you can't send text messages. Boom.

>> *Send TTS Messages:* If you have members that rely on Text-to-Speech to receive messages, this option will grant that to any message using the /tts command in the chat field.

>> *Manage Messages:* If you have messages in channels that you would prefer *not* to be online or if you want messages to be pinned at the top of channels for whatever reason, this permission allows for that. This should be a privilege only allowed to moderators.

>> *Embed Links:* This allows for posting and sharing of links in posts.

>> *Attach Files:* This allows users to attach media to their posts.

>> *Read Message History:* If this permission is not enabled, then Discord members can only read threads within a current session. If you log out, close a window, or quit the mobile application, then a session is terminated. By having this on, server members can track back in a conversation. (This is good to have enabled for all roles.)

>> *Mention Everyone:* Anyone with this permission can use the *@everyone* and *@here* notifications. This permission should be limited to members carrying an administrative role.

>> *Use External Emojis:* For servers that are integrated with Twitch or servers that use custom emojis, this permission offers your members the ability to use other emojis in your server channels.

>> *Add Reactions:* Pictured in Figure 3-9 are Reactions, which appear as small emojis underneath a post with a small counter. Server members click Reactions to add to the sentiment. (Think of Reactions as Likes on Instagram or Twitter.) This function either enables or disables that feature for roles.

I will be covering the remaining voice permissions for Discord when I cover audio and video in Chapters 5 and 6.

REMEMBER

FIGURE 3-9:
By clicking the Reactions icon, located on the right side of a post, you access a drop-down menu of various emojis — both standard and custom — that can be used as a variety of responses to a post.

Perhaps you want to disable sharing of media if the media being shared is not up to your standards. (Yes, your server should have standards.) Perhaps you want to leave yourself as the sole moderator with a different authority role that has *some* of the responsibility but not *all* the responsibility. Remember, this is your server and users should be following your rules as well as the rules established by Discord. You can review Discord's Terms of Service at https://discordapp.com/terms, which is a good template to follow when taking your first steps into community management.

At this point, you should have full control over what will be your virtual coffee shop or Members Only treehouse club. And no, I would not be surprised at all if you have started tinkering with the audio and video features presently. But in the words of one of history's greatest sidekicks: *Don't worry, m'lord. I have a cunning plan.* My own cunning plan with Discord is to teach all the details of text messaging so the basics are covered.

So what's next? We're going to take all this communication and step it up to the next level. We're taking our server on the road.

2

Communication in Discord beyond Text

Chapter **4**

Discord beyond the Browser

O ur journey through Discord has been working with the communication tool through a browser. Doesn't matter the browser on your computer — Chrome, Firefox, Safari, or otherwise — Discord is working to help you build a community online, all rallying around your cause, whether it is your Twitch channel, your charity, or your tech service. And if you don't mind one more tab open in your browser, then working with Discord through your browser is more than okay.

As my friends will attest to, though, I am one of those people when it comes to working online. I think my record for leaving tabs open was 48. No, that's not a typo, nor is it an exaggeration. *Forty. Eight.* It's not necessarily something I am proud of, and yes, I get endless grief for it. I'm surprised friends and family have not staged some sort of intervention over it. The good news is, though, I am taking steps to try to break this habit.

One way Discord helps me keep my open tab habit in check is offering its platform accessible through means other than a browser. I don't think Discord is doing this for my benefit, mind you. I do think this is just par for Discord's course. Discord goes out of its way to make things easy. And you know — I dig that.

Using Discord on Your Desktop

If you have access to Discord on your browser then why bother with an app? A legitimate question that deserves a legitimate answer, and one that reaches back to my many decades (I'm old. Get over it. I do . . . every day.) working with computers, the Internet, and browsers.

When Netscape Navigator (now *there's* a blast from the past) first came on the scene, it had a pretty simple job: download and display websites. And in the early days of the Internet, that was a piece of cake. Then came the introduction of audio, video, and animation. Better, more powerful browsers were needed to keep up, and so came the emergence of more familiar players like Firefox and Safari. Then web designers collaborated with web developers to create *dynamic web content* where the displayed page would not only change in real time but the outside world could interact with said content. At the time of this writing, Google Stadia (https://store.google.com/us/product/stadia) launched with the promise that you could game whenever and wherever you wanted provided you have Google's controller, a Wi-Fi connection, and a powerful browser like Google Chrome (https://www.google.com/chrome). This kind of content delivery would have been thought impossible back in the time of Netscape Navigator. This is nothing short of amazing.

This is also asking a lot from your browser. *A. Lot.*

All this is why there is still a demand for stand-alone applications for web-based services and platforms like Discord. For example, I can watch *Twitch* (https://www.twitch.tv) on my laptop, and I usually do when I am watching from anywhere other than home. When at home, I am watching Twitch on the stand-alone app on AppleTV. Why? Outside of better picture and sound, a lot of performance demands are taken off my browser if I use the stand-alone app, allowing my browser to do more on other websites that lack a stand-alone component.

As a stand-alone app, Discord frees up your browser to do more while still offering you all the features of the browser-reliant app. (See Figure 4-1.) Even the app's interface is identical to the browser's. (Note the menu bar, unique to Discord, as opposed to your browser.)

What's even nicer is the transition between running the Discord stand-alone app and what you have learned up to this point is just remembering not to go to the browser but going to the Discord app. The UI is identical.

1. **Launch your browser of choice, and go to** https://discordapp.com.

   Discord offers you two options: Download for your OS or Open Discord in Your Browser.

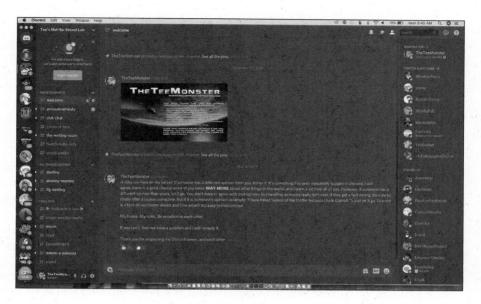

FIGURE 4-1:
Discord as a
stand-alone app.

2. **Select the Download for your OS option.**

Your browser should automatically recognize what your current operating system is, so click away. Depending on your security settings, you may be asked to confirm you're downloading something from www.discordapp.com, which, yes, you should allow.

3. **Once the Discord download concludes, open the package, and follow the steps to install it on your desktop or laptop.**

(Try not to blink. It's that quick and simple.)

4. **As soon as the install is complete, launch Discord, and log in with your credentials.**

After you are logged in, welcome to Discord. If you have a browser tab running Discord, feel free to close the tab. You won't need it.

Preferences ⌘,

Although you may think nothing is that easy with technology, that is all it takes to make the jump from browser to stand-alone app. All the menus, functions, and features discussed in previous chapters are still located where they were in the browser version. One little shortcut to note, though, is that your Account Preferences can now be accessed by the Preferences option in the menu bar.

From this point, we will be working with either the stand-alone app for your desktop or laptop, or working with the mobile version of Discord. Their features are all identical to the browser version, but if there are any differences, I will let you know.

Working with the Desktop Discord

Moving forward with Discord, it will really be your preference as to whether or not you want to work with the browser app or the desktop app. For myself, I prefer working with the desktop app as it frees up the browser from a few additional demands. (Especially in light of my bad habits.) Find a workflow that works best for you, and stick with it.

Let's say you decide that in one of the channels, sharing images may not be appropriate or is blurring the focus of the channel's topic. You know where to disable images on your server, but you don't want to necessarily disable images for *all* your channels. Just this one. Is that even possible?

Again, Discord is working hard to make sure you know "Oh yeah, we got this."

1. Take a look at your Discord app, and confirm you are in your server by checking the sidebar menu of servers you have joined off to the left.

A small white line should be to the left of your server's avatar, and the title of your server should be across the top of the column of channels.

2. Roll your cursor slowly over your channels.

You should notice the channel light up with two icons appearing off to the right. The one that looks like a person's silhouette is the Invite Friends option, while the gear wheel is the Edit Channel option.

The Invite Friends option is yet another shortcut to inviting friends in your Friends list or creating an invitation URL for your server. The Edit Channel option, which is what we will be focusing on in this exercise, allows us to grant or deny permissions that the server has but you may wish to change for an individual channel. Anything you change here only affects the channel as opposed to an entire server.

3. Select a channel and click its Edit Channel option. Take a look at the Overview for this channel, seen in Figure 4-2.

Overview offers quick, basic details of a channel. Under this option, you can set up a few parameters that will affect the channel, but not the server on a whole:

- *Channel Name:* The title of your channel. Regardless of what you call your channel, it always appears in this format. If you want to rename your channel, it's here.

- *Channel Topic:* A quick summary of what the topic of this channel is.

- *Slow Mode*: If traffic gets a little too busy, Slow Mode puts a time limit on the amount of times someone can post within a pocket of time. This is a great deterrent for anyone attempting to spam a channel with content you would rather not share.

- *NSFW Channel:* In case you are setting up a channel that may offer up content that might make your grandmother — or as NSFW suggests, associates at the office — the NSFW (which stands for *not safe for work*) Channel will have anyone visiting the channel offer up a warning about the content shared here before viewing the channel.

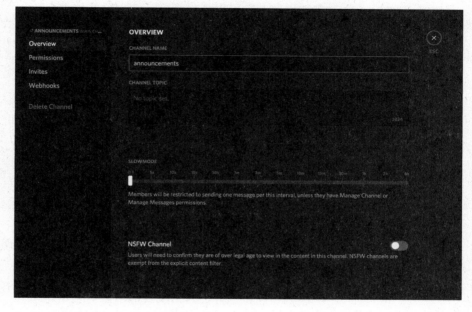

FIGURE 4-2: The Edit Channel option is a series of preferences, allowing you to make individual changes to channel behaviors without affecting the entire server.

4. **Click the Permissions option, and scroll to review the various options available (see Figure 4-3).**

   If these options look familiar to you, it's because you worked with them in Chapter 3. These are a repeat of the Permissions you dealt with earlier, but with a slightly different interface. Instead of the On/Off switch, you have three options:

   - *Permission Denied:* Permission is denied for this action.
   - *Permission Neutral:* The permission, by default, is allowed.
   - *Permission Granted:* Permission is allowed for this action.

   As you can assign to individual channels moderators or any of the other roles you have created for the server, you can now designate which roles have certain permissions over others. If you are not assigning individual roles by channel, you can leave these permissions on the neutral setting, granting that permission to everyone or every role present.

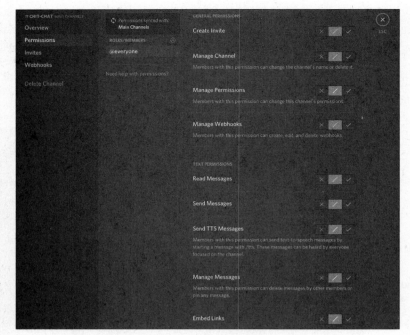

FIGURE 4-3:
When editing a channel, preferences and roles can be assigned without affecting the server on a global level. This allows for delegation of responsibilities for the various roles you create.

5. Click the Invites option to review any invitations sent from this channel.

6. Click the Webhooks option to review any active or applied webhooks specific to that channel.

Based on the activity of a channel, you can go through your server and designate specific roles as you would for the entire server, only make the roles specific for that channel. For a review of roles, skip back to Chapter 3. Roles, you may think are limited to just assigning someone a Moderator role, but some Discord server take roles to a higher level of organization.

A good example of channel-specific assignments is best seen with Twitch Streamer and Discord diva, SheSnaps (https://mindofsnaps.com), and her incredible community. (See Figure 4-4.) Snaps on her Snap Pack server offers channels covering pets, fashion, music, photography, working with disabilities (both physical and mental), affirmations, relationships, men's and women's issues, LGBTQI+, food, self-care, theatre, movies, and . . .

Wait, was that a kitchen-sink channel I saw?!

With more than 75 channels of content, it's a wonder that Snaps has time to manage her Discord server along with making time for her wellness and gaming streams, her awareness advocacy for mental health, her photography, and all of her many multifaceted pursuits in life. Well, she doesn't. She turns to her community for help. Members of her community like me.

FIGURE 4-4:
Jessy a/k/a
SheSnaps is host
of a massive
Discord
community, and
reaches out to it
on occasion when
she needs help in
moderating
channels.

I got a message from Snaps asking if I would be interested in taking on a moderator role for her #creative-writing channel. Always happy to talk shop, I went on and agreed. Snaps then went on and established me as a mod *specifically for this channel* dedicated to writing. Had this feature not been available, she would have needed to grant me moderator privileges over *all* her channels. While Snaps does trust me, even that would be a leap to take. With Discord proactive strategy on channels and moderators, I only hold mod privileges in one channel.

Thanks, Discord!

As you can see here with the desktop app there is no difference between working with it and the browser version of the app. At least, there's no difference *that you can see*. Working independently of the browser, you can now allocate more or less memory to the application as you deem needed. You're not placing more demands on your browser which will make the browser on a whole perform more efficiently, and your Discord will also perform more efficiently when standing on its own. Depending on how busy Discord keeps you, you can find your preference of having Discord either as a stand-alone app on your desktop or as an open tab on your browser.

The demands on your browser are not so rough when you are using Discord for text communications and media sharing. When you add in audio and video, though, you are pushing its limits considerably. If you know you will be turning to audio and video on Discord, then download the stand-alone app in order to allocate the resources you need for smooth and clear communications. I cover audio and video in Chapters 5 and 6, respectively.

That phrase *depending on how busy Discord keeps you* is something to consider the larger your community grows. Although SheSnaps's Discord looks and sounds overwhelming, she is not an anomaly. There are quite a few busy, robust Discord servers online, and when you are managing an active, busy server, you need to keep an eye on it. That can be hard, even with the stand-alone app, if you are not close to a computer.

But if you have solid data connection, Discord is still available to you, just in case your community comes a-calling.

Using Discord on the Go: Mobile Options

Our first steps with Discord have kept us tethered to a laptop or desktop machine. Not uncommon, but in today's mobile device climate where data is demanded at a moment's notice, it would not be a bad thing to expect the same kind of delivery of our server.

And Discord delivers for iOS and Android, without fail. The mobile app, much like the stand-alone and browser app, offers

>> Sharing of URLs, video, audio, and images

>> Push notifications

>> Invitations from servers and channels

>> Multiple server and channels support

>> Audio and video chat (group and private)

>> Private text messaging

The mobile app offers a lot of the features you find in the desktop and stand-alone app. While there are some features unavailable with the mobile app, the biggest difference between it and the desktop/stand-alone app is how features are accessed.

Let's work with organizing your servers along the left side. You'll not only learn an organizational skill but also be introduced to how to manage your way through Discord's smartphone app.

REMEMBER

Although "mobile devices" covers iPads, Surfaces, and other tablets, the apps for tablets are identical to the stand–alone desktop apps. Tablets have a bit more screen real estate to play around with. The jump from desktop to tablet app is easy. Here, we are focusing on smartphones as screens are smaller, making app developers conceive ingenious ways to offer the same options as their desktop counterparts.

1. **If you haven't already, go to where you normally download mobile apps (Apple's App Store, Google Play, and so on) and download the latest version of Discord for your smartphone.**

2. **Once installed, launch the Discord app and sign in.**

When you first log into the Discord mobile app, you should notice the *UIs* (user interfaces) are identical to one another. If, however, you are looking at only text, Discord is picking up in the mobile app where you left off in the desktop or browser app. Simply touch the top-left icon of *Server Lists* (it will be three lines, marked sometimes with an alert for unread messages across all your servers) to reveal all channels in your active server as well as a list of servers you are a member of.

3. **With your list of servers visible in the mobile app, tap and hold one of the servers you have joined, drag the selected icon up and down along your listed servers, and place this server on your list in an order of priority you want to give it.**

The sorting you give servers is more for your benefit. Messages will still come in on a first-come-first-serve manner, and @mentions to you will be sorted and signaled accordingly. Organizing your servers here is a visual aesthetic.

4. **Repeat Step 3 to sort all your servers into an order that best suits your evolving workflow on Discord.**

5. **Tap and hold one of the servers you have just sorted, and drag the selected icon on top of another server.**

A small gray box should appear behind the server icons.

Release the server to see it grouped with the other server.

Group folders (see Figure 4-5) are used to sort servers in a way that will be easy for you to organize servers by handy, custom categories when your network begins to grow.

6. **Tap and hold another server, and drag the selected icon into the group folder you just created.**

FIGURE 4-5:
To adjust settings
in group folders,
open the folder
and then tap and
hold the folder
icon to view the
options menu.

7. Repeat Step 6 until you have grouped the servers you want to have grouped.

8. Repeat Steps 5–7 until your Discord server list is organized accordingly.

TIP

If you have grouped a server but prefer to move or remove the server from that particular folder, tap one of the folder collections you have created. Tap and hold the server you want to move, and drag the selected avatar out of the group.

Whenever you see a folder icon with server avatars underneath it, this means you are looking at an open group folder.

9. In the group folder you just opened, tap and hold the folder icon.

An options menu slides into view.

10. Tap the Folder Settings option.

11. In the Folder Name field, come up with a name for this particular grouping.

12. Tap the swatch of color under Folder Color, select a new color, and tap Save to accept this selection.

13. Tap Close in the upper-left corner and then tap the folder icon to close the group.

14. Repeat Steps 9–13, selecting different colors for each grouping.

In all versions of Discord, your group folders are now color-coded.

If you want to access any of the preferences of your Discord servers, tapping either the + or ⋯ icon will reveal the various options I have already covered in this book so far. As you see with this particular exercise, you can touch and hold an icon (a group folder, for example) and access additional options. Working more and more with the Discord app reveals there are minor differences between the browser app, the stand-alone app, and this mobile app. Discord has worked really hard to make the transition from browser app to stand-alone app to mobile app seamless. It's really well done and very easy to navigate. You can create channels, organize them into categories, and manage servers however you like. You can even join and create new servers, and upgrade your server to Nitro.

There are a few subtle differences between the mobile app and its counterparts. At the time of this writing, though, the mobile app cannot access the Activity feed. Rollover hints and, as shown in Figure 4-6, labels for your various group folders are visible on the browser and desktop versions of Discord, but not so much on tablets and smartphones are there is no "cursor" available. Moving back and forth between the three interfaces though has been designed to be easy. The more you work with the smartphone app, transitioning will come easier.

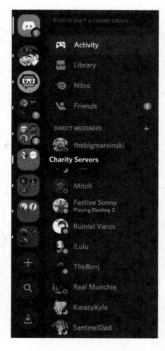

FIGURE 4-6: On the desktop and the browser app, different group folders reveal their labels when you roll your cursor over them.

You can also make your Discord experience better by something mentioned only a paragraph ago — *upgrading to Nitro*. Exactly what does that entail and why would you even want to make that jump?

Leveling Up: Discord Nitro

The more you work with Discord, the more you realize just how robust and powerful this free platform is. So many possibilities and applications come to mind the more you engage, the more you share. It's pretty cool.

Then you see references to something called *Discord Nitro*. (See Figure 4-7.) You may see it when attempting to upload media. You may be nudged to upgrade if you want to try uploading animated emojis. Discord Nitro is a special subscription service that grants special perks to a server and comes in two flavors — *Nitro* and *Nitro Classic*. Although you still have all the features Discord is known for (channel discussions, audio and video chat, direct messaging), Discord Nitro Classic offers servers:

>> Animated avatars

>> Custom number tags (in order to make them easier to remember)

FIGURE 4-7: Discord Nitro levels up your server with more emotes, better bandwidth, and optimized file sharing, all for a monthly subscription price.

- ➤➤ Full use of your custom emotes (Twitch emotes, as an example) in other Discord servers
- ➤➤ Higher-quality screen sharing
- ➤➤ Uploading of files up to 50MB (default is 8MB)

WHEN YOU GIVE YOURSELF A BOOST

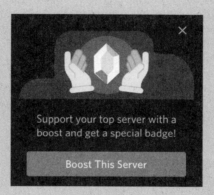

Exactly why would you give a server a boost? It does feel like something of a rabbit hole where you are spending money on something you were originally was told was free, right?

Well, it still is. Discord still offers you at no cost audio and video chat, the ability to share media between one another, and other cool things we have covered. However, *server boosts* allows you to do more with the basic features, the community rallying around servers (yours, your best friend's, your mom's, you get the idea . . .) and unlocking various *level perks*. With each level perk, your server unlocks new features. For example, you can stream directly from your Discord (called *Go Live*, which I discuss in Chapter 6) at a stream quality of 720p (the dimension of your stream, based on horizontal pixels) at 30fps (frames per second). With a Level 1 boost, your stream quality goes up to 720p/60fps. At Level 2, your resolution goes up to 1080p/60fps. There is a big jump between 720p/30fps and 1080p/60fps, and this is if you are streaming. Other perks include Vanity URLs, higher audio quality for media shared, unlocking of custom emoji slots, and more.

Think of the boost as upgrading from a PS4 to a PSPro. It's a step up in ways you may not see, but still benefit from.

Discord Nitro, the upgrade to the upgrade, along with all of the above offers:

>> Exclusive Nitro game perks that ramp up your experience on participating gaming titles

>> Server boosts where your server achieves level perks, unlocking new features

No, you don't have to upgrade your Discord to Nitro in order to carry out your plans for world domination, but just with the increase in the uploading cap, those plans to hack the planet have become far easier to achieve. How much media you are sharing on your server, and on others, may play in the deciding factor on whether or not you want to make this jump. If you are a gamer and want more out of your experience in Warframe, Minion Masters, or other games partnered up with Discord, then you may want to invest. Whatever your reasoning, Discord makes the upgrade pretty simple. And yes, affordable.

1. **Go to your Discord mobile app, look at the bottom menu of options, and tap your avatar at the far right to access your Account Settings, as seen in Figure 4-8.**

   You can join Discord Nitro on any version of the Discord platform, but as we are focusing on the smartphone app, let's use it to upgrade.

FIGURE 4-8:
In your Account Settings, found by tapping your avatar at the far right of the mobile app's menu, you can upgrade to Discord Nitro by tapping the Get Nitro option.

2. **Tap the Set Status option, and choose any of the options offered.**

   While we are in our account profile, let's take a look at our status. The following statuses we can set for public view on Discord:

   - *Online:* This shows if you are logged on an active. Selecting it here will keep you showing as Online even if you are inactive.

   - *Idle:* When you are online and inactive, Idle indicates that you are either *AFK* (**A**way **F**rom **K**eyboard) or online but just quiet. You can tap this option to make it permanent instead of reliant on Discord to turn it on and off for you.

   - *Do Not Disturb:* You're online, yes, but you are in an interview or having a private conversation. This option is the polite "Not right now" reply to people who want to engage with you.

   - *Invisible:* Sometimes you want to be online, but sometimes you don't want people to know. Welcome to Discord: Stealth Mode.

   - *Set Custom Status:* This allows you to create your own status. You can say you are "Working hard and hardly working" or use a "You're pretty awesome!" affirmation to make someone smile.

3. **When your status is set, tap your Profile in the background to return to it, and tap Get Nitro to begin the upgrade.**

   While your Set Status option is showing as Online you will see your Custom Status appear just underneath your Discord ID.

4. **Review the terms of Discord Nitro at $9.99 per month or Nitro Classic at $4.99 per month.**

   There are discounts offered if you select yearly contracts. It is up to you how much you want to invest in a Nitro account, and (of course) which plan you want to try.

5. **Tap the option you want to activate for your server and then complete the transaction steps.**

6. **Once your transaction is completed, provided you purchased Discord Nitro, boost your own server by returning to Server List at the far-left of your smartphone app's menu, or returning to your Account Settings main menu, both pictured in Figure 4-9.**

7. **Under the Server List view, tap the name of your server at the top of your screen to access server options. Tap the pink diamond to boost *your* server.**

FIGURE 4-9:
Boosting a server
can either be
accessed from
your Server List
(left) or Account
Settings (right).
(*Note:* Under
Account Settings,
the Get Nitro
option now reads
Manage Nitro
after you
subscribe.)

SERVER LIST
VIEW

ACCOUNT SETTINGS
VIEW

8. **Under the Account Settings view, tap the Server Boost option to boost
your server *or someone else's* server.**

When you purchase Discord Nitro, you are automatically rewarded two server
boosts to use for yourself or for other servers. Additional server boosts can be
purchased at a discount by Discord Nitro and Nitro Classic subscribers.

Once you finish the purchase, Discord announces on your general chat channel
that the upgrade has occurred. The effects are similar to throwing a switch, and
for the next month, you and your server should have the features discussed here.
Play around with animated emojis and avatars. Try uploading larger files. You
have a month to experiment with all these new add-ons to your server. If you like
what you can do with Discord Nitro, then you can renew your subscription or
invest into a full year of the extra bells and whistles.

An investment in Discord Nitro really is up to the individual. Deciding factors in it
may be in how you game or how much media you share. If you take advantage of
the streaming features coming with Discord (covered in Chapter 6) then that will
also lean you in direction or another.

Use of the server also will direct you in what kind of server you want to develop
and what kind of server you will eventually be hosting. One size does not always
fit all, and Discord may become for you or for your business something of a hub
for all your communications. This is why Discord comes to you in different flavors.

Serving Up Awesome: Server Types in Discord

The current server that you run on Discord is the most basic of servers. At this point of your education with it, you know that this server offers you a lot straight out of the box. Text chat, audio and video chat, private discussions, media exchange — these are all features we have covered or are about to cover in Discord, and now we have discovered that you and your community can reach out and help your server grow with a boost.

Another way your server can change, grow, or evolve is to be designated into a specific class or style of server by Discord itself. It is not necessarily something you hear server mods and Discord admins talk a lot about, mainly as this pertains to more behind-the-scenes management of a server. A really good Discord server never shows the man-behind-the-curtain unless they want you to or if they are offering you the opportunity to be the person at the Captain's Wheel.

Public servers

Right now, you are the admin for a public server. The public server is exactly what it sounds like. Even though you need an invitation to join a server on Discord, the server itself is still considered open to the public. The same features are there as you would find in any other server, and you can opt into Discord Nitro in order to unlock more features within your server. A public server is everyone's Square One when they join Discord. What happens once you turn your server on depends on the discussions you entertain in the various channels you create. Like any social media platform, a server's popularity rests on those involved in maintaining it. Each day offers you a new chance to invite new members into your growing community; and maybe — just maybe — cross those social streams, which wouldn't be so bad. I know, maybe Egon Spengler showed a lot of concern over crossing streams, but in the case of Discord, it's a good thing I'm telling you!

WARNING

When subscribing to servers, it may feel like you can join limitless servers but there is a limit. Discord allows you to join 100 servers. Once that limit is reached, you cannot join any additional servers unless some are purged off your current subscription list. Why 100? Apart from having a difficult time to manage 100 servers and their various channels (I struggle with the ones I am following at the time of this writing, and I lost count after 20!), the 100-cap is in place to avoid unscrupulous types from joining thousands of servers and suddenly spamming content, be it innocuous URLs to images that might make your grandparents blush. Your maintenance grows with each server you join so be aware that even Discord has limits.

Private servers

So, if the majority of Discord is running on public servers, then why do you hear some groups talk about their "private server" on the platform?

Well, technically, we set the groundwork for a private server back in Chapter 3.

Although we all start by default with a public server, a private server actually comes from administrators setting up preferences and permissions, and creating a Members Only role independent of the @everyone default role. (See Figure 4-10.) It is still the same server and same quality as described above, but administrators have taken steps to lock down the server in order to make it a very swish Executive Club server, velvet ropes and massive bouncer with just-visible South Pacific tribal tattoos optional.

And if all this sounds familiar, yes, you did this back in Chapter 3 concerning roles.

1. **Go to your Discord stand-alone app, tap the drop menu to the right of your server's name, and select the Server Settings option.**

   As you are making serious adjustments to a server here, it would be best to work with the stand-alone app.

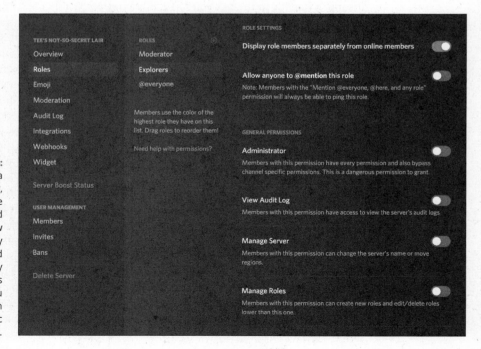

FIGURE 4-10: When creating a private server, the @everyone role is replaced with a brand new Members Only role (pictured here, from my own server, as "Explorers") you create with specific permissions.

2. **Go to the Roles option, and disable all permissions for the @everyone role.**

When you are done with Step 2, no permissions should be granted to this role. Make sure to check and double-check that all permissions are off for this role.

3. **Create a new Members Only role.**

4. **Start from the top of the Permissions, and begin granting the new Members Only role specific privileges.**

For this example, I have granted anyone in this role permission to

- Create Invites
- Read Text & See Voice Channels
- Send Messages
- Send TTS Messages
- Embed Links
- Attach Links
- Read Message History
- Add Reactions
- Connect
- Speak
- Use Voice Activity

You can either follow this recommendation or grant privileges you think are suitable for a base membership in your server.

When you launch a new server, you can go on and leave it as is, and the @everyone role applies to anyone who is not a Moderator or officer in your organization. By creating this default member role, however, you add an extra layer of security, and lay down the groundwork for additional "exclusivity" for other roles in the future. It all starts with how secure you want to make your server. Sometimes, sticking to what's simple works best. If, however, you are thinking ahead to how you want to manage your community, then consider making a jump from public to private in your server setup.

Verified servers

Anyone can make a server, and that server can be anything it wants to be on Discord. Let's say, however, that you and your server start to gain traction. When I mean traction, I mean thousands *on thousands* of people joining your corner of the Internet. Whatever your strategy is for Discord, in this particular hypothetical, it is working like gangbusters.

YES, IT'S PRIVATE, BUT NOT *THAT* PRIVATE

Perhaps in your own research independent of this title, you may have found that Discord does not necessarily emulate perfect harmony. There have been some servers created that promote toxicity, a problem often encountered when setting up a social platform. Everyone should have a voice; but when that voice turns malicious, what happens?

Discord, on August 15, 2017, drew boundaries.

The *New York Times* reported (https://www.nytimes.com/2017/08/15/technology/discord-chat-app-alt-right.html) Discord banning several communities known for promoting hate. "We unequivocally condemn white supremacy, neo-Nazism, or any other group, term, ideology that is based on these beliefs," said Eros Resmini, Discord's Chief Marketing Officer. "They are not welcome on Discord." Adding to this sentiment, Discord board member Josh Elman stated Reached after Discord's decision to ban alt-right groups, Mr. Elman said, "I believe every communication channel — public or private — has a responsibility to investigate and take action on any reports of misuse including harassment, inciting violence or hate, and other abuse."

Discord is a place where you make the rules. There is no perfect balance or ideal Nirvana here. People will be people, frailties and all. What is important is to remember is there are consequences with words and within the Community you encourage. Much like on your Channel, you have to decide what your rules in Discord are and how you intend to enforce them. Yes, the First Amendment is a right; but with that right comes a responsibility.

With success on the Internet, though, comes the inevitable: imitations and knock-offs.

Brand management is a cornerstone for whatever business you want to carry out, be it online, in the waking world, or both. People want to make sure they are working with the real Tee Morris, or actual *For Dummies* representatives, or a specific entity behind the foundation of a Discord server. Basic brand management involves a guarantee to people that if you are at a specific location or working with specific people that you are dealing with the brand represented, whether it is an individual or a large company. Are you at the official Discord for Bungie? Are you at my Discord? Are you at the Discord for iLulu? Are you at an official Discord representing *Fortnite* or *Call of Duty*?

If you are concerned about brand management, and have concerns about imitators tapping into your audience, then a verified server may be what you need.

Verified servers are similar to verified accounts on Twitter. When you reach a certain level, you can visit `https://discordapp.com/verification` and complete the application. There are a few basics that you should have covered:

>> The applicant must be an official representative of the individual or group as well as the owner of the server.

>> The applicant should be ready to offer detailed information on the individual or group necessary for verification.

>> The applicant should use a formal email address (not Gmail, Yahoo!, or even Hotmail) related to the individual or group and indicating that the applicant does, in fact, hold an official position with the individual or group.

>> The server submitted for verification should have active categories, channels, and both Channel and Role structures in place.

Provided you meet these four simple requirements, you are on your way to a verified server. Oh, yeah, there's more to applying for the verification than what's featured above, but with the above points covered, you are on your way. Once verified, your server will receive a few distinctions, like *Destiny*'s badge, pictured in Figure 4-11, which assures visitors and members of your community that, yes, this is the official server for a specific group of developers, a rock band, or a particular individual that has carved out a place for their fam online.

A verified server is definitely a worthwhile investment of time and resources if you want to assure your brand remains protected and trusted by those visiting Discord. Especially if you are a game development company, a performance group, a non-profit, or a corporate entity, the Verified Server separates the conversation occurring on your server from fan speculation and offers news straight from the source.

Partnered servers

If a verified server is an opportunity for your community to grow all while protecting your brand, then a partnered server is where Discord works with you to take your community to even greater heights all while Discord treats you like the superstar that you are.

Many of the perks you receive with a verified server you also receive with a partnered server, along with a few really cool extras:

» Exclusive partner badges, even more distinguishing than the verified badge

» Discord Nitro, provided by Discord on the house

» Improved audio servers, offering higher quality and stability in performance

» Exclusive Discord hoodies, as pictured in Figure 4-12, setting you apart from other Discord admins, provided you're not somewhere hot

» Revenue, generated from Discord Nitro transactions happening on account of your server's success

FIGURE 4-12: Getting partnered in Discord is not an easy feat. This is why when it does happen, Discord offers perks — including exclusive gear — to set you apart from the pack.

You are more than just a host with a partnered server. You become something of an endorsed representative of Discord, an example that other Discord communities should strive to emulate. It's a big deal, not to mention an achievement earned by a lot of hard work invested into making your server outstanding among the thousands on thousands on thousands of servers currently active on the platform. Sure, becoming partnered in Discord is a long and sometimes difficult road to navigate; but if you are looking for a destination in your own personal journey with Discord, here it is.

And even if you don't reach partner with Discord, think of the good times you will have on Discord along this journey. Whether you reach that goal or not, you are here, building relationships, communities, and friendships. Pretty cool, huh?

With servers defined and the various ways you can access Discord, you have the tools at the ready to build and develop a means of communications between you and your community. You can also look ahead to the potential of your server, and set goals for your community. Discord is offering you a place to cavll home on the Internet, and now you can access that community from everywhere and anywhere in the world, provided you have the data connection to do so.

So what do you want to say? What do you want to talk about? Think about what you want to say and what you want to share, then express yourself. And welcome to your growing community.

Chapter **5**

Audio Check

We have been spending the first four chapters of this book delving into the bare basics of this platform, and on the risk of sounding like a broken record — and with the resurgence of vinyl, I no longer have to worry about sounding old when using that turn of phrase — there is a *lot* to Discord. We've covered a lot of solid ground, and if you flip back through the previous chapters, you'll see we've been getting very familiar with all the various things we can do with text, with media sharing, and with the overall performance of our individual server. Let's just call it like it is: Discord is one amazing app.

But we haven't even touched on the features of *why* Discord was created. We've waited long enough then. Let's talk about *audio and voice chat.*

As mentioned at the very beginning in Chapter 1, Discord was originally created to offer to gamers an alternative to in-game networks. What Discord has evolved into is a clear, easy-to-mix, reliable audio communication platform for large groups. Discord offers an upgrade from other VoIP offerings, whether it is for game comms, audio conferences, or any other need for a group to convene from a variety of remote locations.

Of course, when it comes to working with audio on a computer, the demands on your computer or mobile device have increased, but resources on even the most basic of laptops and smartphones can handle the needs of Discord when working with real-time audio connections.

Sound Strategy: Audio on Discord

Setting up an audio conversation is pretty simple. We're going to take this basic approach and build on it, of course, but in most cases, everything you need is ready to go. Your laptop or tablet will already have a built-in microphone, and your smartphone had *better* come with a microphone, lest it is the *dimmest* smart-*phone* ever! So long as you know where everything is on your computer, what you will be using to carry out audio communications, and how to control it, figuring out the audio features of Discord is easy.

Making the call: Audio conversations

While we have one by default, we're going to create an audio channel just to get into the practice of the process. It's easy to set up and host a voice channel on Discord, but this is something of a two-part process. First, we are going to walk through the setup and engagement of a voice chat, then talk a bit about how to manage people coming in and out of your audio channel.

1. **Launch Discord on your computer or smart device of choice.**

2. **In your own server, scroll down to the Voice Channels section, and single-click the + icon to create a new channel for this category.**

3. **Select Voice Channel as the Channel Type, and give your new voice channel a name.**

   Call this new channel Open Comms, Game Comms, or some title that reminds you that this will be your main channel for voice chat. (For this exercise, as seen in Figure 5-1, we will use *Voice Comms* for the name of this new channel.)

4. **Click the Save Changes button, return to your Discord, and click the name of your voice channel to connect to it.**

   If you have not accessed your microphone before for any reason, you will be prompted to grant Discord permission to use your laptop's or smart device's microphone.

 5. **Once you see your own name appear, click the Create Invite icon at the right of Voice Comms, and invite someone (preferably who is online) into your chat room.**

6. **When your friend joins you in Voice Comms (by repeating Step 4 on their side), right-click (Ctrl+click in macOS, Alt-click in Windows) your guest's username to access the User Options menu (see Figure 5-2).**

   Many of the options should be familiar to you already, but this menu gives you full control, including the ability to connect through private messages or even private audio conversations.

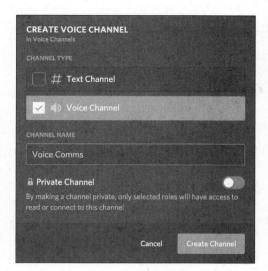

FIGURE 5-1:
Creating a new voice channel is easy. You create a new channel as you would in any category but designate it as a voice channel and keep it public so that any role can join it.

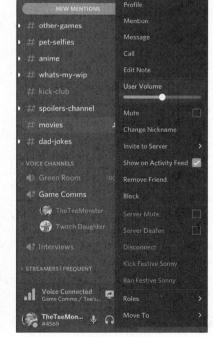

FIGURE 5-2:
When others join your server's audio channels, you can access details on that Discord member and manage that individual from here.

TIP

Perhaps the most celebrated feature in this menu is the User Volume option. Unlike other gaming platform audio networks where users are either audible or muted completely, User Volume allows you to manually mix your guests in voice channels. The volume slider can either boost weak signals or soften audio signals that overpower others in your group chat.

7. Chat, as you are now live with your guest.

Even as you make adjustments (if needed) to your guest's audio, you are still connected and interacting in real time.

8. When you wrap up your chat session, click the Disconnect icon (a phone receiver with an X next to it) to end the conversation and leave the Voice Comms channel.

Without disconnecting, you will remain in the channel. Make sure to disconnect if you want to leave.

REMEMBER

The conversation, similar to real life, can go on without you. When you want to leave an audio chat session in Discord, you can simply disconnect. But even though it is your server, your guests can remain in the channel, continue to hang out and chat, and keep the conversation going, regardless if you are still present.

9. Return to Voice Comms, and click the Edit Channel option (the gear wheel) to pull up the Channel Options window.

10. Move the User Limit slider (Overview section) to 10 Users, as shown in Figure 5-3.

If you want to manage the amount of people you host in a single channel, this feature will limit how many people can join a channel at one time. If the slider is all the way to the left, there is no limit to how many people can enter the channel.

WARNING

The more participants you host in a channel, audio or video, will test the limits of a server. Consider a realistic number for a chat session and set Voice Comms accordingly.

11. Click the Save Changes button.

To the right of your channel's title, you will see a counter keeping track of how many people are currently in your channel.

Welcome to the wonderful world of audio. This was why Discord was created, but as you can see, it offers many more options than just audio. You now have the ability to create solid, reliable communications with your fireteam, invite friends playing other games to hang out, coordinate conferences with associates and co-workers either in your office or from remote locations, and set up interviews for streams, podcasts, and other media. Discord, in real time, can easily become a powerful tool for event planning and productivity.

One thing to remember about Discord, though, is how it is designed to bring people together. It's a digital open door for anyone and everyone wanting to talk about a specific topic. This could be problematic if you want to keep a semblance of organization to your comms only to have random members of your Discord dropping in to say *"O HAI!!! Wat u do now?"* which will usually happen when focus is crucial. This is also a huge problem when you are streaming content. Currently, your voice channels are open for anyone who wants to come in and completely derail your train of thought, or worse, take hold of your conversation and monopolize it.

This is why the importance of a holding area or *green room* is essential.

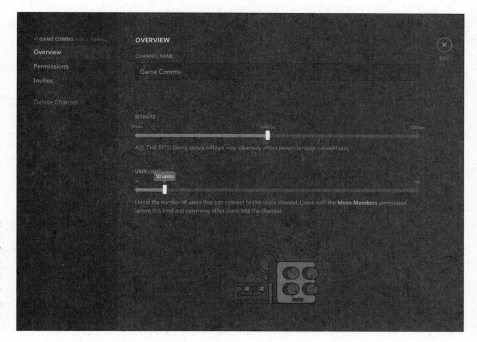

FIGURE 5-3:
The Channel Options window allows you to name your voice channel as well as set the maximum number of users in a channel.

Holding pattern: Creating a green room

What exactly is a green room? It's something of a tradition from the entertainment industry, but a *green room* is the place in a theater (once upon a time, always painted green, but nowadays any color) where guests on a talk show or members of a cast wait to make an entrance. It's something like the air lock between the main hull of your spaceship and The Black. (Keep flying, Browncoats.) While you stand by in a green room, a stage manager or assistant escorts you to the stage. This is a great method of keeping control of people coming and going.

We're going to make a green room for our main communications channel.

1. **In the Voice Channels section, click the gear wheel by Voice Comms, or right-click (Ctrl+click in macOS, Alt+click in Windows) your Voice Comms, and select the Edit Channel option.**

2. **In the Edit Channel window, go to Permissions.**

3. **Scroll down to the Voice Permissions section, and click the @everyone role.**

4. **Click the red X to the right of the Connect option, as seen in Figure 5-4.**

   As elsewhere in Discord, there are a lot of permissions to cover, but some of them will sound familiar to you:

   - *Create Invite:* Similar to the text messaging of Discord, this permission refers to keeping invitations exclusive.

   - *Manage Channel:* This permission, when granted the green check mark, grants the ability to create, edit, and delete audio channels. Much like this permission with text channels, this should be managed closely.

   - *Manage Permissions:* This is where you grant (or revoke) specific administrative responsibilities and privileges specific channels should have.

   - *Manage Webhooks:* If you recall, webhooks work with other websites to generate URL messages that will automatically pop up on your Discord server. This is for webhooks specific for channels, not servers.

   - *View Channel:* This permission grants users the ability to view or interact with the contents of a channel. In the Neutral setting, anyone can view it.

   - *Connect:* Specific for audio and video channels, this allows members to connect to a channel. In the Neutral setting, anyone can connect to it.

   - *Speak:* Specific for audio channels, this allows members to talk within a channel. In the Neutral setting, anyone can connect to a channel.

   - *Mute Members* and *Deafen Members:* For audio and video, the Mute option silences a speaker, while the Deafen option puts attendees in a virtual soundproof booth.

   - *Move Members:* This permission allows those granted this permission to be moved from one channel to another.

   - *Use Voice Activity:* If active, people in an audio or video channel need to use the Push to Talk function to use audio.

   - *Priority Speaker:* When active, this permission grants roles it is assigned to the ability to lower other audio signals in a channel when this role is speaking.

   - *Go Live:* This grants roles the ability to stream in Discord.

   Setting Connect to Denied for the @everyone role means no one can randomly enter a voice channel.

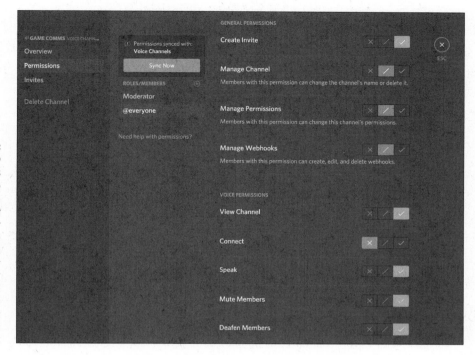

FIGURE 5-4:
By denying @
everyone's
permission to
connect to a
channel, you now
need another
channel to serve
as a green room
so other
moderators or
roles with the
permission to
Move Members
can grant them
access.

5. Select the Moderator role, and click the green check mark for the Connect permission.

6. Return to your voice channels, and click the + option to add a new voice channel.

7. Call the channel Green Room and then click the Create Channel button.

8. Click Green Room's gear wheel, or right-click (Ctrl-click in macOS, Alt-click in Windows) Green Room and select the Edit Channel option.

9. In the Overview option, set the User Limit to 10 in order to allow only ten users in the green room.

10. Click the Save Changes button.

11. Leave all the green room permissions at their default settings.

12. Invite people into your voice channel's green room, or tell members of your community to wait in the Green Room.

13. Once you recognize names of those you have invited, click and drag guests from the green room to Voice Comms.

14. Enjoy the chat!

REMEMBER

The above exercise is working with @everyone as the default role. If you have read Chapters 3 and 4 and created a new Members role as your default, you can simply repeat the above exercise for Members so both roles have this permission.

Now when people want to join you in your conversation, they arrive on your Discord via the green room. As you are in your Voice Comms (or whatever you choose to call your primary audio channel), you will not have any audio for the green room. You can see who is in there, but you do not hear what they have to say, nor does their audio come out in your conversation as you are not in their channel. The addition of a green room gives you more control over who is coming into your voice channels.

We have our first channels for audio communications. You can now create other channels similar to Voice Comms. You can have one for interviews, another for fund-raising and charity events, and another for Destiny and Halo fireteams. All of these rooms will take advantage of your green room, offering a decorum of control over your audio channels.

Now that you can manage your various audio channels, let's talk about the audio itself. Presently, we are using the built-in microphones of our laptop and smart device. These microphones are usually butted up right next to speakers, which can, in most cases, cause problems with the quality of the audio captured and reproduced. Unwanted, unwelcomed interference. Tinny sound. When you're starting out, it's more than okay to work with these as the quality still isn't bad. You don't need to upgrade straightaway.

When you do want to upgrade, though, here are a few ideas to consider.

The Mystery of Microphones

I have been writing about microphones for nearly two decades. No kidding — 15 years of podcasting teaches you a lot of things. In the first edition of *Podcasting For Dummies*, I wrote with Evo Terra about the various microphones that were available to the public. Across three more editions with Chuck Tomasi, I have watched microphones change dramatically both in their capabilities and their affordability.

In this magical mystery tour of podcasting, recording, streaming, and audio and video editing, one thing hasn't changed at all: the value of questions. Before running out and dropping a lot of cash on a new, shiny toy, which could easily become about as useful as a paperweight if you don't know what you're looking for or what you need, it's good to ask questions. Often.

>> **What do you want this mic to do?** Capture your voice? All microphones do that, sure, but if they all do the same thing then why are there so many different microphones out there? Well, there are some mics that work better in wide spaces. Some are good in a small studio. Others may have the ability to capture live music while recording your voice. Before purchasing a microphone, consider what your intentions are for this microphone. Are you going to use it just for gaming and Discord? Or are you thinking about different kinds of content creation in the future?

>> **What's your budget for a microphone?** If you find a microphone on the cheap, then there is a chance you will get what you pay for. The price tag is more than just a gauge of how well the microphone works; it is also tied into the quality of its construction, its durability, and its range of capabilities.

>> **What's your budget for the microphone's accessories?** So you have a microphone, but did it come with a shockmount? Do you need a shockmount? Or a stand? Will the stand be a desktop stand, or were you wanting to use a boom microphone to leave your desk clean? If you are planning a different setup for your Discord, then what will you need?

Even after narrowing your options, there are so many microphones on the market. After a while, the manufacturers, makes, and models all start to give you that kind of brain freeze you get when you suck down a Slurpee too fast. Allow me to give you the lowdown on the mic that's right for your budget and even make a few *sound* recommendations along the way.

Come on. They call me Twitch Dad, after all. You should be used to my Twitch Dad Jokes™ by now.

USB mics

The most prevalent microphones for any sort of online comms are microphones that use *USB (Universal Serial Bus)* connections. Figure 5-5 shows three types of USB microphones you can use with Discord. You can go online to any computer equipment or audio gear retailers and type "USB microphones" in their respective search engines. The results will range from headsets to desktop microphones to portable recorders, all of them ranging in price, features, and included accessories.

REMEMBER

You don't have to sell a kidney to invest in a professional-quality USB microphone. The SADES L9Plus gaming headset, pictured in the center of Figure 5-5, for example, is priced just under $25USD and captures high quality audio. Start with a modest budget, and when you are set, start looking at the more expensive options.

Gaming headsets

While usually associated with video games like *Halo, Destiny, Fortnite,* and *Call of Duty, gaming headsets* are far more versatile than people give them credit. Most gaming headsets are *closed-ear headphones,* headphones that fit around the entire ear (as opposed to *earbuds* which go inside the ear) and reproduce audio with stereo separation and frequency depth. Gaming headsets also offer microphones that vary in quality but on average capture clear audio. Many brick-and-mortar electronic stores do offer headsets on display, giving consumers an opportunity to try out a variety of headsets before purchasing. Personally, I was sold on the Corsair Void Pro Wireless Headset (shown in Figure 5-6) when a vendor pumped in actual gameplay audio from *Overwatch* into the headset. If you are on a tight budget, gaming headsets are an option worth considering and a great first step.

Desktop mics

Higher-quality, built to last, and an overall performance improvement, *desktop microphones* offer users options beyond Discord. While gaming headsets work fine for basic communication and even streaming, desktop microphones like *Shure Microphones' MV5* and *MV51* (both shown in Figure 5-7) offer professional-quality audio packaged in a sleek retro design for fun. Features with these models include

>> Digital signal processor (or DSP) presets

>> iOS and USB connectivity

>> Built-in headphone jack and volume adjustment for real-time monitoring

>> Quick-and-easy plug-and-play capability

>> Large-diaphragm condenser capsule offering wider audio range for recording

FIGURE 5-6:
The *Corsair Void Pro Headset* offers audio quality and ergonomic comfort, their sound quality considered one of the best on the market for its price.

FIGURE 5-7:
Shure's MV5 (left) and MV51 (right), part of the MOTIV series, offers Discord users high-quality audio capture as well as potential expansion to other creative endeavors.

The MV5 and MV51 promise simple setup and recording, and quality and durability also suited for podcasting or streaming. This audio gear can help you make that jump far easier. Prices for these kind of microphones range from $100 to $200, a major investment for a microphone dedicated to Discord. However, an investment like this is more about expanding your audio setup for projects beyond community management.

One advantage headsets have over a desktop microphone is that your mouth is always the same distance away from the microphone. If you're an animated gamer (*ahem*, like your author), this may be useful. On the other hand, they can be very sensitive to breathing sounds. If the mic is in the wrong position, the slightest breath from your mouth or nose will sound like an EF5 tornado passing by. The more you work with audio equipment, the easier it is to know what you need and when you're just indulging in overkill. Don't break your bank for the hottest or latest and greatest, unless you really see yourself growing beyond Discord.

XLR microphones

While it feels like we're talking that money isn't an issue here and that a quick check between the couch cushions will land you a nice microphone, allow me to assure you we're not. Even with my bylines in fiction and nonfiction, I work on a budget. Still, it can be frustrating. You can go on the cheap and pick up a mic for as little as ten dollars, but let's be honest here: When you're in game comms, you sound like you're talking on a $10 mic. When you feel like you've outgrown that first microphone, it's time to shop for an upgrade.

Before you do so, you might want to hold on to something. Microphones that are not USB-powered range in price from roughly $70 to an incredible $3,600! (No, you're not seeing a typo involving an extra zero.) So what defines a microphone? Price? Manufacturer? Look?

What truly defines a microphone is how *you* sound in it and how it reproduces incoming audio signals. Usually, the best mics are *XLR microphones,* considered the industry standards. Shure. MXL. Audio-Technica. These are all manufacturers that create audio equipment recording professionals rely on.

REMEMBER

When you purchase a higher-end microphone, keep in mind that you probably will receive no additional cables for hookup, a jack that does not fit into your computer, and no stand. That's because you're upgrading to *professional* equipment. The manufacturer is assuming that you already have the bells, whistles, and extra doodads needed to make this mic work for you. As far as what else you need for XLR microphones, continue to the end of this chapter.

Yes, professional-quality microphones may be considered too much for Discord. If you are looking to level up your gaming with podcasting or streaming in the future, you might want to seriously look into the durability and reliability of an XLR microphone. But as G.I. Joe said back in the '80s, knowing is half the battle.

And after writing four editions of *Podcasting For Dummies* and the first edition of *Twitch For Dummies,* trust me — there is *a lot* to know about the XLR microphones.

Dynamic mics

When someone mentions the word *microphone,* the image that comes to mind is probably a *dynamic microphone.* These mics work like a speaker in reverse. Sound enters a dynamic mic by speaking directly into it, vibrating a *diaphragm* (a small plate) attached to a coil which, in turn, creates a small electric current. This *signal* runs through a *preamp* or *mixer* where the original sound is re-created. This system sounds complicated (and if you've ever looked inside of a microphone, trust me, it is), but the internal makeup of dynamic microphones is such that they can take a lot of incoming signal and still produce audio clearly.

Perhaps the most common and reliable of this classification of microphone is the *Shure SM58* (pictured in Figure 5-8). The SM58 is the textbook definition of a dynamic microphone. It is seen everywhere — concert stages, public speeches, and anywhere a voice needs to be heard. The Shure SM58 is so durable that when you see people "drop the mic" it is usually the 58 you see hitting the floor. Listed at an affordable price (under $100), the SM58 remains the best of starter microphones for many streamers and podcasters.

FIGURE 5-8:
The Shure SM58 is an XLR dynamic microphone, considered an industry standard on account of its durability and ease of use.

WARNING

Yes, the SM58 is a workhorse of a microphone, but *under no circumstances should you literally drop a mic.* Go back and read that section on microphones on diaphragms, coils, and so on. Even as durable as an SM58 is, a severe impact like an impact to a floor could jostle one of the many components inside a mic, rendering it useless. So, please, *never literally drop the mic. Never. Never! Never!!!*

Condenser mics

Another classification of XLR microphones you may come across when shopping is a *studio condenser microphone.* The inner workings of a condenser microphone look very different from a dynamic one. The diaphragm of a condenser mic is suspended in front of a second stationary plate that conducts electricity. As a signal enters the microphone, the air between the diaphragm and the plate is displaced, creating a fluctuating charge. With the addition of something called *phantom power* (explained in a sidebar later in this chapter), the charge becomes an electrical representation of the incoming audio signal.

If you thought the setup of a dynamic microphone sounded precarious, a condenser mic is ridiculous. These particular mics are so sensitive, they are usually transported in padded cases and, when in use, are suspended in a suspension frame called a *shockmount* (as seen in Figure 5-9). If manhandled or jostled around (or worse, dropped — see my Warning above), internal pickups can be knocked out of whack, causing problems in reception. The advantage to this delicate setup is that condenser mics are far more sensitive to sound, picking up a wider spectrum of audio. The end result is studio-level audio quality, depending on where you are using this microphone, of course.

FIGURE 5-9:
MXL's Overstream Bundle comes with everything you need to effectively stream audio or record audio for podcasting. The bundle even includes an XLR-to-USB adapter.

I am a big fan of condenser mics from MXL. My first microphone was an MXL 990, a model I still podcast and stream with to this day. MXL has broadened its offerings to include the *Overstream Bundle* (http://www.mxlmics.com/microphones/podcasting/overstreambundles), which includes

>> Desk-mounted, hinged-arm mic stand

>> Integrated all-in-one shockmount and pop filter

>> Choice of either the 990 Blizzard or 990 Blaze

>> MXL Mic Mate Pro (defined in the section "Thingamajigs, Whammerwhips, and Doodads: Audio Accessories," found later in this chapter)

NO POWER LIKE PHANTOM POWER

You might notice that condenser mics (such as the 990 and BCD-1) are *phantom-powered*. To reproduce that superior sound, condenser mics need an extra kick of electricity. Some condenser mics use batteries to get this kick, but when batteries start to die, so does the audio quality. (A word to the wise: Always check your mic's battery level before any event and have fresh batteries on hand.) As phantom power comes from an exterior source (a mixing board like the GoXLR pictured here, an adapter, and so on) through its connecting cable, it supplies a constant boost. No batteries or stress over how good your batteries are required. If the source of phantom power is on, your mic is working, and you are live.

MXL bundles like the Overstream can also be found at online vendors like BSW (https://www.bswusa.com). BSW sells podcast bundles (perfect for the ultimate audio setup for Discord) featuring another MXL microphone, the *BCD-1*. With each bundle offering new accessories, cost and features go up, but the quality sound that the MXL line captures remains the same.

You now have a good idea how to shop for a new microphone, something that takes your online communications to a new level and perhaps open up a few possibilities for you beyond Discord. However, as I mention in the "XLR microphones" section, higher-end microphones — unless you are investing in a bundle like the Overstream — lack a few of the other things you might need to complete your setup.

Thingamajigs, Whammerwhips, and Doodads: Audio Accessories

Purchasing a microphone is not always a one–shot deal. Depending on what you pick up to upgrade your Discord setup, some accessories may be necessary to finish that upgrade and help you produce solid audio:

>> **Cables:** As mentioned earlier in this chapter, your spiffy-new microphone may arrive without any cable — and buying the wrong cable can be incredibly easy if you don't know jack (so to speak). The standard cables for dynamic and condenser microphones are a three-prong connection: a three-pin XLR male plug connecting to a three-pin XLR female plug, as shown in Figure 5-10.

To plug a microphone into either a mixer, adapter, or preamp, you want a three-pin XLR-to-XLR male-to-female cord. These cables begin at $9 and work their way up, depending on the length of the cord and quality of the inputs.

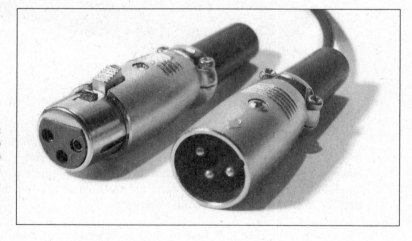

FIGURE 5-10:
XLR male (right) and female (left) plugs are standard plugs for phantom-powered microphones.

>> **Microphone stands:** On receiving the microphone and possibly its shock-mount, you may notice the attachment for a mic stand . . . but no mic stand comes with your new mic. It's your responsibility to provide one, and although that may sound like an easy buy, your options for mic stands are many, each with their advantages.

A simple desktop mic stand, the most basic of setups, can run about $10 A boom mic stand that suspends the mic over your desk is priced around the $100 range. The type of mic stand best for you depends on how you are working with Discord.

>> **Pop filters and windscreens:** Pop filters and windscreens help soften explosive consonants (percussive ones like *B* and *P*) when on a voice channel. A windscreen can also reduce some ambient room noise. Using *both* a windscreen and pop filter on one mic could be overkill, but these are terrific add-ons to your microphones.

>> **XLR-to-USB adapters:** As you are considering the investment into dynamic or condenser microphones, this would be a good time to mention how these microphones connect with computers. In many cases, these connections happen through either mixer boards or preamps which provide phantom power for these microphones to work. These options are good for podcasters and streamers who are hosting multiple people in a studio. However, as we are working with Discord, all you need is a single connection for yourself. This is when an XLR-to-USB adapter such as *MXL's Mic Mate Pro* or *Shure's X2U* (see Figure 5-11) comes into play. Adapters provide an XLR connection, a USB connection, and phantom power. Other features include a ¼-inch jack for headphones or hard-wired earbuds, gain control, and both monitor and volume control. XLR-to-USB adapters open up a wider variety of microphones that can make your voice channels pop.

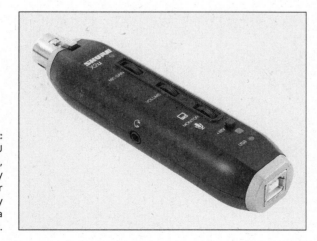

FIGURE 5-11: The Shure X2U provides a simple, plug-and-play connection for XLR mics to any computer with a USB port.

There is a lot to Discord's audio, and the possibilities promise creative pursuits aplenty. If you enjoy hosting friends and colleagues on Discord, maybe a podcast is in your future, or maybe you will want to take on streaming your favorite video game(s), if you aren't already. You have a lot to explore creatively with audio and Discord, and it can be a fun ride, especially with all the *extremely cool audio tech toys* out there.

With audio effectively covered, it's time to turn our attention to video. We've been connecting with others and establishing reliable comms with audio through Discord. Now we go to video and take advantage of Discord's videoconferencing features.

Chapter **6**

Ready for That Close-Up: Video on Discord

The advancement of digital video never ceases to boggle my mind. I know that sounds like a dad thing to say (am I right, Markiplier?), but let me explain . . .

In 1996, I edited my first video on a computer. The Apple computer I was working on had been upgraded to its limits, the video capture card alone matching the size of my forearm. I had taught myself Adobe Premiere. The external drive was a massive 8GB drive, which, I discovered, was just enough for a 30-minute short film, although today it would be called a *vidoc*. And this was for 4:3 SD (standard definition) video; 16:9 HD (high definition) video didn't exist back then.

Geez, I'm old.

Over the years, I have watched digital video improve in resolution, in data size efficiency, and in integration with computers and other devices. The ability to stream video over the Internet went from something resembling bad stop motion animation to flawless playback. Video is now *expected* to run without fail on desktop and laptop computers, along with smart devices of all makes and models.

I love it. I absolutely love it. And now I'm getting to play with video on Discord.

Moving Pictures: Video on Discord

In stand-alone applications and online services like Skype, FaceTime, Zoom, and Discord, *video calls* is the feature that introduces video integration. Straight out of science fiction, your laptop's built-in camera is now a connection to the outside world with others either using cameras built-in or connected with their computers, or tablets and smartphones.

But this is where video with Discord *starts*. There are a few more tricks this platform has up its sleeve when it comes to this medium.

Setting the stage: Video settings

Before jumping headlong into action, complete with lights and camera, we need to make sure the connections are all working properly. Cameras need to be sending signals, lighting needs to be adjusted, and (of course) your Internet needs the bandwidth to support a video chat.

1. **Launch Discord, and click the User Settings (gear wheel) icon next to your username and avatar, located in the lower-left corner of the UI.**

2. **Under the App Settings settings, select the Voice & Video option.**

   Voice & Video allows you to not only test (and, if something isn't working, troubleshoot) your audio, but also check your video settings.

3. **Scroll down to the Video Settings option, and select which camera you would like to use from your available video resources.**

   Depending on how many cameras you have connected to your desktop or laptop computer, the *Camera* menu will vary on what video sources are available. If a specific camera you want to use is not on the drop-down menu, check the camera first to see if the camera is on. If the desired camera is on and connected, but not available on the menu, restart your computer.

4. **In the Preview section, click the Test Video button to run a quick diagnostics of your camera and its connection, as shown in Figure 6-1.**

5. **Once you have a clear signal, both for your audio and video, either press the Esc (Escape) key or click the X in the upper-right corner of the Settings window.**

TIP

Most computers come with their own built-in cameras, but if you need to work with a different one, external webcams are USB-powered, easily incorporated into your system, and affordable.

VIDEO SETTINGS

CAMERA

FaceTime HD Camera

PREVIEW

FIGURE 6-1:
Video Settings options offer a test for your incoming video sources to make sure that your signal is coming in loud and clear.

With your audio and video settings all checking out, it's time to start talking with friends, family, and associates on Discord. Before you fire up your camera, make sure your surroundings are not overly distracting. Check what you're wearing (like pants — pants are always good), and be certain you are not backlit. When a subject is backlit, the light source is coming from behind you, making you appear like a shadowy figure in front of the camera. So long as you can see yourself in the test video, you're good to go.

You have to be there: Video conversations

For video calls, you don't need to set up a new channel as you do with audio or text. What you need for a video chat is to establish a private conversation or private group chat (discussed in Chapter 3), then open up the call from the discussion.

So how about we get some interpersonal communication going on Discord?

1. **Click the Home icon, and review the list of direct messages you have previously started.**

2. **Click one of those names in your Direct Messages log or click the + icon to the right of the Direct Messages label to create a new group DM.**

   A *group direct message* or *group DM* not only gives you group communications between multiple people, but it also allows you to host audio and video conferencing.

3. **In the upper-right area of the Discord app, you will see four icons all pertaining to private messaging (from left to right):**

   ● Start Voice Call

   ● Start Video Call

- Pinned Messages (pertaining to that specific DM)

- Add Friends to DM

Click the Start Video Call (camera) icon to begin your call.

TIP

In the same vein as with private messages, before launching into a video call with someone you may not know very well, it is a good idea to ask in a text message if a video call would be welcomed. Consider it a courtesy.

4. **Under the participants of the video call, as seen in Figure 6-2, a set of options appears (from left to right):**

- Start/Stop Screen Sharing

- Start/Stop Video

- Leave Call

- Mute/Unmute Audio

- User Settings

Continue your chat, clicking any of the featured options as they are needed.

5. **When your call reaches its conclusion, click the red Leave Call button to end the conversation.**

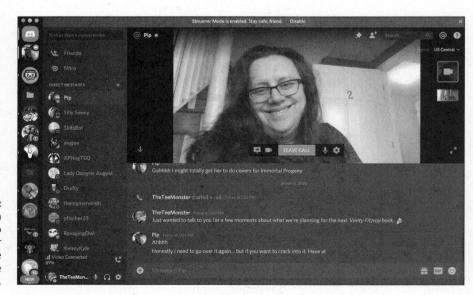

FIGURE 6-2: Video calls on Discord tend to be a private affair between those invited to the discussion.

Video conversations, unlike voice channels, are neither open to all nor even managed with a green room solution. These are more of an invitation-only meeting where you decide who has access. The maximum amount of participants in a Discord video chat at the time of this writing is ten people; but, as discussed in Chapter 4, the stability of that video call with ten participants will vary from a test of will to rock solid, depending on the status of your server and the bandwidth of your Internet connection.

Video conversations can improve in stability if some of your participants turn off their video (simply by clicking the *Start/Stop Video* feature, seen in Figure 6-2) but in my own experience, the call's ability to remain reliable depends on more than just the status of a Discord server. Other factors affecting the quality of a video call are:

>> Time of day/week

>> Activity on Discord servers

>> Participants' Internet connection

Granted, a ten-person chat is something of a rarity (unless you are using video comms for a *Dungeons & Dragons* outing), and Discord's reputation for one-on-one video chat is solid. There is plenty you can accomplish when working with people through Discord's video chat.

But remember, I said video conversations are just the start for what you can accomplish with Discord. You have heard me discuss *streaming* throughout the book. Just in case you are not sure what that is or what it entails, let me introduce you to streaming media and how Discord fits into all of it.

A Go for Launch: Using Discord's Go Live

Streaming is the creation of content in real time with friends or simply on your own and sharing this creation with the Internet. You tend to see streaming happen on other platforms like *Twitch* (`https://twitch.tv`) and *Mixer* (`https://mixer.com`), and in most cases a video game is involved. If you are familiar with one of my other titles, *Twitch For Dummies,* you know that streaming goes well beyond video games. From creative endeavors to cooking to a simple online chit-chat with your community, streaming is one of the fastest growing platforms of communications, serving as a gateway for another passion of mine: *podcasting.*

Discord now offers its own platform for streaming to your community.

While this feature is a groundbreaker for Discord, it is in Beta at the time of this writing. Currently, *Go Live* is only available through the Windows desktop app with spectating Go Live streams only available through desktop clients (both Mac and Windows) and the Chrome browser. However, as Discord is always looking to up its game (pardon the pun), more platforms and devices will become available.

Going Live with Go Live

1. **Create a new audio channel.**

2. **In the Overview settings, call the channel [YOUR NAME] LIVE and leave the User Limit slider at the ∞ icon.**

3. **In the Permissions section of the new audio channel, click the + icon to create a new role, and select Moderator if you have one already created for your Discord.**

By default, you are designated as a Moderator in Discord. These permissions you are about to set up pertain specifically to this new audio channel you are setting up.

4. **Make sure the Moderator role is selected, and set these permissions:**

   - View Channel: granted (green check mark)

   - Connect: granted

   - Speak: granted

   - Move Members: granted

   - Go Live: granted (see Figure 6-3)

5. **Click the Save Changes button.**

6. **Select the @everyone role, and set these permissions:**

   - View Channel: granted

   - Connect: granted

   - Speak: denied (red X)

   - Mute Members: denied

   - Deafen Members: denied

7. **Click the Save Changes button.**

The @everyone role is your default role for members. If you have created a "new members" role, apply that role to this exercise.

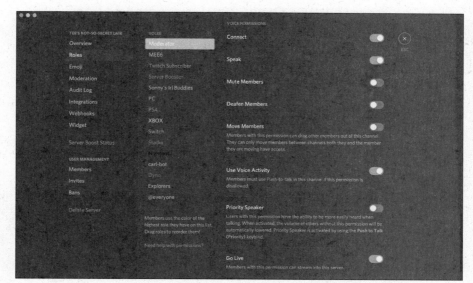

FIGURE 6-3:
Keep the Go Live permission reserved for Moderators and roles that you trust in streaming video from your Discord server.

8. **With Discord still running, launch your video game of choice.**

Just above your name, you should see the video game you are playing. To the right of your game is the Go Live icon, which will show a Stream [YOUR GAME] tag.

9. **Click the tag for setup.**

For streaming on Discord to work, your game has to be recognized. If you need to double-check if your game is recognized, choose User Settings ⇨ Game Activity to confirm.

REMEMBER

Console game systems will not be detected by Discord. Streaming only works, at the time of this writing, with PC games.

The Go Live options window comes up.

10. **Confirm here what game you are playing and which Voice channel you're streaming from, and then click the Go Live button.**

Your activity appears as inset video. When you roll over the new video window, you will see (as pictured in Figure 6-4) the various tools you need to manage your stream:

- *Invite Viewers:* Send out invitations to others; let them know that you are streaming content.

- *Number of Viewers:* Similar to other streaming platforms, this tool tracks how many are watching you.

- *Stream Settings:* This icon allows you to access your stream settings. You can easily change your settings as you stream to improve or downgrade your stream. When you are streaming, a red marker will indicate you are live.

- *Stop Streaming:* When you are done streaming, you simply click this icon to end your stream.

If you need to change anything in your stream (aside from the gamer itself, of course), this is a control panel to use.

FIGURE 6-4:
When using Go Live, your activity appears as inset video while Discord runs in the background.

11. **Play your game.**

Keep an eye on Discord, and feel free to interact with anyone chatting with you in a text channel, or feel free to unmute guests to your voice channel.

TIP

When you double-click the inset video of the stream, the stream takes place of the main chat window. In the lower-right corner, you can enter the stream's full-screen mode by clicking it. Click any channel — text or voice — to return the video to inset mode.

12. **When you're ready to end your stream, click the Stop Streaming icon.**

This is streaming with Discord, and the promise of turning your community into your Chat Stream as you would have with Twitch, Mixer, or some other platform, is evident. This is a cutting-edge development worthy of some attention.

Growing Pains: Limitations with Go Live

There is real potential in being able to stream directly within Discord, and considering how close a relationship Discord has with streamers from all the aforementioned platforms, this new feature is pretty exciting.

But let's state that one more time: Go Live is *new* to Discord, which means — unlike the tried and true platforms of streaming media — there are a few things to consider with this newcomer:

» **Streaming off a voice channel:** To stream in Discord, you need to stream off one of the voice channels you have created on your server. This could be Discord wanting to keep streaming as part of your game comms, but having the voice channel as the channel where you are inviting people can make things a little hard to manage. In the above exercise, I have you set up the voice channel so that only moderators have the ability to talk. If you are thinking, "Eh, I'll leave the voice channel open to all," it could get noisy if you have ten people joining you. If your channel grows in popularity, and you have 20 or 30 watching you, then it becomes like THAT PARTY AT COLLEGE WHERE YOU'RE SHOUTING OVER THE PARTY MIX TO BE HEARD! YOU KNOW, LIKE THE ONE BACK IN CHAPTER 3? IT'S STILL HAPPENING! WOW, THIS DJ IS A FREAKIN' MACHINE! DROP THAT BASS, BRO!!! With the permissions I've outlined here, you can manage it, but it may be hard to interact with guests who are muted in one channel and chatting in another.

» **No second camera or elements available:** Streaming on other platforms incorporates a second camera so you can see the gamer in action, as pictured in Figure 6-5. Other platforms also offer the ability to introduce overlays and various interactive elements to give the stream a snappy look or offer opportunities for the audience to interact with the streamer, also seen in Figure 6-5. Presently, when you stream content using Discord, none of these options are available. Go Live is pretty bare-bones which is not out of the ordinary for some beginning streamers and their channels; but if an audience follows you from Twitch to Discord, the sparse look may be a bit jarring.

If you are like me and *really* want those elements that Streamlabs and other streaming software packages offer, you can — with a multiple monitor setup and some unconventional thinking — stream a game with inset video using Open Broadcasting Software, or OBS (https://obsproject.com). For more on this, look at the "Building on the Basics: Video Accessories and Upgrades" section later in this chapter.

» **Dropped frames and lag in game:** When you look back in Chapter 4, I talk about the various types of servers Discord offers. With its various upgrades, be it Nitro or verified servers, Discord ramps up bandwidth capabilities, especially for audio and video. With my server running on Discord Nitro, I set my stream settings to the maximum — Source/60fps — to see what would happen. It didn't take long to notice a sudden slowdown in my game's performance, the action on-screen appearing less than fluid even with uncapped frames. While my own server is at a modest Level 1 at the time of this writing, it guarantees a stream at 720p/60fps. You could give up a few frames and stream at 1080p/30fps, but you're pushing Discord's resources when trying for anything higher. So unless you want to invest in more server boosts or getting promotions in your server's status, your first few streams may have to run at the basic settings lest your game's performance takes a hard hit in quality.

FIGURE 6-5:
Streaming with Twitch is commonly a two-camera setup with gameplay as the primary content and the gamer as inset video.

>> **Awkward interface:** So you decide to take advantage of Go Live and you click the Start Streaming icon. This takes you to the Stream Settings window (see Figure 6-6), where you have to confirm *Yes, this is what I wish to stream* and *Yes, this is the channel I wish to stream from*. Then you need to get viewers, and viewers need to have access to the Voice channel and see that you're live. On seeing you live, they should have a visual notification that you're live, and then they either join the stream (which is happening on the same channel as you are in) or they can double-click your name and join the stream. I would describe this whole process with a lot of words, but "graceful" wouldn't be one of them. These little trip-ups will probably be easily smoothed out with time. However, when established streaming platforms — even Facebook Live — feel easier to work with than Discord, why stream here?

Why stream here? It's a very good question to ask of Discord. If you want to find out more about streaming on a whole — particularly streaming with Twitch — I recommend you take a look at my *Twitch For Dummies* title. But as for streaming on Discord, we can take a serious look at exactly why Go Live is a terrific feature, especially when working with smaller groups.

Check this out: Using Go Live as a screen-sharing app

The Go Live feature is more than just an opportunity to share your gaming experience with your audience, but you now have the ability to share your screen with a select audience. Why limit your content to just gaming? Have something you want to demo? Want to host a webinar from your server? Screen-sharing makes a presentation online very easy. The steps to get to our webinar going will be a bit like launching our gaming session, but with a quick left turn in the process.

1. In Discord, go to the [YOUR NAME] LIVE audio channel, and go into its settings.

2. In the Overview section, set the User Limit slider to 10 users to keep your group manageable.

3. Save these changes; then go to Permissions, and change the permissions for @everyone to allow for open discussions.

4. Save those changes when you're done.

   A manageable group is really judged by you, the host. I went with 10, as that is a group easily moderated; but limits you set in the end.

5. **Enter the [YOUR NAME] LIVE audio channel, and click the Go Live icon to the right of your Connection notification.**

   The Go Live options window comes up, pictured in Figure 6-7. Unlike when you confirm what game you are playing, the Go Live options will give you either the Applications or the Screens tab.

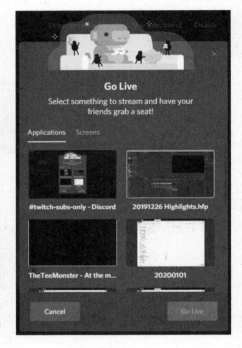

FIGURE 6-7: The Go Live window, when games are not running, looks for what monitors are connected to your PC and what applications are running.

6. **Make sure the Applications tab is selected.**

   The Applications mode detects open windows and desktop clients you have running. (As you see, when the client is a game, Discord automatically recognizes it as a game.) Whether it is a browser window or a desktop client like HitFilm Express or PowerPoint, the selected application is the focus of the stream. Screens mode detects how many monitors you have running. The monitor selected becomes the focus of the stream.

7. **In the Applications options, click an application or a presentation you want to share with viewers; then click the Go Live button.**

   The stream will now show your selected application as you work with it. When you are in the featured application, the inset video on Discord will dim out, displaying a message that your stream is still continuing but has been dimmed in order to be economic on resources.

8. **Give your presentation.**

Engage guests in your voice channel at various points to see if anyone has questions. In Figure 6-8, for example, I am giving a "How to create a highlight reel using HitFilm Express" demo in the Tee Morris LIVE audio channel.

9. **When you're ready to end your screen share, simply click the Stop Streaming icon.**

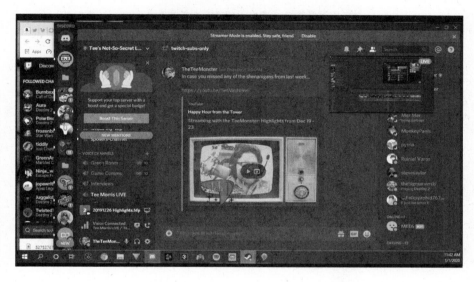

FIGURE 6-8: Screen-sharing, another feature of the new Go Live feature, allows you to run demonstrations (pictured here, a small demo of PressFilm Express), host webinars, and give presentations on Discord.

With the power and versatility of Discord behind you, screen sharing opens up your application of this platform beyond gaming. You can host webinars, offer support to other members of your community with various applications ranging from video editors to audio editors to photo editors, and even give presentations on topics of interest.

Discord is always improving and upgrading, Go Live being a prime example of how the devs are working to make the app even better. Upon logging into or launching Discord, a screen might appear giving the latest news and upgrades. These *change logs*, a recent one pictured in Figure 6-9, appear in order to keep you tied in and up to speed on what big changes have happened with Discord. Change logs, also accessible under User Settings, appear automatically whenever upgrades happen.

It's not often we talk about mobile improvements on desktop; we're changing it up for the end of the year and wanted to highlight all the improvements we've made to our iOS app throughout 2019 with a video. A lot of our mobile releases are quieter and happen quickly, and we don't often celebrate them like we do for desktop.

After our work over the last year, the app is faster, more reliable, prettier, and rid of a ton of bugs. We're committed to keeping your mobile experience, both iOS and Android, equal to desktop as we enter the new year and beyond.

PHONES SHMONES

- **Added timed muting.** Right click to temporarily mute group DMs, channels, and servers for set amounts of time because the only time the group chat wants to talk is when it's 11:55pm and you have work due at 11:59.

- **Our chat bar is now, as the engineer explaining this to me described it, -rich-.** See formatting like **bold**, *italics*, mentions,

Missed an update? Check out our previous change logs

FIGURE 6-9:
When upgrades and changes like Go Live happen in Discord, a change log will appear whenever Discord launches. These are the upgrades devs can't wait to tell you about.

The upgrades I cover here you won't find in changelogs. These are upgrades as featured back in Chapter 5. With video, there are a few neat add-ons out there for you to consider.

Building on the Basics: Video Accessories and Upgrades

When you were looking over the various audio upgrades in Chapter 5, I can imagine what you were thinking as you looked over the various accessories I introduced. I still remember exploring the various gadgets out on the market that were around in 2005. With each edition of *Podcasting For Dummies,* the gadgets just got cooler.

Then I got into streaming. Wow! I had only scratched the surface of cool gadgetry out in the audio-video market.

So here's where I have to whip out the bucket of ice water and douse you, but only because I love you. Much like we did with audio gear and accessories, there are questions we have to ask before laying down the greenbacks.

And yes, they may seem very familiar:

>> **What's your budget?** There is no point in dropping a lot of cash into the coolest gear if you know you are not going to need it. For example, why invest in a steady cam (costing around $150) if you can only stream with the desktop app. Before considering accessories of any kind, make sure you can afford new gear but more importantly, make sure you are able to use the new gear with Discord and its current capabilities.

>> **Where will you be using Discord?** This may not seem to be a big deal; but when it comes to upgrades, this is *important*. Where will you be hosting audio and video chats? A good chance your Discord activities, particularly when it comes to video, will be happening in a studio of some description. These kinds of logistics are going to be important to keep in mind when looking at upgrades and what will (and won't) work.

And speaking of what will and won't work . . .

>> **Would this upgrade work with Discord?** You can incorporate a new camera to improve the quality of your video calls, but how necessary would it be to set up a light ring? Sure, a light ring would improve the quality of a video call, but unless you can stream video of yourself through Discord, a light ring may be something of overkill. The same could be said for other accessories like a deck switcher, which streamers on Twitch, Mixer, and other platforms have a powerful need for. As Discord only reads one source presently, a deck switcher would not have much use in this setup. Always ask yourself if an upgrade really works.

Once you have answers to your questions, you're ready to go shopping. It may not be as big of a list as you would find for audio gear or for someone putting together a streamer's studio, but the gear listed here will help you in putting together sophisticated streams for Discord.

Video cameras

In 2019, film director David Leitch (*John Wick, Deadpool 2*) shot and directed *Snowbrawl* for Apple, an action short film completely shot using an iPhone 11. This is an example of how far video quality on smartphones has progressed. Basic cameras on smart devices and laptops are good, but upgrading a camera to capture a little more detail can be both easy and affordable. Logitech's C920, shown in Figure 6-10, captures full high-definition (HD) 1080p resolution at a cost of around just $50.

FIGURE 6-10:
The Logitech
C920 webcam,
priced at just
under $50, offers
streamers full
1080p video,
built-in
microphones
with automatic
noise reduction,
and automatic
low-light
correction.

As cameras go up in price, resolution and frame rate quality increase. So do other features like color correction, low light correction, and so on. Depending on whether or not you are incorporating audio accessories, you can use the camera's on-board microphone as your audio input. Before investing into an external webcam, make sure first that you have a place for the camera itself. Will you be mounting it on top of a screen or a small desk tripod (another $10, but a worthwhile $10 spent), and from what angle?

Start economically. Small steps. The more demands you have for video in Discord, the easier it will be to upgrade, if needed.

Open Broadcasting Software (OBS)

So here is a serious workaround for streaming on Discord, but incorporating inset video of yourself gaming in time with the action on screen. Open Broadcasting Software (also known as OBS, at https://obsproject.com) is well known amongst streamers as it transforms your computer into a broadcasting control room. OBS sorts both incoming and outgoing audio and video sources, and allows you to mix and arrange by layers these sources, creating a sophisticated look to your stream.

Making OBS work with Discord requires a bit of prep work, though. For this to work, you need:

>> An understanding of OBS (and if you're looking for a book in that, take a look at *Twitch For Dummies*, written by yours truly)

>> A dual monitor system

Setting up a second monitor may sound a little tricky, at first; but it is super-easy to set up, and your PC's operating system should be able to detect a new display source without fail. With these prerequisites all in place, let's go!

1. **Download OBS by going to** `https://obsproject.com` **and selecting the Download for Windows option.**

2. **Run through the steps to install OBS and then launch OBS.**

   At the top right of each tool set and control panels is a small pop-out window.

3. **Pop out all these windows, and move them to a secondary monitor.**

4. **With one window dedicated to your feed, begin to build a scene by adding in a source from a webcam and either a game or another source, placed behind your webcam.**

5. **Return to Discord, and select the Go Live feature.**

6. **In the Go Live options, select the Applications tab.**

7. **In the Applications options, click the OBS window; then click the Go Live button.**

   You can now stream your game or give your presentation while featuring inset video.

8. **Stream your game or presentation, as seen in Figure 6-11.**

9. **Once you finish your stream, click the Stop Streaming icon.**

FIGURE 6-11: Using OBS, you can emulate the full streaming experience, complete with inset video and other elements featured in streams seen on other platforms.

WARNING

This is a work-around. The end results are . . . okay? I will admit, this is a *hard push* to get Discord's streaming feature to emulate streaming platforms. At this point, I would simply say stream elsewhere as Discord's Go Live feature needs work. Or just go with the basics and do the bare-bones stream. While I have proven you can re-create the streaming experience, I think Dr. Ian Malcolm said it best: "Your scientists were so preoccupied with whether or not they *could* that they didn't stop to think if they *should*."

If you decide that incorporating OBS with your Discord is the direction you want to go, then there are a few more accessories to think about working into your setup.

Green screen

Sometimes called privacy screens the green screen is exactly what you're thinking: a backdrop of a lime green color that, when well-lit, removes the background from your video, leaving only you visible. To achieve this effect:

1. **After setting up your green screen, go into OBS, right-click the Video Capture Device source, and select the Filters option.**

2. **In the Effects Filters window, select the Chroma Key option.**

3. **Accept the Key Color Type Green.**

   Leave it alone. This is what you want.

4. **As lighting and green screens can vary, play around with the various settings in this window.**

   If you are struggling in making a clean separation between you and your green screen, add more lighting.

   When working with green screens, make sure you have plenty of light on your subject. Also avoid *any* shades of green, both in fashion and in makeup.

5. **Click the Close button.**

The main reason for incorporating a green screen into your Discord stream would be to reveal more of your presentation, on-screen demo, or your game. If you do invest into a green screen, know you're going to have to experiment with lighting, space, and comfort. There are many benefits to employing a green screen into your studio setup, but it is an extra step that will come with a learning curve. If you want to make your Discord stream more like a traditional stream, make sure to be patient in navigating that learning curve.

Already mentioned in the above tip, lighting can help in making a green screen work. Consider, then, adding into your setup a solution that streamers of all backgrounds swear by.

LED ring lights

LED ring lights have quickly flooded the market *(See what I did there?)* with different sizes, shades, and features. As shown in Figure 6-11, ring lights are exactly what they say they are: an LED light source that helps to add and balance the lighting of your studio setup. Some of these ring lights are built into a tripod, leaving an apparatus for a webcam or a phone to be secured at the center of the ring. Other ring lights vary in tint, color, and brightness controls. The tripods included with many of these rings can be low, also pictured in Figure 6-12, built to sit on a desk surface while others are free standing boom stands, similar to boom mic stands. With LED ring lights, unlike conventional lighting setups seen in photographer's studios and movie sets, heat is also manageable.

FIGURE 6-12: LED ring lights, like the Aixpi 10-Inch LED Ring Light here, provide balanced, controlled lighting for your video content.

What Discord is doing with video and where it appears to be heading with it promises a lot for everyone involved with the platform. It does not matter if you are enjoying the benefits of this free communications tool or if you are one of the Partnered Servers enjoying all the benefits of what comes with that distinction: Discord is now looking ahead with opportunities and applications that video can afford its community.

However, as this platform is a familiar platform with gamers, Discord is also a must-have accessory with streamers. I have been referencing these other outlets throughout this chapter, and Chapter 9 even goes into the ways streamers use Discord to build their community. The creative minds at Discord get that. Because we're focusing on video and we're talking about streaming, let's look at how Discord integrates with Twitch to keep the pace going after a stream wraps for the day.

One More Thing: Integrating Twitch with Discord

What exactly does *integration* mean, particularly with respect to Discord and Twitch? To understand how this relationship — and that is what *integration* means here — between these two platforms, we first have to understand what it means to be a *subscriber* (or a *sub*) on Twitch. When you become a sub to a streamer, you pay a subscription fee to that streamer. It's your own investment in that content creator, in the hopes that your subscription (and yes, subscriptions from others) might help that content creator stream more content in the future. From the streamer's perspective, subscriptions offer an incentive, whether it is emotes, sub-only Chat sessions, or other perks. This is the relationship between streamers and subs.

Discord is part of this relationship, offering integration with Twitch to offer little perks as well.

To get this integration up and running, you first must connect your Twitch and Discord accounts. After these connections are set, we can then talk a bit about what they do for us.

1. **Go to your User Settings by clicking the gear wheel to the right of your username.**

2. **Click the Connections option. (See Figure 6-13.)**

   To review, the various apps you can integrate with Discord include (from left to right):

   - Twitch

   - YouTube

   - Blizzard.net

   - Steam

- Reddit
- Facebook
- Twitter
- Spotify
- Xbox

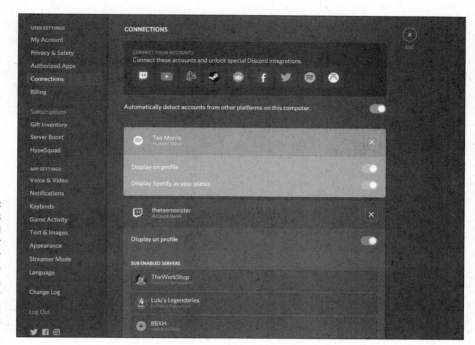

3. **Click the Twitch icon and follow the steps to connect your server to your Twitch account.**

   At the time of this writing, the only streaming platforms recognized by Discord are Twitch, YouTube, and Facebook.

4. **After the connection is made, activate the Display on Profile option.**

5. **Return to Discord, and go to your server settings.**

6. **Select the Integrations option and confirm that the Sync option is checked.**

7. **As pictured in Figure 6-14, set the Expired Sub Behavior to Remove Role, and the Grace Period to 7 Days.**

8. **Make sure the permission for Discord users to use Custom Emotes is activated.**

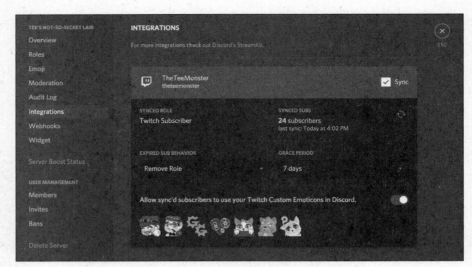

FIGURE 6-14:
After Twitch is integrated with your Discord, you can grant extra perks to your subs when a Twitch subscription happens; and you can manage some of those perks from here as well.

Exactly what does integration do for you and your subs? By setting up this connection and syncing (either manually or automatically), Discord offers Twitch users the ability to join servers of its supported streams by going to Connections found under User Settings. There, they will see all the various servers they are subbed to, and can simply click the Join button to join that respective server. Discord also automatically creates a Twitch Subscriber role and then assigns that role to any new server member who subscribes to you. Finally, you might notice a subs-only channel created, complete with permissions catering to your Twitch Subscriber role.

REMEMBER

Integrations cover more than just streams from Twitch and YouTube. Share what you're listening to on Spotify. Let people know what your game of choice is at Steam. Explore what each integration offers your server and find out what works for you.

The relationship between Discord and content creators like your humble author here has always been a close one. Podcasters, streamers, and artists of all backgrounds have found this platform to be a healthy, positive place to build a community around their content, and video only helps you create content that feels more personal, more intimate. With Discord's ability to stream still in Beta yet with such incredible potential, the future of video on the platform looks exciting.

Now that we have video covered, it's time to take all of this and begin to incorporate final touches to the server. We engage bots to help us do more with a #welcome message, then we look at how to enforce rules and engender good, positive vibes, and finally we start to work on a routine. A community can build itself, but when its founder takes an active role in its development, the community grows faster. That happens with a reliable schedule and an incorporation of this new platform in your established ones.

Chapter **7**

Setting the Stage: Making Discord Your Digital Hangout

What a ride this has been. We have worked through all kinds of tips and tricks, and just wrapped up talking in-depth about adding video into your Discord routine. Right now, you should be feeling like you have received a solid introduction to everything that makes this platform go, provided you have been reading this book from cover to cover.

And seriously, thanks. A lot of love goes into these *For Dummies* books, and if you are hanging on my every word, that means a lot.

But maybe, like some folks who are in a pinch for time and want to cut to the end of a good whodunnit — and far be it from me to judge, but yeah, I'm *totally* judging you — you may be using *Discord For Dummies* more like a reference tool. You're jumping in and around the chapters, looking for those solutions you need, hopping from the Index to the reference cited. *"This is the Way."* as *The Mandalorian* taught us. Kinda.

Point is, if you are already up on your audio settings, your video settings, and all the intimate settings for text, roles, and servers, you may have jumped directly to this chapter, in which case, *"Hi, how you doin'? My name's Tee, and I'm here to help you with Discord.*" We have a server up and running, but we lack some of the details you may need to add after its "soft opening." These are the finer details that involve access to your server, and laying down the groundwork for what you, the server's founder, deem as appropriate behavior. Whereas Chapter 8 goes into the details of good behavior, this chapter focuses more on making it clear this server is "your house, your rules" and not some trendy mob scene at Studio 54 on one of its wilder and weirder days.

First impressions mean a lot. It should be where people take note of the kind of server you run and how to be the best kind of member of this particular community.

Greetings, Fellow Programs: The Value of a #Welcome Channel

Some Discord servers drop newcomers right into the middle of the action. It is difficult to know exactly where to go on arriving, especially if you are new to the platform on a whole. The good news is, there is a trend on Discord to ease newcomers into a person's or group's server: the *#welcome channel.*

What exactly is the welcome channel, and why do people in other channels sometimes use hashtags specific to your server's channel? And why are we reviewing it? We covered this in Chapter 3. Well, yes we did, but back in Chapter 3, we were working with formatting primarily. Here's we're looking at tone and intent. Each Discord server has its own set of rules, all depending on the various hosts of a channel and their expectations of a community. Some people keep their intros short and sweet. Others take their welcome pages very seriously, outlining rules of engagement and orders of conduct so there is no risk of hearing *"Wait, I didn't know that I couldn't say . . ."* when someone finds himself on the business end of Mjölnir's cousin, Fluffy the Ban Hammer. Both approaches to a #welcome page are valid. What matters is making clear the foundation for what to do and what not to do in a channel.

Ya basic: Putting together a simple #welcome channel

There are two ways you can set up a "hello" to all the newcomers to your server. It just takes a little bit of time to write out what you want people to know about your server and what they can expect while they are there.

1. **Launch Discord and in your server, go to Main Channels and click the "+" icon to add in a new channel.**

2. **Call this new channel Welcome and make sure Text Channels is selected. Click the Create Channel button when ready.**

3. **Go to the #welcome channel and click-and-drag it to the top of your Main Channels section. Click the gear wheel to go into the Channel Settings.**

4. **In the Permissions options, set the following:**

   - **Create Invite — Granted (green check mark)**

   - **Read Messages — Granted**

   - **Add Reactions — Granted**

   - **All other settings — Denied (red X)**

   These settings lock down the page so that people can read and react to it, but not post anything that will move the Welcome message out of view.

5. **Accept the changes and return to your #welcome message by clicking the "X" icon to the upper-right or by pressing the Esc key.**

6. **In the text field, enter in the following text as your official welcome to the server. Follow the formatting as shown here:**

   A little law here on my server: If someone has a different opinion from you, honor it. It's something I've seen repeatedly happen in Discord. I will agree, there is a good chance some of you know *way more* about other things in the world, and I learn a lot from you. However, if someone has a different opinion than yours, let it go. You don't have to agree with said opinion, but needling someone really isn't cool. If they get a fact wrong, then try to kindly offer a course correction, but if what they get "wrong" is someone's opinion (example: "I have hated Season of the Drifter because I hate Gambit."), just let it go. Discord is a text-driven comm device, and (like email) it's too easy to misunderstand.

   My house. My rules. Be excellent to each other.

   If you can't, then we have a problem and I will remedy it.

   Thank you for respecting my Discord server, and each other.

TIP

If you have a lot of text you are going to post, it would be best to compose the message in a word processor first, as checking for errors will be a lot easier. Once you have it ready to go, copy and paste it into your Discord message field.

7. **Add to your message an appropriate image. It can be your streaming schedule, an animated GIF welcoming people to your server, or whatever you think matches the personality of your server.**

   Remember to keep the image within the limits of Discord's terms of service. Images from favorite media, memes, and the like are permissible, but overtly violent or sexual images could be problematic. Just think before you post.

8. **Press the Enter key to make your #welcome channel live, as seen in Figure 7-1.**

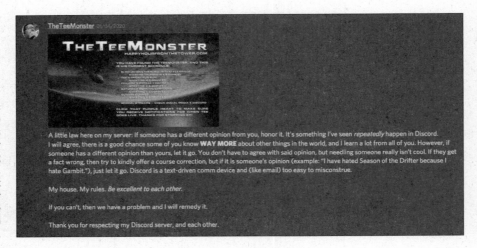

FIGURE 7-1:
A simple welcome channel lays down the law for everyone arriving to your server. Rules are set here by you for everyone to make nice with each other.

That was pretty simple, now wasn't it? A few thoughts jotted down on Discord and maybe an image representative of your server to go with it. But #welcome channels, no matter how fun or welcoming they are, can sometimes go overlooked like the Terms of Service concerning our favorite social media platforms. (Yes, as a matter of fact, Facebook *does* have permission to know what you're doing.) So how do you make sure that you have people actually reviewing the rules of your server when they first arrive to your server?

Oh, don't worry — I've got your back on that with a little help from my buddy, Carl. No, not Carl (pronounced "CORAL") from *The Walking Dead* who knows Glenn's favorite cartoon character was Popeye. No, this is Carl-bot (https://carl.gg) and he's here to offer you an extra layer of security to your server.

Access granted: Putting together a #welcome channel with Carl-bot

Mal Reynolds: "Listen up! We comin' down to empty that vault!"

Vault Guard: "You're gonna have to give me your authorization password."

Jayne fires off several rounds into the vault

Vault Guard: "Okay."

—Joss Whedon's *Serenity*

In building a community on Discord, understanding the rules of your server may be a little thing you want, and sometimes the best way to make sure people know what your server is all about is to deny them access to that after signing up for your server. That may sound harsh, but as Tony Stark once said about himself ruling Asgard, "I will be fair but firmly cruel." Sometimes, to get what you want, you have to make tough calls, and people by nature crave access. Gaining access to a location, exclusive content, or something along those lines is kind of a rush. It's a bit like being an executive or a VIP, knowing that there are no limits between you and wherever you want to go.

What is also satisfying is that when people gain access to your site, they have gone through a simple confirmation that the rules have been acknowledged in some way. As the administrator and moderator of an online community, you know the rules have not only been read but also understood and agreed upon, and that there is a binding agreement about those rules between you and the members of your server.

So how do you guarantee that?

"Guarantee" is something of a big promise, but what we are going to do is set up our #welcome page to act as a verification page. Once you have verified yourself here, the server's channels will unlock and appear, thus "guaranteeing" that this #welcome message has been read. We will be getting very familiar with roles, permissions, and hierarchies in this exercise, and these are all steps in improving our server.

Setting up roles and permissions for the #welcome channel

Our modest welcome channel is a good start, but we need to do a little more to it in order to give it this extra level of security and confirmation. And let's be honest, this "enhanced" server *is* a level of security. Before granting any newcomers full access to your server, we're asking for "one more thing" before getting to know the group. We're asking for an assurance that you've read the rules.

So, with @everyone being the basic role offered by default to all members of your server, and your only other role being for moderators, let's begin.

1. **Go to your server's name in Discord and access the drop-down menu. Select Server Settings and click the Roles option.**

2. **Click the small "+" icon at the right of Roles and create a Confirmed role.**

   At a basic level, anyone joining a server is designated with the @everyone role, but @everyone is not an official role. So you will be establishing Confirmed as a basic role, and depreciating the accessibility of the @everyone role on your server.

TIP

   You can name these roles whatever you like, so long as the permission you grant here is consistent. For example, in my screen captures, I have labeled my confirmed role *Explorers*. If you have a Member role active like the one we created in Chapter 3, you can use that one as a confirmed role.

3. **Grant the Confirmed role with the following settings and permissions:**

   - Display role members separately from online members
   - Create Invite
   - Change Nickname
   - Read Text Channels and See Voice Channels
   - Send Messages
   - Send TTS Messages
   - Embed Links
   - Attach Files
   - Read Message History
   - Use External Emojis
   - Voice Permissions: Connect
   - Voice Permissions: Speak
   - Use Voice Activity

4. **Go to Role Color and assign it an easy-to-identify-at-a-glance color.**

5. **If needed, click and drag the new Confirmed role from the list of roles in your server and make sure it is just above the @everyone role, as pictured in Figure 7-2.**

   Order is important because some roles affect other roles based on their hierarchy. Because we want to make sure Confirmed is a basic role but not an entry role like @everyone, we want to make sure both roles are at the bottom of the hierarchy with @everyone at the bottom and Confirmed above it. A basic role for your server members, such as Explorers pictured here, should be above the default @everyone role but underneath Moderators. This way, Discord knows which role takes priority over another.

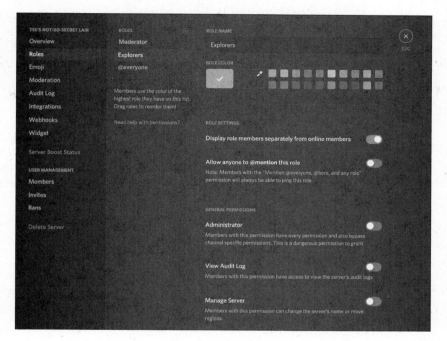

FIGURE 7-2: Hierarchy in your roles matter.

6. Save changes to return to Discord.

7. Launch or return to your browser and go to Carl-bot at https://carl.gg and log in with your Discord credentials. Follow the steps to link up Carl-bot with your server. You should see both yourself and your server in the upper-right of the dashboard, as seen in Figure 7-3.

8. Return to Discord and return to the Roles option of your server. Make sure that the newly created Carl-bot role is above both the Confirmed and @everyone roles. Click-and-drag it above Confirmed and save changes, if necessary.

9. Before changing permissions for the @everyone role, go to Members in the User Management section and assign existing members of your server with the Confirmed role.

FIGURE 7-3:
Carl-bot, found at
https://
carl.gg, offers
your Discord
added capabilities
to your server,
some requiring
custom code
whereas others
are simple
point-and-click
options.

This could be a time-consuming process if you have been up-and-running, and actively promoting your server. If your server is still relatively new, then you can take a few minutes to do so. Otherwise, when you change your @everyone settings, you are locking them out of the server, because we are making @everyone the entry-level role that needs verification.

10. **Return to Discord and go to your User Settings, located at the bottom-left of the app. Go to Appearance and scroll to the Advanced section. Make Developer Mode active.**

11. **Return to the #welcome channel and single-click the Edit Channel icon. Click the Permissions options and, for the @everyone role, grant the Read Messages permission. Make sure all other options are on the neutral (slash) setting. Save changes if needed.**

12. **Click the Confirmed role and deny the Read Messages permission. Make sure all other options are on the neutral (slash) setting. Save changes if needed.**

A lot going on here, huh? What you should be feeling is a strong sense of accomplishment as we have successfully set up the groundwork just for our new-and-improved #welcome channel. Now we need to take a look at the other channels and categories of our server.

Setting up roles and permissions for the rest of the server

1. **If your #welcome channel is grouped into a category, drag it out of your Main Channels to the top of the server's directory, on its own.**

Back in Chapter 2, we talked about the advantages of categories for servers that have many servers. As we are making the #welcome channel something of a stand-alone element, we can go on and move it to stand on its own.

2. **Right-click on your first category of channels (in Figure 7-4, this is Main Channels, as found on my server) and select the Edit Category option.**

FIGURE 7-4:
By going into your server categories, you can make global changes to permissions for all the channels grouped there.

3. **Click the Permissions option for Main Channels and click the @everyone role. Deny the Read Text Channels and See Voice Channels permissions. Make sure all other options are on the neutral (slash) setting, as seen in Figure 7-4. Save changes if needed.**

4. **Click the "+" sign and add the Confirmed role. Make sure Confirmed is above the @everyone role. Grant the following permissions:**

   - Read Text Channels and See Voice Channels
   - Send Messages
   - Send TTS Messages
   - Embed Links
   - Attach Files
   - Read Message History
   - Use External Emojis
   - Add Reactions
   - Voice Permissions: Connect
   - Voice Permissions: Speak
   - Use Voice Activity

Make sure all other options are on the neutral (slash) setting. Save changes if needed.

5. **Save changes to return to Discord. Click the channels in your Main Channels category and check Permissions to assure that your roles are all set.**

You can always do a quick sync for channel roles in categories by clicking the *Permissions Synced With* feature, located at the top of your Roles roster.

6. **Repeat Steps 2-5 for all your categories.**

7. **With all of your categories and channels set to hide channels for @everyone and reveal all channels for Confirmed roles, return to the Main Channels category. Create a new #about channel.**

We want to have the rules still visible and accessible as a reference once members are confirmed, so we will make a duplicate #welcome channel with different permissions.

8. **Go to the #welcome channel and copy the message.**

9. **Go to the #about channel and paste the message into the text field. Check the formatting to make sure everything is how you want it to look. Feel free to edit, if needed.**

10. **Place an appropriate image with the post, if desired.**

When a post is copied, the image associated with it will not be. You will need to attach the image again.

11. **Post your welcome in the #about channel.**

This may feel like a lot of prep work, but the payoff will be worth it in the end. We are now in the backstretch and are about to get into the development part of this with Carl-bot. Oh yeah, strap in, Sparky — we're about to go into Developer Mode with Discord.

Setting up Carl-bot for the server confirmation

You're probably thinking *Wait, this is a Dummies book and I'm about to do code as in hardcore dev code?* Well, kinda. CORAL-bot — I'm sorry, bad habit. — *Carl*-bot is going to do a lot of the heavy lifting for you. This will be a bit of a cakewalk, but it's still working in Developer Mode. And with Carl-bot, this is just the first step in having your Discord do some pretty cool things.

1. **Go to your browser, return to** https://carl.gg, **and get back to your dashboard.**

2. **In the left sidebar, click the Commands option. Along the top of commands are a variety of features and options. Click Roles and make sure the Reactrole option is active. (Its switch should be green.)**

By default, Reactrole should be active. If it isn't, click its switch to the lower-left to make it so.

3. **In the left sidebar, look for Utility ⇨ Reaction Roles and click the Create New Reaction Role button to begin. (See Figure 7-5.)**

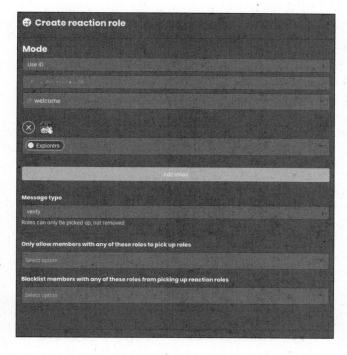

FIGURE 7-5: With Carl-bot, we will create a reaction role that uses the basics of programming to make verification occur at our #welcome channel.

4. **Under the Mode menu are three menus. Click Post Embed and select Use ID from the drop-down menu.**

5. **Go back to Discord and your #welcome channel. Click the More option (the "•••" icon) in your welcome message and select Copy ID from the menu.**

As you now have Developer Mode active in your account, the *Copy ID* option is now available. When working with bots, you will find these features both handy and essential.

6. **Return to your Carl-bot dashboard and paste in the #welcome message ID in the field into the Please Enter Your Message ID option.**

7. From the Please Select a Channel option, select #welcome from the menu.

8. Click the Add Emoji button and select from menu whatever emoji you would like to use as your confirmation reaction.

If you are a streamer and have Twitch integrated with your server, as discussed in Chapter 6, you can use your emotes as enable buttons for this command.

9. In the Select Option menu, select the Confirmed role as this will be the role assigned to users.

10. Proceed to Message Type and from that drop-down menu, select the Verify option.

With the Message Type established, Carl-bot will assign the role of Confirmed to users when they click the designated emoji as their reaction.

11. Click the green Create button to activate this command.

Refresh your browser and you will see that Carl-bot now has your command up and running. If you return to your #welcome channel, you should notice the entry now has the emoji you have designated as the reaction icon.

For clarification, it's not a bad idea to let people know they don't have to go hunting for the right emoji or emote. Just tell them the emote is there, waiting for them to click it.

So when newcomers come to your page, they will see Figure 7-6:

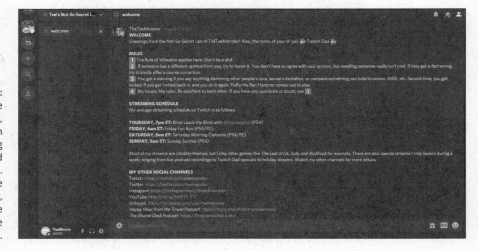

FIGURE 7-6:
Tee's #welcome channel, complete with rules, streaming schedule, and other social links. Note in the left-hand menu, only the #welcome channel is visible.

As soon as a new member to my server clicks on the designated emoji to confirm that the rules have been read and understood, the server is unlocked, as we see Figure 7-7:

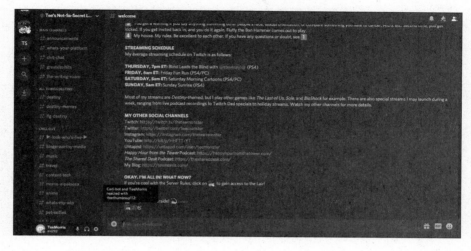

FIGURE 7-7: When the emote is clicked, the server is unlocked. Note in the left-hand sidebar, #welcome is now invisible (but you can still access the rules in the #about channel).

You did it! Not only did you survive a deep dive into permissions and bots that you didn't expect for a basic *For Dummies* book, you have the benefits of the end result: a slick verification process by which you are assured visitors have reviewed your rules and are ready to honor them.

It's also a great first impression. You know how to Discord like the best of them.

You now have two ways of greeting people to your channel, and whether you decide to go with the simple approach or something a little more sophisticated, the idea is to make people feel welcome at your server. Whatever you do to make it happen is what matters.

But what do you do with newcomers and returning visitors to your Discord after you've welcomed them? That should be the easy part — the hardest, at least in my own experience with Discord, is trying to be found. Getting found is not easy at all when you consider all the other talented people out there launching their own servers. But when you have people coming by, saying hi, and settling in, what do you do then?

I would never say community building and management is easy, because it isn't. Discord is there to help you make the most of it and to get out of it what you're putting into it. So let's look closely at how we're going to build on that welcome.

A LITTLE HELP FROM DOWN UNDER

When I set out to write this book, my main intent was not only to teach readers how to get the most out of Discord, but also to broaden my own skill set when it comes to this platform. I set out to create a book that was as comprehensive as I could make it. Thing is, though, Discord has *so much* to it. Sometimes you need some help from others to fill in the blanks.

And that why Y0kenB (pronounced Yoh-can-bee) from Australia is somebody I want to introduce to you. He has so much in his head about Discord, he's bursting at the seams.

Y0kenB offers at his YouTube channel at a wide array of videos about Discord, from the basics to the advanced. Y0kenB shows you how to work with bots like Dyno, Mee6, and others, and he deep dives into what makes Discord work as a platform. Then, for the admins, mods, and devs curious about webhooks, he offers instruction on applying webhooks with Discord, Twitter, and other apps with open APIs. When you feel like *Discord For Dummies* has given you as much as it can, I recommend giving Y0kenB a visit, either on YouTube or on one of his many social media platforms. He taught me at `http://bit.ly/yoken-discord` how to make the welcome page we just completed.

And sometimes he plays video games. His current game of choice? *Destiny*, it turns out.

I think this is the beginning of a beautiful friendship . . .

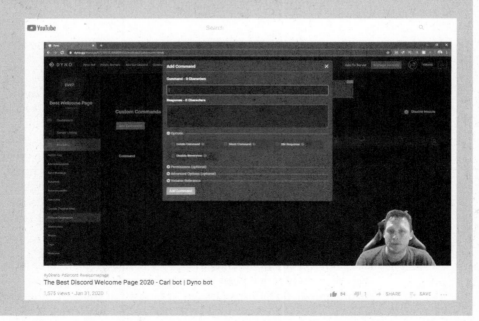

Attention, All Personnel: The Value of an #Announcements Channel

With the #welcome channel, you laid down some house rules for everyone to follow, and with a little help from Carl-bot you also set up an #about channel to make sure people understand the rules still apply, even after you say, "Hey, I'm all good with this. . ." and then start causing problems. Our server now needs to keep people in the know. After all, this is your corner of the Interwebs, or at least a corner belonging to a group or business that you're in charge of. What makes a community grow is open, robust communication, and this is why the #announcements channel is so important to you. Although the #welcome channel opens the door for your community, the #announcements channel keeps people in the know.

What designates the difference between the #welcome channel, the #chit-chat channel, and the #announcements channel all comes to approach. As we said earlier, the #welcome page is the first impression. No need for any real discussion. If you did want to ask something specific about the rules, the #chit-chat would be the best place as it is the general social space. People are hanging out, enjoying time together, making new friends, and reconnecting with familiar faces all on a variety of topics. So yes, you do want discussion there. The #announcements channel, much like #welcome and #about, is a space *specific to you,* and only your comments should be present there. It is in the #announcements channel, my own pictured in Figure 7-8, you share any changes to your server's own set of rules, details on where you are hosting a "Meat Space" meetup, or post notifications that you are going live on your streaming platform of choice should appear. This way, when people see the #announcements channel highlighted, they know that something worth the community's time has just gone live.

Setting up Mee6 on your #announcements channel

As we have already worked with bots previously in this chapter, you have an idea of exactly what these additions to your server are capable of. So let's go on and take a look at another bot, Mee6 (https://mee6.xyz). This digital assistant, inspired by Justin Roiland's Mr. Meeseeks from *Rick & Morty,* is a *"Can do!"* helper that's anxious to keep your community informed. We will be incorporating Mee6 with our #announcements channel in order to let people know here when an event online is taking place.

1. **Go to Discord. Create a new text channel called #announcements in the Main Channels category and make sure it is Read-Only.**

FIGURE 7-8:
An #announcements channel can be manual posts, bot-driven posts, or a combination of both, all working to keep your channel in the know.

If you have created the interactive #welcome channel where you assign roles on joining the server, you do not have to worry about duplicating those permissions for a new channel. The new channel will automatically take on the permissions as you established them with the category.

2. **Click-and-drag the new #announcements channel up to the top of the Main Channels category or place it underneath your #about channel.**

3. **Go to Mee6's website at** `https://mee6.xyz` **and follow the steps to authorize your account with it. When completed, click the Setup MEE6 button to begin.**

4. **After you have authorized Mee6 with your server (yes, a second time), you will be rerouted to the Plugins page, as seen in Figure 7-9. Select the Twitch option.**

5. **In the opening field, enter your Twitch channel's URL. If the URL is legitimate, Mee6 will find it.**

   If you are not a streamer, you can always enter in a streamer you follow on Twitch, Mixer, or YouTube here. Mee6 works with these platforms and a host of others. The idea behind this exercise is to show you how an assistant like Mee6 works for you and your #announcements channel.

FIGURE 7-9:
Mee6 (http://
mee6.xyz) allows
you to send out
on designated
channels
automatic
notifications of
events, like
Twitch streamers
going live.

6. **With Mee6's Twitch plug-in, a simple message is posted when the Twitch feed goes live. Edit the message to read:**

   Hey, @everyone — did you hear? {streamer} just went live on {link} so it's _Game Time!_ Don't miss out on the wicked plays, close calls, and shenanigans because, yes, there **WILL BE** shenanigans!

   You are allowed up to 2,000 characters. Because this is an auto-message, it is best not to make the post specific to one game or anything specific. Details will appear in the accompanying link.

REMEMBER

   By using the @everyone tag, your entire server is tagged and notified that you are going live. Some streamers use the @everyone tag in their Mee6 messages, whereas others use it more sparingly across their server. Consider the pros and cons, along with alternative strategies, when using the @everyone tag. (Or note the sidebar immediately following this exercise.)

7. **Under the Post In Channel menu, make sure to select the #announcements channel, as seen in Figure 7-10.**

8. **Click the Save button to accept the parameters for your Twitch command.**

You now have a simple notification cued up and ready to appear in your #announcements whenever you or your favorite streamer goes live. This is handy for getting the word out about a live stream, and there are other platforms and services you can funnel into here; but what other content would be good for an #announcement channel?

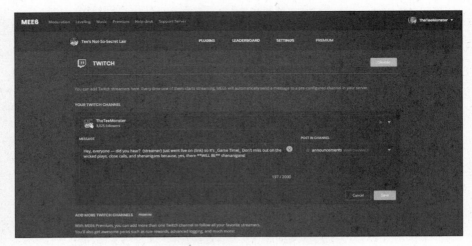

FIGURE 7-10:
Mee6 makes
automatic
notifications of
when you are
going live
extremely easy.
Hard coding is
taken care of with
simple, basic
menu options.

Posting an announcement (manually) on your #announcements channel

This channel doesn't necessarily need a bot to power it. You can simply work with it as a bulletin board of quick news and special events. Let's take a look at how you would do this if you're planning to stream a podcast recording, and you want your community to know about it.

1. **Go to your #announcements channel and type in the following:**

Got questions about _Destiny_, _Sea of Thieves_, or streaming on Twitch? What about hosting a 24-hour stream for St. Jude Children's Hospital?

@ZGphoto#5987 is coming to _Happy Hour from the Tower_ tonight at 5pm ET! Join us as he talks about all this **AND MORE!**

Because we don't want every announcement here to carry the @everyone tag, we're keeping this one simple. New postings are marked with highlighted channel titles, so this announcement should not get lost.

2. **Post the announcement about your upcoming podcast recording. Then click on the GIF icon located to the right of the text field.**

This menu of GIFs powered by https://tenor.com is a library of ready-to-use animated clips to add some fun to posts or instigate a GIF war, whichever you choose.

3. **In the Search Tenor field above the categorized GIF's, enter "Be there" as your search parameter. Pick a GIF you think works for your podcast post and click it. The GIF appears just underneath your post, as seen in Figure 7-11.**

FIGURE 7-11:
Announcements
can sometimes
be a combination
of text and
animated GIFs, a
simple combo
that yields
eye-catching
results.

4. **In a word processor, compose the following for an announcement:**

@everyone Good morning, Monsters! I had something of a bumpy end to what was a **solid** week of streaming. I'm taking steps to remedy that, so expect next week to have a few "training sessions" which should make for some fun montages.

Edits for _Discord For Dummies_ will be starting in earnest this week, so that means I will be running another "Editing with Twitch Dad" stream, because the tester stream seemed to be something of a hit with viewers. I didn't expect that, so let's run with it again. As for my Twitch Dad stream for February, I will still do one. I had hoped to do this before Valentine's but I can still make it work. If not, I'll run two Twitch Dad streams in March.

Here's how this week is shaping up:

THURSDAY, 7pm ET: Blind Leads the Blind with @stevesaylor#4811 and _Destiny 2_ (PS4)

FRIDAY, 6am ET: Friday Fun Run with _The Last of Us_ (PS4)

SATURDAY, 5am ET: Saturday Morning Cartoons (and Private Crucible Training) with _Destiny 2_ (PS4)

SUNDAY, 5am ET: Sunday Sunrise with _Destiny 2_ (PS4)

SUNDAY, 7pm ET: _The Shared Desk_: RECORDED LIVE!!!

Watch this channel and my social media avenues for any unannounced streams and last-minute changes. And take a look at this week's Highlight Reel at https://youtu.be/nppSm3BsF00:dizzy: See you all starside! :dizzy:

5. **Save this file to use as a template for future schedule postings.**

   This kind of announcement, while specific to a streamer, could apply to a musician or an author on tour, a business planning a variety of meetings and meetups throughout March, or a professional speaker making an appearance at an event. The above is an example of the kind of information you can share on your #announcements channel.

6. **With a final look for spelling and grammar, copy this message.**

7. **Paste this message into your Discord text field. With one last look at the message for any errors (because you can never be too careful), post your announcement.**

REVISITING THE @EVERYONE TAG STRATEGY

I touched briefly on the concern of using the *@everyone* tag, but it wouldn't hurt to give this another thought or two, especially from a strategic point-of-view.

Although, yes, you want to make sure that everyone sees something important coming from you, the idea of having a bot send out automated messages carrying the @everyone tag could get a little problematic. With the cautionary tale of "The Boy Who Cried Wolf" in mind, not every item posted on your #announcements channel can be regarded as top priority. You have to consider what is more important, where the emphasis on attention should be. I recommend not having the automated or even the spur-of-the-moment postings carry the @everyone tag. Instead, save these tags for the schedule postings. By reserving the "Now Hear This!" rally call, this tag could spotlight a post that would feature:

- A weekly schedule
- Relevant links to your weekly schedule
- Links to other media ("Best of" video, relevant podcast, and so forth)

This approach lends itself to your community sitting up and taking notice of the occasional @everyone post, featuring details and relevant supporting media instead of an onslaught of posts all screaming for attention.

Of course, there are always exceptions to the rule; but your own application of Discord and the ways you want to best leverage your community should help guide you in determining the best time to let fly with the @everyone tag.

There are a variety of ways to utilize an #announcements channel, either by taking advantage of bots, working with the animated GIF library in order to grab attention, or just using the channel to post weekly or monthly schedules. Keep in mind that the management of an #announcements channel means making sure the voice going out on it is your voice and yours alone. The #announcements channel should not be a location for discussion, chatter, or debate. You are making sure details are going out to the public. This is where you inform people and, hopefully, kick up a little hype.

Hype away, and hype hard!

On the topic of the @everyone tag, you may have noticed that your phone has become more and more greedy for your attention with each server you have joined. This is a somewhat inconvenient truth and an uncomfortable reality of Discord — there is a lot of traffic on popular servers, and the constant alerts you receive at worst can be distracting to you and to everyone around you, and at best can chew through your smartphone's battery.

Discord is on top of this and has something for you concerning all that traffic: control. There will be those channels, and sometimes those servers, that need a time out in the Sin Bin, or a complete ejection from the game. In the end, you have the power to decide what to respond to, what not to, and when to turn the volume all the way down to zero. (And you can ask the guys from Spinal Tap, that's a far away location from 11.)

But that's the point. No matter how much you enjoy Discord, you need to make certain you are in control of it. Not the other way around.

Getting in the Last Word with Discord

The "chirp" notification alert Discord is known for is pretty subtle, and I would know because I was of the time when Twitterific (https://twitterific.com) would announce new tweets with a chime *and a bird call*. It's charming and always brings a smile — that is, until you forget it's on and the app goes off at a particularly tense moment in a meeting.

Yes, that's happened to me before. Not proud to own it, but own it I will.

While there are worse alerts than the Discord chirp, the alert has made me flinch once or twice when it gets into a rapid-fire mode. Suddenly, that low-key alert becomes something akin to fingernails on a chalkboard. And if you have been playing with Discord on your various devices, you know what I mean by the machine gun-like chirping that gets underneath your skin.

Let's gain a little control over that, shall we?

1. **In Discord, go to your User Settings, located at the bottom-left of the app. Click the "gear wheel" icon and select the Notifications options.**

   Notifications covers all the various sounds that come out of Discord. As seen in Figure 7-12, you can decide how you want to be notified and if the notification comes with sound or not.

REMEMBER

   These options depicted in this exercise are only accessible with the desktop or browser versions of the app. The mobile versions of the app do not feature the details depicted here.

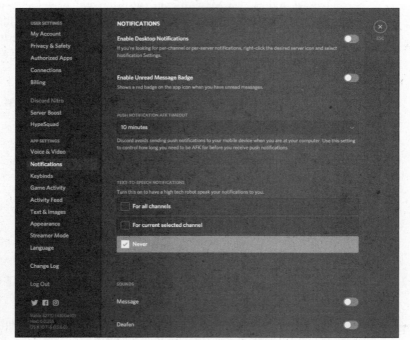

FIGURE 7-12:
The Notifications option is a global look at how you are alerted to incoming messages, either from a visual alert, an aural alert, or both.

2. **Click the Enable Desktop Notifications option in order to activate a small alert with the Discord user's avatar and a portion of their post.**

   These subtle alerts are also known as *push notifications*. Although they're unobtrusive on a desktop or laptop computer, push notifications can sometimes be viewed as distracting on mobile devices. You can always deactivate push notifications on Discord, or go into your device's own Notifications Settings and disable these alerts for just that particular device.

3. Scroll down to the Sounds section of Notifications and roll your cursor over one of the sound effects. A speaker icon appears. Click it to sample the sound. Go through the list to either activate or deactivate the alerts.

If the signature "chirp" from Discord is working on your last nerve, disable the Message alert. You will still receive notifications, if enabled, but they will just be silent.

4. When you are done, return to Discord by clicking the "X" to the upper-right or pressing the Esc key.

5. If you have Discord running on a mobile device such as a tablet or iPad, look in the lower-left for User Settings, which is the gear icon similar to the desktop app. Tap the User Settings icon and scroll down to the Notifications option.

If you are not using Discord on a tablet, skip to Step 10.

6. Tap the Notifications option.

7. Tap Get Notifications Outside of Discord in order to review where you are granting access for Discord. You can revoke Discord's access to these apps or change the way notifications arrive to your tablet.

8. Tap the Back or Discord option in the upper-left corner of your device in order to return to Discord. Disable notifications, if desired, by tapping the Get Notifications within Discord switch, off to the left.

9. Tap the Back option to return to your User Preferences, then tap Close to return to Discord.

10. If you have Discord running on a smartphone, look in the lower-right for the icon of your avatar. This is Discord's User Settings on a smartphone. Tap the User Settings icon and scroll down to the Notifications option, as seen in Figure 7-13.

11. Tap the Notifications option.

12. Tap Get Notifications Outside of Discord in order to review where you are granting access for Discord. You can revoke Discord's access on these apps or change the way notifications arrive on your smartphone.

13. Tap the Back or Discord option in the upper-left corner of your smart-phone in order to return to Discord. Disable notifications, if desired, by tapping the Get Notifications within Discord switch, located to the left.

14. Tap the Back option to return to your User Preferences, then tap the far-left icon at the bottom of the screen to return to Discord.

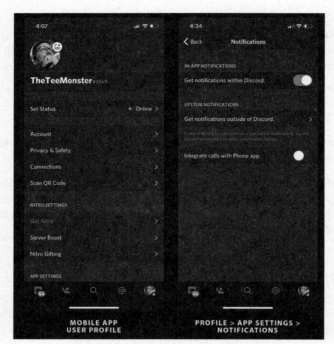

MOBILE APP
USER PROFILE

PROFILE > APP SETTINGS >
NOTIFICATIONS

Changing your Notifications preferences can turn down some of the noise in the signal you are creating in Discord, both from your own server as well as from other servers you have joined. However, you might find there are some servers you visit that tend to be noisier than others. There's nothing wrong with that. Some places online are like pubs, taverns, and hookah bars. You might visit a few that are incredible chill whereas others are BLASTING HOUSE MUSIC TO SET A TONE FOR THOSE WINDING DOWN FROM A NIGHT OF CLUBBING! I MEAN, YEAH, THIS WAS A GREAT IDEA TO CHILL OUT HERE AFTER THAT PARTY WE VISITED IN CHAPTERS 3 AND 6!!!

Right . . .

You want to make sure your server is taking top priority over the other servers you have followed. You don't want to leave those servers because they have a resource or a connection you want to keep working with, but the chatter from other channels have you questioning the value of that server. Presently, we have taken control over how Discord notifies us, but these next steps allow us to take control of exactly who will notify us and who won't.

1. Go into your Discord on your browser or desktop app, and find a channel you think is okay to "time out" due to excessive or distracting traffic.

For this exercise, I'm choosing my #meme-a-palooza channel. I've got nothing against memes. I love them, maybe a little too much. For the sake of this exercise, though, let's say this content has been something of a distraction.

2. **Right-click on the channel to access the Options menu, and then click on the Mute Channel option.**

   As seen in Figure 7-14, a submenu appears offering time blocks:

   - For 15 minutes

   - For 1 hour

   - For 8 hours

   - For 24 hours

   - Until I turn it back on

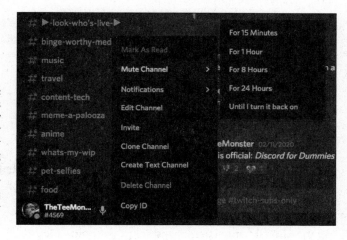

FIGURE 7-14:
If a channel is getting too noisy either on your server or elsewhere, using the Mute Channel option is a better option than leaving a server completely.

3. **Choose for how long this channel is to be muted.**

   With the exception of the Until I Turn It Back On option, all notifications and updates from this channel will be muted. When you visit other servers, the menu is identical except for a few missing options (because you are not the administrator there). The process for muting a channel is no different from server to server.

4. **Now look over your server, or a server that you are a member of, and find a category in the left-hand sidebar. Right-click on a server category to access the Options menu.**

5. **Click the Mute Channel option and review the submenu of time blocks:**

- For 15 minutes
- For 1 hour
- For 8 hours
- For 24 hours
- Until I turn it back on

6. **If desired, choose for how long this *category* is to be muted.**

7. **Right-click on the name of a server at the top of the left-hand sidebar of categories and channels. With the Options menu visible, repeat Steps 5-6.**

   As mentioned before, Discord developers are granting you control on all levels of the platform. So you can either muter individual channels or categories outright, or completely mute a server.

8. **Return to your own server and mute three random channels for 15 minutes. When you're done, go to your server name and click it to reveal your Server Preferences menu.**

9. **Select the Hide Muted Channels option.**

   When silencing channels, you have the option of hiding them from view. This is just an aesthetic change, but it can cut down any clutter in your Discord UI if you have muted channels for a long period of time.

10. **Go to your smartphone and launch the Discord app. Find a channel in your server you want to mute and hold your finger on it. An Options menu slides up from the bottom. Tap the Edit Channel option.**

11. **In this screen, tap the Notifications Settings option.**

12. **Tap the Mute [channel name] and select your time block.**

13. **Return to Discord's main interface on your smartphone and press and hold your finger on a category in your server. From the Options menu that appears, tap the Edit Channel option.**

14. **Repeat Steps 10–11.**

REMEMBER

   Muting channels and categories from mobile devices only works with servers that you are moderating. You can only mute entire servers from mobile devices, but that's all.

15. **Return to Discord's main interface and tap the More option (the "•••" icon) and access the Server Options menu.**

16. Tap the Notifications icon and repeat Steps 10-11 to mute the server, as pictured in Figure 7-15.

Although the path to get there differs slightly, the options for muting channels, categories, and servers are the same from desktop to mobile.

FIGURE 7-15: Discord developers have worked within the desktop and mobile environments to make sure all options are available for your Discord experience.

With this chapter, you should now feel something of a sense of control, more over the Discord environment than over your community. That sort of control is always a work-in-progress; and on some days, it is better than others. The control covered here is more about controlling the signal, making sure you are notified when you want to be, and being able to turn down the volume if the noise gets too intense. When cultivating a community, it is only beneficial to know when chatter is becoming a distraction. You need to make certain that you and your community understand one another, and communicate efficiently and effectively.

With control over the noise, you can't stop the signal.

» Hosting interviews on Discord

» Prepping for interviews and live recordings

» Using OBS to record Discord sessions

Chapter **8**

Discord in Name Only: Etiquette

D iscord is truly all about communications. Sure, it was invented, developed, and distributed by the gaming community in order to provide a solutions for better in-game comms (which, if you have ever used in-game comms, you know how the demand for something like that is real); but watching how it has progressed just in the time I've been using it, Discord is a platform dedicated to people connecting with one another through text, audio, and video. A lot is happening here, and it's very cool to be a part of it.

But every day on Discord is hardly a picnic. Some days, it rains. Like heavy downpours.

Along with sharing what you love and herding ca — I mean, organizing volunteers for an online event, this platform centers itself around managing people. That may sound a little cold, as I have grown to know truly wonderful people through Discord, but this is the truth of it. You are moderating your own server, interacting with those who are taking part in it, and keeping the conversation positive and friendly, and you have to manage people as you are the host of this server at the end of the day. If there's a problem, you or your moderators need to take care of it.

And it's a good practice to show other servers how you yourself would like to be treated on your own.

As I've done in other titles concerning social media and its platforms, I want to provide a guide to not only creating and managing a solid Discord server but also embody a voice welcomed on other servers. So maybe this chapter isn't for those who set out to be dillweeds (because they will never read this section, if they bother to read at all). This chapter is for those of you who want a better understanding of what is perceived as good behavior, positive attitudes, and excellent community management.

Bye, Felicia: Causing Discord on Discord

If I were to tell you, "Everyone on Discord is just overflowing with awesome," then I should also add that when you join my server, you get a free pony and a lifetime supply of smoked chicken and bacon. It's a nice fantasy to think we exist in a perfect world online where open minds and open hearts prevail, but let's be honest: There are some really nasty people among us, some either managing mayhem from their office cubicle, from the basement of their mom and dad's house, or from the patio of a bistro overlooking the Potomac. Sooner or later, these people will find you and your server.

Many of the bad people you will come across, fortunately, are easily categorized. The way you deal with them can sometimes be tricky, though, or creative, depending on your approach. While some of these offenders consciously set out to make an impact on someone's server, most of the time the lapse in etiquette is purely unintentional. In most cases, infractions can be easily avoided. It can just be a matter of common sense.

It's those other times, though, when you just have to brace for impact. And hopefully, I can give you something of a strategy here.

You know, over on my server . . .

In Chapter 2, I cover every conceivable way of promoting your server. Streaming platforms. Twitter. Your blog. You have a lot of options.

Except one.

This approach you see on Twitch a lot, and it still befuddles me that people think this is the *best* way to invite people to their server, but it happens. And I wish I knew where people got this tip as a great way to promote your server and build your community so I could go up to that wellspring of misinformation and punch them in the throat.

It usually happens like this:

[Challenger approaching – **Random New User** has joined your server!]

Random New User

Want more lively conversations. Why not join my server and join in on the fun!
[Discord Server URL]

The message may be worded differently, or it may just be the link all by itself, but there is no reason whatsoever to do this on anyone's server. And truth be told, it makes you look like a complete and utter nimrod.

REMEMBER

The difference between self-promotion and spam is the self-promotion comes at an invitation from the host, either encouraged by the host in a channel or a channel labeled #self-promotion where people are encouraged to promote what they are working on. Spam is usually random, never welcome, and inappropriate for unrelated channels.

Unwarranted, unwelcome self-promotion doesn't work. Never has. Never will. Not on *any* platform. (And yet, for whatever reason, people still do it.) Many spammers attempting to hop from server to server usually are cruising the Internet various streamers, be their platform YouTube, Mixer, Twitch, or otherwise. Once sufficient server invites have been selected, the server-hopping begins, joining a server, dropping the same message, and moving on to the next unsuspecting server. This doesn't count as networking or a promotion, but it does count as a shortcut to getting banned.

It's a better idea to find a channel that invites people to promote than randomly promote yourself and your server. Otherwise, ask the host if it would be permissible to promote your server on specific channel.

I hate everyone: Dealing with trolls

No, it doesn't make a lot of sense when people pop into a discussion about *Destiny, Fortnite, Overwatch,* or some other game, and they say something like "People still play this game?" Well, if you're in a specific game channel, yes, people are still playing this game. It gets worse, though, when saying, "Well, this is why your [Character Class] sucks. It's because . . ." Such a helper. Thanks for stopping by.

Or maybe you're having a solid conversation with a number of people based on your own skillset (writing, art, music, and so on), until someone creeps out of the woodwork and opens their rebuttal with *"Well, actually,"* and then proceeds to contradict you and everyone else chiming in. But hey, everyone needs an armchair quarterback, especially when they are busy taking notes on a conversation 20 posts long. Appreciate the critique, Sparky.

Then you have those even-more-charming individuals who think saying the same thing over and over *and over again* . . . and one more time for good measure . . . are making a contribution to your server. Or instead of a textual post, an individual drops in the same URL and the link appears dubious in nature. Or worse, it's content you wouldn't want to share with your daughter or your mom. And if it isn't comments or URLs, it's images of stuff that you tend to find only in corners of the Internet that require a Silkwood-style shower to cleanse you free of them; and yet, neither that nor all the brain bleach you can muster will erase those images from your memory. And yet, these folks think repeatedly posting images like this is funny.

Ah, yes, welcome to the wonderful world of Internet *trolls*.

The mission of a troll is a simple one: Rattle a community, derail the good juju, and make everyone feel uncomfortable. It's your mission — should you choose to accept it — to succeed in scoring what trolls hate the most in losing: *the last word*. There are several ways you and your mods can do this:

1. **When the offending comment appears in a channel, right-click the offender's username.**

   The menu that appears is a Server Member Options menu for the individual's account. (See Figure 8-1.) Instead of affecting a channel or a server, this menu directly displays an individual's account details.

   There are three options for dealing with a troll:

   - Block
   - Kick
   - Ban

2. **Choose the Block option to serve as a warning shot.**

   The user can still see posts in the server, but cannot post until you unblock them.

   Two other disciplinary options, Mute and Deafen, are for offenders on audio and video channels.

3. **If, on unblocking the individual, an offensive user returns and continues harassment, right-click the offender's username and select the Kick option.**

   When you kick someone off a channel or server, that user is booted from the channel or server where they are a member. They can be invited back by other members who have permissions to send out invitations. On responding to a new invite, the kicked member can return.

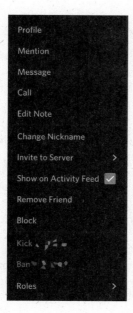

FIGURE 8-1:
The Server
Member Options
menu, accessed
by right-clicking
on a username in
a channel, offers
you a variety of
ways to interact
with the
individual.

4. **If an offensive user is invited back to your server and they still continue harassment, right-click the offender's username and select the Ban option.**

    The Ban option is the nuclear option. That user is removed from the server and cannot rejoin, even with an invitation. An administrator can choose to clear any and all of the offending user's messages remaining on the server.

WARNING

Some trolls may establish a new user profile under a different name and return to your server to pick up where they left off. Best for you and your moderators to remain alert.

The important thing to remember about trolls is that *you* get in the last word, not vice versa. As you have heard repeatedly throughout the book, this is your house, your rules. No matter how nasty a troll's intent is, it is up to you and your mods to protect this house! Don't hesitate to do so.

Hate speech

Beyond the trolls described in the preceding section are another group of haters that say things they would never be brave enough to say to you in public. Behind a keyboard and monitor, there is a lot of swagger and swearing, and even though you have it clear in your rules that you really don't want that sort of talk in your stream, these chatters somehow think of themselves as exempt of the rules.

Ugh, this game is AIDS. (Um, no, it's not. It's just a bad game.)

I hope these game developers die in a mass shooting. (This actually was said in my chat. I was able to explain to this member of my server this was not acceptable here, on my Twitch channel, or anywhere in real life. Even as a joke.)

What are you? Some kind of fa— (Okay, I think we're done.)

This kind of toxic talk will wind up on your server at some point in time, and there is no real standard trigger for it. Sometimes, people think they are being clever. Other times, people might be quoting movies, thinking they are being clever, when out of context, the quote is just wrong. Sometimes, people are looking to start up drama. Hate speech is up to you to manage. Preferably, the best way to manage these corrosive personalities is towards the nearest exit.

This is why we have the rules of a server, addressed in Chapter 7, and pictured in Figure 8-2. These rules are to make sure that those new to the community understand the boundaries. Other servers may be more liberal when it comes to what they do and don't allow, and that is their business. It doesn't have to be yours. What happens on your stream falls under your standards. Make sure to stick by them and adhere to them.

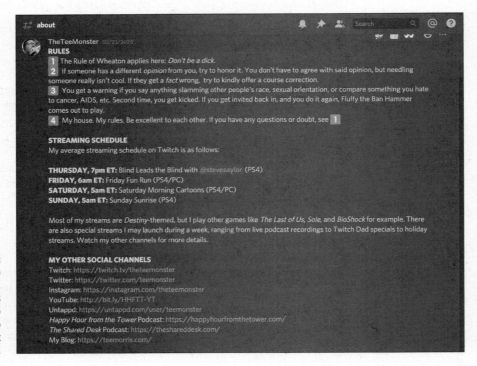

FIGURE 8-2:
When you set up rules for a server, sometimes it is best to go into detail in order to make clear what is not tolerated.

I'LL TAKE THE FIRST: FREE SPEECH VERSUS SLANDER

Words carry weight. Sometimes, those toxic souls on Discord forget this. Words spoken in the heat of the moment or off the cuff can (potentially, at least) get you into a world of trouble and unwanted attention. I'm not a lawyer, but I have pulled up for this sidebar the legal definition of *slander:* "a verbal form of defamation, or spoken words that falsely and negatively reflect on one's reputation.

So where does Discord fit into all this? Discord, like any platform on the Internet, be it podcasting, streaming, or any other social media, is a make and manner of a public space. Think about it: Before you open your mouth and begin a slam-fest on someone you don't like or go on a personal attack of someone you work alongside, remember that your little rant is reaching a *worldwide* audience. Don't ever assume that nobody's listening. It doesn't take but a moment *before* you open your mouth or click the Send icon to really think about what's on the tip of your forked tongue. The best hard rule about trash talking of any kind is to keep others' names out of your mouth unless you are talking about these people in a positive light. Trashing others may attract attention, sure, but it's the kind of attention you will not want. The possibility of long-term success coming from toxic chatter doesn't happen. And while yes, you may have a First Amendment *right* to say it, with that right also comes the responsibility of consequences.

Keep it positive, or just keep it to yourself.

Along with making sure others are keeping themselves on the right path of getting along with one another, you as a moderator and administrator to your server should look at how you are coming across to other you invite into your digital hangout. Discord is, as we've mentioned before, something more than just a platform for you and your fireteam to get their comms on. If you are a podcaster or a streamer, you can also use Discord as a platform for interviews. The audio and video quality found in Discord provides real potential for you to hold roundtable discussions or more intimate one-on-ones with people.

But interviewing is more than just having someone connect with you on your server, and then having a chit-chat. There is a subtle science to how interviews go, and some hazards are out there you should be aware of.

Getting Your Gab On: Interview Tips

A guest could be your dad, your mother-in-law, your best friend, or the man on the street. It could also be the friend of a friend who can get you on the phone with your favorite author, actor, or athlete. When you're interviewing, you have a second voice to share the focus with on your Discord.

Interviews with subject matter experts and special guests are not only just plain fun to do, but when video is involved, you can observe body language, facial expressions, and reactions to questions and answers. Depending on who you talk to, the subject matter at hand, and the questions you ask, interviews can be informative and invocative. The difference between an interview that knocks it out of the park and an interview that goes over like a lead balloon stems back to how you carry yourself.

Rules for guests and hosts

With Discord, interviews can happen just about anywhere. If, however, you are having guests at your home — unlikely, but just in case — make them feel at home. Offer them something to drink. Offer to take them on a tour of your humble abode. Introduce them to your family. The point is to be polite. And tidy. Depending on your house cleaning skills, you want your house to be ready for guest. Straightening up may *not* be enough.

And if you're having in-studio interviews, it's also a good idea to have your studio clutter-free and ready for guests, as seen in Figure 8-3. Make sure you and your studio are presentable. While streaming in my pajamas on Saturday morning, as I'm flying solo and it's Saturday morning, is allowed, that's one thing. If other streamers, authors, or other outstanding individuals in their respective fields are coming over to the house for an interview, don't think for a minute I'll be greeting them in my *Star Wars* jammies and Dogfish Head Brewery slippers.

Okay, maybe I *would* greet them wearing the Dogfish slippers, but I would be bathed, groomed, and dressed and the house would be ready to receive royalty. The key word here is *guest.* Treat your guests, be they in person or on the other side of a webcam, as such. Be cool, be pleasant, be nice. And if you're a guest on someone else's Discord channel for a podcast, stream or both, the same rules apply. Don't prop your feet up on the furniture, don't demand hospitality, and please *don't be a jerk during the interview.*

FIGURE 8-3: When having guests over for interviews, make sure you can handle the traffic, both on Discord and in your studio.

An interview, be it an in-studio visit or all online, is an audition for both guest and host. If the guest is abrasive, abusive, and just plain rude, chances are good that the guest will never be invited back, no matter how well the interview goes. Flipping the script, if a host asks unapproved questions, continues to pry into personal matters that have nothing to do with the interview, or seems determined to take over the interview spotlight as if trying to impress the guest, said guest may never return, even if extended several invitations.

Off-the-cuff interviews

On account of the Discord app and some really ingenious gadget out on the market, you take your studio on the road. You may find yourself at another person's home, a place of business, or some neutral ground from where you are hosting this interview. And if you are quickly composing questions in your head (as the opportunity might not present itself again), you're practicing, for the lack of a better term, *guerilla journalism*. Maybe you don't think you're ambushing unsuspecting people with hard, probing questions, but to people not expecting to be interviewed, this can be a little intimidating. Make certain to show respect to your guests, wherever you are when the interview takes place.

A good approach for getting good interviews is to ask permission of your guests, be they passersby or experts at their place of business, to interview them. If the guest you want to interview has a handler or liaison, it's good protocol to follow the suggestions and advice of the guest's staff, as outlined earlier in this chapter.

If you start out with a warm, welcoming smile and explain what you're doing and why, most people open up and are happy to talk.

REMEMBER

Before going mobile, test your equipment. You're now out of the controlled environment of your home studio; you have to deal with surrounding ambient noise, how well your interview is recording in the midst of uncontrolled background variables, and of course how good the Internet connection is. Power up your laptop and portable gear, and perform a quick test to see if you have everything you need out of your control under a semblance of control. When you have your setup good to go, you're ready to get on to your interviews.

And although this may sound a bit pessimistic, be ready for things to go wrong. Guests might not show up for interviews. New high-tech toys, if not given a proper pre-interview shakedown, may not come through. It's is always good to have a Plan B for when things go horrendously wrong.

Interview requests

The courage to submit an interview request comes simply from your interest in the interview subject. Script or compose an email to ask your favorite author, actor, sports celebrity, game streamer, podcaster, or whomever you want for an interview. You may need to submit the request multiple times, and sometimes you may have to work through numerous people simply to get a no as your final reply. That happens. It doesn't mean that individual is mean, a rude person, or otherwise. They just don't do interviews. For every no, you will find ten others who will enthusiastically say yes.

Here are some things you should keep in mind when working on the interview request:

>> **Market yourself and your show.** Your interview request needs to sell your services to the prospective interviewee. Large listenership numbers are always helpful. It's also a good idea to let people know how long your show has been running. Have you done interviews before? If so, do some name dropping.

>> **What can I do for you?** The person (or the person's agent) is going ask What's in it for me (or my client)? You need to ask yourself questions like: Does he or she have a special charity event they wish to promote? Perhaps he or she is

about to launch a special product? Do you have a book or an album (or both!) coming out? Find an angle and work with it.

» **Be flexible.** Remember, you're asking for their time. There may be restrictions in your schedule and theirs. Sometimes you can get an interview within 24 hours or you have to schedule it weeks or months in advance. You may have to take time off work from your regular job or rearrange other plans, just like the interview subject who is taking time out of their day to chat with you.

So if you wanted an example of an interview request email, it may look something like this:

Good morning/afternoon/evening, [name of interview subject].

My name is Tee Morris, and I am currently writing *Discord For Dummies*. I'd like to talk to you about how you build your community and manage it. Here are questions I have for you concerning you and your Discord server:

» When did you first launch your Discord server?

» You are a streamer but it appears that your Discord is geared more for [angle on the individual]. What brought about that evolution?

» What drives your community? What is it about your server that keeps people coming back?

» What do you think is the greatest challenge starting a Discord server?

» What is your proudest moment with Discord? Is it sharing your gaming experiences, sharing creative ideas, or discovering new tools from your community that help you accomplish creative tasks?

» What is the life lesson that Discord has taught you?

If at all possible, I would like to talk to you sometime on [suggested date], if that is convenient for you and your schedule. If you could let me know by [deadline for notification], I would appreciate it. We can narrow down details by then. We can either conduct our interview through Discord (on your schedule) and I would record it. You can reach me at this email address if you have any additional questions.

If you are curious about me and my background, I am an award-winning Science Fiction and Fantasy author, as well as an award-winning podcaster. In 2005, I was asked to write *Podcasting For Dummies* alongside Evo Terra. Since then, I have written several titles covering social media, including *All a Twitter, Sams Teach Yourself Twitter in 10 Minutes,* and *Social Media for Writers. Podcasting For Dummies* released its 3rd edition in October 2017 (and slated for a 4th edition in 2020), and I released with Wiley in January 2019 *Twitch For Dummies. Discord For Dummies* will be my fifth title with Wiley Publishing.

Thank you for your time and attention on this. I hope to hear from you on this.

All my best,

Tee Morris

Author, Podcaster, Streamer

Use this letter as your own template, adjusting it to your voice and your needs. This can serve as your go-to for when you want to reach out to people you want to interview on Discord. Before sending out the interview request, carefully check the letter to make sure there are no artifacts (references to previous recipients, or elements from the original template) and that questions pertain to the person you are sending the request to.

WARNING

If you are going to be talking to streamers, gamers, professionals in the gaming industry, and perhaps the odd podcaster or to will know Discord. You may be asked by some people outside of these tech-nerd circles "What's Discord?" Hopefully, this book will change that; but if there are those interview subjects that are not comfortable with or do not know Discord, you may have to switch to another interview platform.

It's All in the Planning: Preparing for Interviews

A few paragraphs back, I was talking about preparing for the worst. Plan B, just in case things don't work out the way you want it to with the interview. Thing is, Plan B should be a contingency; and it should be the kind of contingency that we know is there but we also know, deep down, we won't need. Because we're ready. We know what we need to do to make this interview a hit with the guest and with those who hear it.

Asking really great questions

Chances are good that if you're new to interviewing people, you've never held an interview quite like this — an interpersonal, casual chat that could get a bit thought-provoking or downright controversial, depending on what you are talking about. The interview may be arranged by you, or it may be prearranged for you. There's a science to it, and here are just a few tips to take to heart so you can hold a good, engaging interview:

» **Know who you're talking to and what to talk about.** When guests appear on your show, it is a good idea to know at the very least the subject matter on which you will be talking about. Let's say, for example, you are having an author appear on your show. If the author has written over a dozen books, be they fiction or nonfiction, trying to find the time to read all of your guest's books would seem an impossibility. So do some homework. If the author guest has written a popular series, go online and research the series. Visit Wikipedia and see if the series has a summary there. If you can only find limited information, find websites relevant to the topic of the series. If the series is steampunk, dig up information about the Victorian era. If the series follows a snarky, sentient robot, look up artificial intelligence. This has two effects: (1) You sound like you have a clue what the writer is writing about and (2) It allows you to ask better questions. These same rules apply for nonfiction authors, and really for guests of any particular background.

It's also a good idea to visit guests' websites or their social media platforms. You don't have to be an expert on their subject matter, but you should be familiar with it so you know in what direction to take the interview.

TIP

» **Have your questions follow a logical progression.** Say you're interviewing a filmmaker who is working on a horror movie. A good progression for your interview would be something like this:

- What made you want to shoot a horror movie?

- What makes a really good horror film?

- Who inspired you in this genre?

- In your opinion, what is the scariest film ever made?

You'll notice these questions are all based around filmmaking, beginning and ending with a director's choice. The progression of this interview starts specific on the current work and then broadens to a wider perspective. Most interviews should follow a progression like this, or they can start on a very broad viewpoint and slowly become more specific to the guest's expertise.

» **Ask open-ended questions.** To understand open-ended questions, it's simpler to explain closed-ended questions. Closed-ended questions are the kind that give you one word answers — for example, *"How long have you been studying plate tectonics?"* Don't count on your interviewee giving a dynamic answer to a question like that. Closed-ended questions make the process harder than it needs to be. Instead, rephrase your question like *"So what exactly got you interested in plate tectonics?"*

TIP

Write down a series of questions that could fill your podcast with brief, one-or-two-word answers. This way, if you find yourself struggling, you have a hidden stockpile of questions to call upon. After a few quick answers, you can always fall back on the *"Would you expand a bit on that please?"* question.

>> **Prepare twice the number of questions that you think you'll need.** Some interviews you hear grind to a halt for no other reason than the interviewer believed that the guest would talk his head off on the first question. You're certainly in for a bumpy ride when you ask a guest, *"Tell me a little bit about your experience at WidgetCo,"* and the guest replies, *"It was a lot of hard work, but rewarding,"* and he stops, obviously waiting for the next question. (Yeah, this is going to get painful.)

TIP

Have a pad and a pen on hand, ready to go. In the middle of your interview, an answer may inspire a brand new question you would want to ask your guest. Jot it down so you won't forget it. Then ask this new question either as a follow-up, or in place of another question you have up and coming. I recommend a pad and pen as keyboards can sometimes get noisy when in an interview session.

>> **Never worry about asking a stupid question.** When asking questions that may sound obvious or frequently asked, remember: Chances are good that your audience has never heard them answered before. Okay, maybe a writer has been asked time and again, "Where do your ideas come from?" or a politician has heard, "So when did you first start in politics?" often. When you have a guest present for a podcast, there's no such thing as a stupid question; what's really dumb is not to ask a question that you think isn't worth the guest's time. He or she may be champing at the bit in hopes you will ask it.

REMEMBER

Leave room for spontaneous questions as mentioned above. Listen to your guest's answers and see if a new path has opened up. They may be tense while answering the same questions for the 50th time, but if you strike a chord and stumble on a piece they are passionate about, abandon the questions for a bit and follow the trail!

How to tick off a guest: Bad interview behavior

Before you start percolating and dream up a few questions based on the preceding tips, stop and think about the interviews you've listened to where things suddenly headed south. Usually the interviewer finds themselves with a guest they know nothing about and they are expected to interview them on the fly, or the host ambushes the guest with questions that dig into something that's out of the guest's scope or none of the interviewer's business. We've piled up the typical gaffes in a prime example of a good interview gone bad.

But no matter your background, it is a little terrifying how quickly a pleasant conversation can turn, and the following blunders should do it faster than an Uwe Boll movie is in and out of theaters:

>> **Ask inappropriate questions.** Keep in mind your interview is not appearing on *60 Minutes, HardTalk,* or even *Dr. Phil.* If you want to fire off hard-hitting-tell-all-mudslinging questions, think about who your audience is, who you're talking to, and whether the question is within the ability of the guest to answer honestly and openly. If not, an awkward moment may be the least of your worries. Inappropriate questions can also be those irrelevant, wacky, off-the-wall, and far-too-personal questions for your guests. *"Who was the rudest person you have ever worked with on a mo-cap set?"* could put a performer's career into jeopardy if answered earnestly. *"What's the worst book you've ever read?"* could drop a writer into hot water with their colleagues. Asking athletes *"You are in fantastic shape. Do you sleep naked?"* could easily derail an interview quickly. Maybe these wildcard questions work for XM Radio shock jocks, but when you have an opportunity to interview people you respect in your field, do you really want to ask them something like, *"Boxers, briefs, or none of the above?"* Think about what you're going to ask before you actually do.

>> **Continue to pursue answers to inappropriate questions.** If a question has been deemed inappropriate by a guest, don't continue to ask it. Move on to the next question and continue forward into the interview. Interviews are not an arena for browbeating people into submission till they break down in tears and cough up the ugly, sordid details of their lives.

Are there exceptions to this exception? We would say, yes, depending on the content you're producing. Just remember: If you're after irreverent material for your show and push that envelope as far as you can, your guests may *not* want to play along — especially if they *don't* get the joke. If that's the case, expect your guests to get up and walk away. Even in the most idyllic situations, guests can (and do) reserve the right to do that.

>> **Turn the interview into the Me Show.** Please remember that the spotlight belongs to your guest. I recall an interview I was listening to where — no kidding — the three-person crew invited a guest on their writing podcast to talk about their books and their methodology of writing. . .only to launch into a 15-minute discussion between themselves on a completely unrelated topic, leaving the guest on the other side of their mic. Silent. For 15 minutes.

When a guest is introduced into the mix, you're surrendering control of your platform to him or her, and that isn't necessarily a bad thing. Let guests enjoy the spotlight; your audience will appreciate them for being there, which adds a new dimension to your feed. One way to avoid the me factor is to think of yourself as a liaison for the listener. Ask yourself, *As a listener, what questions would I ask or information would I be looking for from the guest?*

>> **Respect your guests. Period.** It has happened to me, both as an interview subject and as an interviewer. I've answered some questions that made me very uncomfortable, and requested hosts to please edit out the question and

related awkward response. In most cases, they respected my request. The others who did not bother to edit their podcasts? Well, I no longer field queries from them. With that experience, I extend the same courtesy to my guests. Why? I want to avoid blacklists. Also, interview subjects talk to their friends. You want them to speak positively of you. Show them respect, and those guests worth your time will do the same.

Feelin' the synergy

One final note on preparing for interviews: I've heard some guests say, *"I'm doing these interviewers a favor by going on their show."* And I've been told by other show hosts, *"We're doing you a great favor with this chance to showcase your work on our show."*

Both of these opinions are not just arrogant; they're just flat-out wrong.

The reality is that host and guest are working together to create a synergy. The interviewer has a chance to earn a wider audience and display mastery of journalistic techniques. The guest has a chance to get into the public eye, stay in the public eye, and talk about the next big thing he or she has coming in sight of said public eye. Working together, guest and host create a seamless promotional machine for one another.

If you decide to take on the art of the interview, keep these facts in mind. You and your guests will have your best chance to work together to create something special.

REMEMBER

If your format allows it, ask your guest for a celebrity show ID that you can drop in from time to time. You've probably heard these before on radio stations:

Hi, this is Rex Kramer, danger seeker. You may remember me from such films as *Airplane* **and** *Kentucky Fried Movie,* **and you're listening to** *The Shameless Self-Promoting Discord Show.*

If the interview guests want to be more creative, let them. These are a great self-promotion tool, a whole lot of fun, and a way to remind your listener of previous accomplishments. Remember to ask politely, and be aware that not everyone will (or can) comply.

You're hosting an interview on Discord. Your questions are set, and with what I've shared in this chapter, you are feeling more confident about hosting this talk about whatever subject matter you and your guest are connecting over. Now, the question is how are you going to record the interview? Discord does not offer (presently) any ways or means to record your interview. Is there a way to do that?

Recording Discord with OBS

One option of recording your interviews is with Open Broadcaster Software (`https://obsproject.org`). What makes OBS appealing to content creators is its availability of the application. With Windows, Mac, or Linux, OBS can record your Discord conversations easily and clearly. Sounds pretty incredible, doesn't it? Well, there's one more thing to know about OBS:

It's free.

OBS is open source software, and always improving in its capabilities on account of the community of developers rallying around this software.

WARNING

There are legal restrictions concerning the recording of calls, video or audio, and these restrictions vary from country to country, state to state, and region to region. Compliance with these laws falls on the content creators. Always ask for permission (or better yet, get it in writing) before recording.

Setting op OBS for Discord

Before going to Discord to bring in your guest(s), you're going to want to get OBS ready. For this exercise, we are keeping it simple and using Discord to record audio. The final file will be a video file, but we are recording strictly for audio.

1. **Download OBS Studio from** `https://www.obsproject.org`, **install it, and then launch the app.**

2. **Go to Scenes window at the bottom left of the UI, right-click the default scene, select Rename, and call this the Recording Booth scene.**

3. **In the Sources window, click the + option to view the Source menu (see Figure 8-4).**

   OBS transforms your computer into a working recording studio, complete with multiple incoming *sources* that create a *scene*. We will be creating a scene for our recording session in Discord.

4. **From the Source menu, select the Audio Input Capture option.**

5. **In the Create New window, label this source Discord Capture, and click the OK button.**

   All input signals and media incorporated into an OBS scene are *sources*. Here, the source is an audio signal originating from Discord.

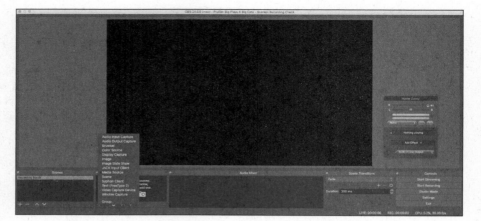

FIGURE 8-4:
OBS transforms
your computer
into a working
broadcast studio,
complete with
multiple input
sources.

6. **Select the Default option, and click the OK button.**

As OBS is recording your audio, you do not need to set up any additional input sources, as you have already done this in Discord. OBS records the default audio, the particular input sources handled by Discord.

7. **From the Source menu, select the Image option.**

8. **In the Create New window, label this source as Background, and click the OK button.**

9. **Click the Browse button, and select an image from your hard drive.**

10. **Click the Open button to drop in the image, and click the OK button to return to the OBS interface.**

Adding the background image is purely optional, but we do so as we are recording and exporting video from OBS once we are done.

11. **Choose Application ⇨ OBS ⇨ Preferences, and select the Output option, pictured in Figure 8-5.**

12. **Review the featured Recording Path. Click the Browse button and designate a new save location.**

Recording Path is where you tell OBS to save any recording files you create.

13. **In the Recording Format section, choose MP4 as your recording format.**

You are now all set and ready to go with OBS as your recorder for this interview. Let's make the magic happen then, shall we?

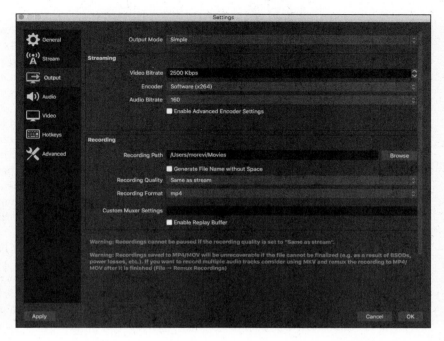

Recording with OBS

To record with OBS, follow these steps:

1. Launch Discord, and set up your interview meeting.

2. With OBS and Discord running, go to OBS, and click the Start Recording button.

3. Return to Discord, and begin your interview.

4. When you are done, click the Stop Recording button.

5. Go to your designated recording path, and find your recording.

6. Import this recording into QuickTime Player, and select File > Export As > Audio Only to pull the audio.

Congratulations! You just recorded your Discord interview.

From here, you can take the audio and prep it for podcasting or whatever you want to do for your interviews. For more on this process, take a look at *Podcasting For Dummies* by me and Chuck Tomasi.

Working with OBS, you can also bring in video sources. If you know your interview subject has a webcam of their own, you can easily set up your OBS for video interviews, and follow the above steps to create audio and/or video podcasts. If you want to know more about OBS, pick up a copy of *Twitch For Dummies*, and go exploring.

If you're doing an interview with multiple participants (known as *conferencing*), it's often best to have the person with the highest-power CPU host the meeting. (So make sure you're that guy or gal.) That person should initiate the call and invite the other attendees one at a time. The better the CPU, the better the conference will run and the better your recording will sound. Also, the conference host may or may not be the same as the person recording the call. Remember, your goal during an interview is to try to minimize the chances for problems.

So now you have a new application for Discord: your gateway to podcasting or streaming. Understanding etiquette and the mechanics behind a good interview can really open up your server to positive personalities and earn for yourself a reputation among other communities that your server is a good server to be a part of. This is what we are striving for when we set up a server — a place people can call their own and enjoy the social time.

In the words of two sage journeymen: Be excellent to each other.

3
Working Discord into Your Routine

Chapter **9**

Building on Your Foundation

I have no doubt you have been experiencing threads, and conversations, and media shares you wish were still continuing. You may also be experiencing those days when you wish you didn't have to take on the responsibility of a server. It's like that from day to day. There will be conversations on Discord that will change your perspective on the world, and then there are servers that make you wonder if "trivial" was redefined just for you. Not every day is going to be an unlocking of the universe's mysteries on your server. Some days, it will be "Hey, there's this actress in that Shudder series, *NoSFR8U*. What else has she been in?" That's the way life goes.

Regardless of the kind of day you had yesterday, you find yourself returning to Discord again and again. When you feel that pull to get back online, that's when you know your community has got a hold of you, and there is nothing wrong with that. There are real people behind those various nicknames, and you are wanting to make a connection with them. During those lulls in your conversations, your mind may wander to what you can do to keep your server active, especially when you visit other servers and note their success. What are they doing to nurture and cultivate their community?

They are constantly working on making a connection, sometimes by just expressing themselves in the most simplest of ways. Baby steps, if you will, before getting around to answering the hard questions of the universe.

Forward Momentum: The After-Show on Discord

Alongside gamers, *streamers* — those creative individuals that I write about in *Twitch For Dummies* — always encourage people in their Chat, especially those new to their stream, to check out their Discord. Offering your Chat a place to visit after the stream wraps, maybe to discuss how you handled the vampiric specter my party faced in the D&D stream pictured in Figure 9-1, is a great way to continue the pace and momentum of your stream with continuing conversations, chatter on the topics covered during your stream, and so on. Starting off on Discord, a lot can be learned in watching other streamers promote their server as well as take an active part in their communities. They are posting regularly on various channels, keeping their name and their digital voice out there so people know they don't consider their Discord a turnkey platform where they set it up and then are never heard from again. People like a host that believes in engagement.

FIGURE 9-1: Streamers create content, and Discord plays into this be keeping the conversation going after the night's entertainment wraps.

But then comes the additional demand on you to create content for your other platform, completely independent of the platform you just finished creating on Twitch, YouTube, Mixer, Facebook, or wherever you are streaming your content from. Yes, your audience is content hungry. One would daresay they are ravenous for new content, and on the heels of several hours of streaming, you are expected to deliver new content to not only keep your audience engaged, but also to make yourself accessible.

Oh yeah, streaming isn't just about playing video games and having people watch you do so. In fact, it never was about that to begin with. It's all about accessibility. How you manage that accessibility is another challenge in itself, something we will be addressing here.

WARNING

If you are new to sharing of any kind — as a podcaster or a streamer, or what is more commonly known as a content creator — it is a good idea to decide exactly how much you want to share on your stream before you ever click Record on your podcast, Start Stream on your stream, or Go Live on Discord. For professional artists of all backgrounds, the lines between the public image and the private image have been long-established and are adhered to pretty stringently. With content creators, the Internet tends to blur those lines. This means you should talk with your loved ones, and perhaps do some retrospective looks with your own self and decide what is fit for public consumption and what is best kept to yourself.

First thing we should do is work with a bot that I mention elsewhere in this book, Nightbot (`https://nightbot.tv`, discussed in Chapters 2 and 11), and we will put together a command for your stream that will send out an invitation, both when prompted and automatically.

We should set up both a command and a timer for our Discord server. This way we can go on and keep people in the know on where to find you after the stream wraps up. Let's begin with setting up a manual command for your Discord.

1. **In Discord, from the drop-down menu associated with your server name, select the Invite People option.**

2. **In the Invite Friends to [YOUR SERVER] window, click the Edit Invite Link located at the bottom.**

3. **In the Server Invite Link Settings window, from the drop-down menu for Expire After, select the Never option.**

   As this link will be one of Nightbot's reoccurring commands, we will need to make this link a permalink.

4. **Click the drop-down menu for Max Number of Uses, and select the No limit option.**

5. **Click the Generate New Link button to create your server's new permalink.**

6. **Click the Copy button to copy the link to your clipboard.**

7. **Return to your browser, go to Nightbot, and review your custom commands in the Custom menu on the left side.**

   If you have never looked at Nightbot for your stream or haven't worked with it for over 30 days, you may have to establish a link between Nightbot and your streaming account. Follow the steps Nightbot provides, and you should have your account synced in no time.

8. Click the blue +Add command button to the right of your browser window to begin creating your command.

The Add Command window is where all your !command messages are created. If you are streaming, this interface should be a familiar one, but to find out more about Nightbot and what it can do for your stream, give my other title, *Twitch For Dummies*, a look.

9. As seen in Figure 9-2, in the Command field, type !discord.

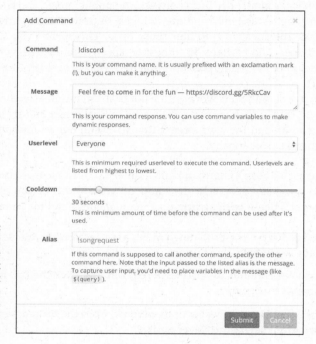

FIGURE 9-2: With Nightbot, you can create commands that quickly post answers to the most-asked questions from your chat.

10. In the Message field, type the following:

Want to meet off-stream for virtual coffee and bagels? Join us at Discord — [PASTE YOUR SERVER'S PERMALINK HERE]

11. Copy this message (and make sure to include your server's permalink invite) to your clipboard.

12. From the Userlevel menu, select the Everyone option.

13. Set the Cooldown slider to 30 seconds so people can avoid spamming this message.

14. Click the blue Submit button to create your command.

If someone asks if you have a Discord server or if you mention "Over at my Discord . . ." while focused on something else in-stream, anyone can type **!discord** into your chat, and the message with the URL invitation will appear. This command, and other answers for frequently asked questions, saves a lot of time for you and your chat.

This command is triggered manually, though. How would we automate this? Well, that's why I had you make a command for starters. Let's now make a *timer* for our streaming account.

1. **Still in Nightbot, in the menu to the left of your browser window, click the Timers option.**

   Timers are !command messages that you want to automatically fire off at timed intervals. Most of these messages are frequently asked questions in your stream or important links or tidbits of information you want your stream audience to see.

2. **Click the blue +Add button to the right of your browser window to begin creating your new timer in a window that looks like Figure 9-3.**

3. **In the Name field, type** Discord**.**

FIGURE 9-3: Timers are automated commands that fire off at intervals you set for the messages to post.

4. **In the Message field, paste the message you created in Step 10 of the previous exercise.**

5. **Set the Interval slider to every 25 minutes to establish when Nightbot will automatically post this in your stream.**

6. **Set the Chat Lines slider to 10 lines so people can avoid spamming this message.**

   The Chat Lines option is how many lines your chat receives before the timer is reset and begins running between the initially triggered timed command. So after your timed command for Discord posts, the time will begin again after 10 new comments in your chat.

7. **Click the blue Submit button to create your new timer.**

Now that we have a command and a timer set for our stream, we are getting the word out about your Discord. Whenever you are live on your streaming platform of choice, you can direct your community to your server for additional content, be it a photo (or series of photos) you want to share, or a video you wanted to share with everyone. You can also keep the conversation going on various channels you have on your server, if you know you have more to say. As you discover, the momentum of what you've created in the stream can continue on your Discord.

The Importance of Your Own Presence on Discord

When you are trying to build a community, it may feel exhausting. You just gave a presentation on your streaming platform of choice and now you want some down-time, but you should swing on over to your Discord to see who is there and what people are talking about. Sounds easy, but it's hard. Why give even more time to your audience as you have just wrapped up your stream for the day? Isn't heading over to Discord for more interaction something akin to overexposure, if not overkill?

The benefits of taking a positive, interactive presence in your server should be considered as an investment into what you want to build beyond your stream and how you want your Discord to grow.

Being on your own server shows that you care

It may seem like a tiny detail, but it speaks volumes about your server. A good example is when I visited a popular streamer's Discord to find out more about her channel and her community. I went to the #announcements channel and found one entry there from September 2019. The particular downer of this is I joined this server in January 2020.

So between September and January, nothing was really important to announce? Considering this streamer's reputation in broadcasting and lively channel banter, that was hard to fathom.

Being a part of your own community — actively taking part in conversations (where you know what people are talking about) and being seen in a server you host — lets people know that yes, this is a place where even the host likes to hang out and spend time. It may sound like common sense, but there are servers where the original host or the people behind its foundation are notably absent, sending a mixed message about the importance of their Discord server. If you are going to promote your server, make certain to clock in time there.

Discord is a platform with a wide reach

It's been said before in this book that when you bring a new platform into your digital workflow, there's going to be a growing pains sort of phase. I know, I know . . . one more platform to concern yourself with.

Discord is different, providing another platform for you to reach out to people and let them know something about you, about your cause, about your product. It is also a kind of platform that serves a somewhat wider demographic than Facebook or Pinterest, and the demographic does tend to lean to a younger crowd, meaning people who support you now will continue to support you in the future, provided the effort is put into your server.

Finally, social media is at its core a reciprocating relationship between platforms, your signal growing just a hint stronger with the inclusion of something new like Discord. While it is true you cannot be everywhere in social media, you can be strategic about where your audience resides and from there build a strategy around how to grow your audience. The more your audience grows, the stronger your community can become.

You might just make someone's day

When you're the host of a podcast, a stream, or a popular, outward-facing platform (like a blog or Instagram), you become something of a celebrity. For a brief time, the term for this was *weblebrity* but has been supplanted for the term *influencer*. Simply put, if you endorse a product, a place, or a person, people listen and react. Sometimes, influencers will back something you believe in (see Blue Yeti X); other times, influencers may put distance between good ideas gone bad (see Fyre Festival). Not all streamers are at the level of full-time influencers, mind you, but there is something to the fact you're creating content for people to enjoy. So when a content creator you respect responds directly to you, there is a little kick up in your day when that happens. Moments like that can also be day flippers for people, so go on and make yourself accessible to your community. You may be surprised how a simple "Good morning" can change a day's direction for someone.

Meet and Greet: Working with Meetups in Discord

Online get-togethers are a lot of fun. That is, after all, one of the more positive aspects of social media. The various platforms up and running today all connect us in some way, these connections reaching back in time for friends from middle-school days or friendships forged across state or country borders.

However, the need to connect in real time, away from a keyboard, is also something special. There's a real value in stepping out of the comfort zone of a monitor and keyboard, and actually meet people you've been corresponding with through this platform. Maybe if you are an introvert, *meetups* — official events sponsored by individuals or groups — are a chance for people to get together, enjoy beverages of all kinds, and clock in some serious social time.

Is there a real science to a solid meetup? Well, yes. For one thing, it's a good idea to find a location with a proper meeting space. Usually, places with rooms available for rent is a good idea (we're talking about official meetups, not a casual "Hey, let's get together for a beer!" kind of event), and the rented space should have some sort of food source, be it a kitchen or a catering service, accessible.

Let's begin with the whole planning process here. How would you make a meetup happen? For this, we're going to use a meetup happening in April 2020 hosted by the Washington DC Community Meetup group, powered by Twitch (`https://discord.gg/twitchwdc`). (See Figure 9-4.) Let's set up a section of our server for organizing meetups, and then break down the TwitchWDC strategy behind it.

1. **Go to Discord, click the name of your server to access its drop-down menu, and select the Create Category option.**

2. **Call this new category Meetups in the Category Name field and then click the Create Category button.**

   There is an option to make this category a private category which will locks all channel within it until you set permission for them. You don't need this option unless trolls become an issue.

3. **Create the following channels for Meetups:**

   - event-planning
   - event-graphics
   - event-photos

   This is a category dedicated mainly for event planning, the exception of that being the Event Photos channels. Moderate these stringently, and keep the chatter on these channels focused.

4. **Make the first Event Planning post read as follows:**

   If you are on this channel, welcome to the Event Planning for our meetups. You have now volunteered your time and attention to helping us plan out the best event we can offer our community. Please keep the posts on this channel related to the event upcoming. If we ask for feedback on a previous meetup, we will ask for it. Otherwise, we are looking ahead to what's coming. Thank you in advance for your help.

FIGURE 9-4: The Washington DC Community Meetup group, powered by Twitch, not only hosts a community on Discord but encourages meetups big and small in the real world.

5. **Pin this message to the top of the channel.**

   You can vary this message however you like, so long as you specify the channel's intent and why idle chatter may not be welcomed. Keep your focus and make sure you're getting work done.

6. **Make your first post, asking for ideas for possible locations.**

   Do not mention dates or times. Just places.

With the foundations set for planning out event on Discord, let's look at what we need to make our event happen.

Find the right place

When you are planning to host a meetup, you want to find a place that's not only versatile but a place that offers you and your group a space for themselves or a place that offers a lot of options for evening entertainment, drinks, and food. If you are working on a budget, you can always organize a meetup at an outdoor venue like a local park. Fire up a grill and go for it. The trickiness at public parks is all in the weather. How hot or cold will it be? Clear skies or rain? A lot of elements come into play, but that is what you pay for with an indoor venue: climate control.

Still, there is nothing wrong with a summer get-together, be it a pool party or a cookout. Work out the food allergies, offer up a list of facilities (number of grills, rest rooms, perks), a menu, and then secure the site. Make sure, too, the site you reserve is truly reserved and not a first come, first serve sort of thing. It's important that the location is agreed upon.

WARNING

The temptation to just throw a meetup at your home or apartment is strong, but if you are new to a group, maybe the notion of a meetup where you live may be a real leap of faith. Also, if you are new to a group and have no idea what the average turnout for an event will be. If you know this is a small group of streamers — say you're holding a special cookout for the Twitch community of Harrisonburg, Virginia — maybe it'll be a smaller group. Just remember you're inviting a new group of people into your house. Get to know them in real life, and gauge how many people attend your local meetups, before seeing how many people you can comfortably fit into your home.

Indoor venues for meetups can cover a lot of different locations. Some apartment buildings now offer open party spaces overlooking stunning views of their host cities. Regardless of the weather, you have a guaranteed place to host your meetup, rain or shine. Indoor venues can include

> » Open social spaces in apartment buildings (usually found in larger cities like Seattle, San Diego, Washington, D.C., and Richmond)

- >> Open work spaces (again, usually found in big cities)
- >> Breweries and distilleries
- >> Restaurants and gastropubs
- >> Barcades and video game centers

REMEMBER

Some of your community may be moms and dads who want to be part of the social hour. Keep in mind how many up-and-coming gamers, streamers, or podcasters who might be attendance; and consider kid-friendly venues as potential meetup locations, or locations that could offer professional sitters.

Something to remember about these kind of spaces is they can be an investment, but then again, if you're organizing a group, there are all different ways to recoup the cost (a cover charge usually the best way) but it depends again on the budget and what you can afford. Open social spaces will be similar to pavilions at public parks where food and drinks will be your responsibility. Other places like breweries and gastropubs may offer a package deal or menus for you and your guests to open tabs and order from. Any options added on to a special reserved space is going to add to the cost. Will there be alcohol served? Planning to card or supply wristbands for people who will and will not be drinking?

Welcome to the wonderful world of event planning.

TIP

Make sure you have bases covered when offering food and drink. Not only should there be nondairy or vegan options, there should also be nonalcoholic options outside of water. Some people don't drink, and that's a good thing.

When organizing meetup for yourself, there's a joy in keeping it simple. You have an RSVP list, you ask a restaurant or a brewery with a large tasting room to hold a large table, and you see who shows up. If, however, you're expecting a larger party, then actually finding a space that can offer you options beyond the open table is better. We will talk about the RSVP process in a minute.

Book the right date

Once you have a place, the next thing to secure is your date. To get a good time and turnout for your event, you may want to consider looking at a time with some considerable distance between the previous meetup. Instead of "Hey, let's do this in a couple of weeks!" go with "Hey, let's do this in a couple of months." In the case of TwitchWDC, their meetups usually happen on cycles of two or three months, giving their membership plenty of time to coordinate and begin talking up on their Discord (and elsewhere) when the next meetup will happen.

But what about the date and time?

When you are planning a large scale social gathering, timing is crucial. You want to enjoy the company, but individuals will want to plan around the event. If you plan the cookout, that can last a good chunk of the day, at least until the food or the beverages run out. For a meetup at a restaurant or brewery, you will want to look at hours of operation and plan accordingly. Weeknights tend to have less expensive price tags than Friday or Saturday nights, but attendance will also be affected by whether or not people will need to leave your early on account of work the next day. In the case of this April meetup organized by TwitchWDC, the call was made to hold it on a Saturday night. This means little pressure about wrapping up in order to work next week (and before you say it, yes, streaming is a job too!) and may open up the event to a wider number of their membership.

But keep in mind this date was secured months out.

The idea is that if you want the event to have a high attendance, you will want plenty of time to send out word that this event is happening. A week? Too soon for something on this scale. A month? Not a bad window to plan around, but having an extra month gives you more time to promote and builds up a bit of anticipation or hype, as you may hear on Discord.

Set up an RSVP

With a time and a place secured for your event, you now want to go ahead and set up an RSVP site. There are several of these event planning sites online, but three in particular to look into and take advantage of are:

>> https://www.meetup.com

>> https://www.eventbrite.com

>> https://rsvpify.com

The idea is that you have an idea of how many people are planning to make your event, and that you stay in contact with your venue to let them know how many they can expect. It reflects well on you and your group when you can give people a heads up on attendance. That was both you and the venue can prepare for the afternoon or evening meetup.

TIP

Another RSVP site worth looking into is the Community Meetups powered by Twitch program located at https://meetups.twitch.tv. This is a Twitch-endorsed initiative that requires new groups to have hosted two previously organized meetups attracting 20 (or more) attendees at each event, involve Twitch streamers and supporters in good standing with Twitch's brand and trademark guidelines, and have (as a group) an existing social media presence.

Each website has its own setup for events and where you enable the RSVP option for said event. Just make sure that when you have the event page up and running, and the RSVP option (as it is usually listed as an option) is active, copy and paste the RSVP URL somewhere easy to access as we will need it for a later exercise coming up next.

Start the promotion

Now comes the time you are going to tell people *"We're having a get-together. You in?"* The idea is to get people involved in your event promotion and circulating that RSVP link you've created. So where to begin?

Ask in your Discord's #event-planning channel if anyone is good with graphics. If no one feel comfortable with Photoshop, Illustrator, or the other open source graphics programs available, ask in your community if anyone was available (for hire) to design a set of graphics for the event. At the very least, two images should be created for your upcoming event:

>> **Banner:** Banners are good to use for Discord and also work well on Facebook (pages, groups, and so on), stream overlays, and blogs. A good size for a web-based graphic is 1800 pixels in width by 900 pixels in height or a 2:1 ratio, as shown in the Twitch WDC image featured in Figure 9-5. Your resolution does not need to exceed 100 pixels per inch.

TIP

The 1800 x 900 image for Discord, Facebook, and blogs works well as these platforms tend to cate to landscape images. However, Facebook Stories, Instagram stories, Snapchat, and Pinterest work best with portrait images. Changing dimensions to 900 × 1800 and redesigning your banner to these specifications will yield better results with these platforms.

>> **Social media promotion:** Most social media platforms, in particular Instagram and Twitter, work better with square or 1:1 ratio images. 1000 pixels in width by 1000 pixels in height with a resolution not exceeding 100 pixels per inch will give you exactly what you need for just about any social media platform solution, save for the exceptions listed above.

WARNING

Investing into *print promotions* — postcards, flyers, magnets, business cards — may be an option, but it is only worthwhile if you know you have an event where you will have a presence and be able to promote your event with time to spare. Rely on digital and word-of-mouth initiatives before considering a visit to Vistaprint.

FIGURE 9-5:
A banner graphic promoting your event should cleanly and concisely convey the essentials of your event: the date, the time, and the place.

Now that you have graphics in place, you need to let people know that your event is a go.

1. **Return to Discord, and in the #event-graphics channel, upload all your newly created promotional graphics there.**

2. **Go to your #announcements channel, and post the following message:**

   We are planning a meetup and we want to see you there!

   DATE: [Date of your event]

   TIME: [Time of your event]

   PLACE: [Location of your event]

   RSVP at [link to RSVP here]

   You can pick up promotional graphics for the event at #event-graphics which you can use on social platforms, blogs or your stream overlays. Make sure to RSVP and we can't wait to see you!

REMEMBER

   One post is not enough. Create a promotional post as a template, then create variants of it every other day on your social media platforms, including Discord. You can always drop announcements in other channels, provided the announcement there is appropriate.

3. **Instead of pinning the message, make sure to point people in the direction of the post.**

   On occasion, compose a freeform post with the URLs from the original posts, as seen in Figure 9-6.

   While you do not want to spam your various social media platforms with the same announcement, you do want to circulate the links you have created for the event. As timing is everything on seeing announcements online, you increase the chances of your links being seen.

4. **If others coming to the event are creating graphics for the event, encourage them to post the graphics in the #event-graphics channel.**

FIGURE 9-6:
Announcements
can either be
formal with the
graphics
specifically
created for your
event, or you can
get clever and
use GIFs to
grab attention
(and make
people smile).

All the parts are now put together for your event. At this point, you now iron out any little details about the event, reach out to potential sponsors who may want to make an impact at your event, or think about any special programming you may want to offer at the event. What matters, first and foremost, is real, genuine connections between you and others in your community.

And when the event is taking place, alongside established hashtags in Twitter and Instagram, you should encourage your community to post photos in the #event-photos channel. (Yeah, one of the other things your event's venue should have: strong Wi-Fi. It'll get a workout at this event of yours.)

REMEMBER

While hashtags work for Instagram, Twitter, and other social media platforms, there are no hashtags in Discord. Anything with the # symbol turns what is typed into a shortcut to a channel in a server.

Other Kinds of Engagement

We have mentioned additional time clocked in Discord following a stream, and we talked about meetups, but are there other ways of using Discord to reach out to your community, build on your foundations whether you are a musician, an author, an artist, or some other creative individual or organization?

When your server goes online, Discord is a blank canvas for you to create your masterpiece upon. As the administrator of this server, how this community grows relies on your interaction and engagement with those present. How you choose to engage with your community does not necessarily have to be as outward-facing as hosting a stream or an epic meetup event. Maybe you're not one for producing a podcast or a stream, or maybe you lack the budget and resources to plan an epic meetup event.

And that's perfectly fine. There are a number of ways you can engage your community all from within your own Discord server.

Creative endeavors

Discord, as you have heard me say again and again, is a social media platform that offers you a place for sharing of all kinds. As you can easily upload media — provided your uploads are within the parameters of your Discord server — this offers a place for your community to share what they are working on as well.

On many servers, administrators will offer a place for their community members to either share their own looks at works-in-progress or advice on a specific creative media. As a writer, I am asked to moderate and give advice on the writer's craft. How do you write in a specific genre? What would I recommend as a good research tip? In this #creative-writing channel on SheSnaps's server, I offer a professional perspective alongside works-in-progress from the community. On Alkali Layke's server, as seen in Figure 9-7, her own #share-creative offers a wide array of projects, from digital art to home improvements to cosplay-in-progress.

If you are an artist, a musician, or a writer, open up your Discord to other artists. Amateur or professional, what matters is a place for your community to share.

WARNING

When you set up a channel for sharing works-in-progress, make sure you set the rules straight on what is allowed. Sometimes, people will look at a place for sharing as a place for open critiquing. If you want to do that, sure, you can; but it could get tense if a disagreement comes up. Establish rules for your channel before you make it live. If someone *asks* for criticism, you may want to keep an eye on how the criticism goes. Make sure it stays constructive.

Spoiler channels

Dude, did you see *The Witcher* series on Netflix? Wasn't that amazing when Geralt [REDACTED]?

FIGURE 9-7:
On Alkali Layke's
Discord, the
#share-creative
channel is a place
where projects of
all kinds — from
cosplay to home
improvement —
are showcased
and celebrated
on completion
with the server.

So, that new series out of New Zealand — *The Dead Lands* — has a scene where **[REDACTED]**. I'm thinking the mother meant that **[REDACTED]** or is that a stretch?

Yesterday, I was watching you play *The Last of Us*. Later on, you are going to **[REDACTED]** because **[REDACTED]**. God, this game is just gut-wrenching!

Spoilers, sweetie. What are you going to do?

Oh yeah, there's the *spoiler* feature, seen in Figure 9-8, you can attach to uploaded media, concealing it from view until it is clicked after it posts in your Discord channel. Everyone's definition of a spoiler is different. For example, in 2020, I started playing the game, *The Last of Us*. The game itself was released in 2014. So, considering how much time it takes to develop a video game, do the understood rules of spoilers apply? For some, yes. For others — and especially for trolls — not so much. When you want to have discussions with folks in an open forum about media consumed and enjoyed, it would be nice to have a #spoilers channel for your community.

A #spoilers channel is exactly what you think it is. Nothing is protected. Everything is up for grabs. You want to talk about the cliffhanger at the end of *Kingdom*? Do it here. You want to talk about some of the cooler moments of the *BioShock* series? Do it here. Got some fun trivia about scenes in *Birds of Prey*?

FIGURE 9-8:
The *spoiler* option
is offered when
you post media
into Discord
channels. You can
use it to either
blur *not-safe-for-
work (NSFW)* or
uploaded spoiler
media.

You get the idea.

The #spoiler channel is guilt-free engagement platform for everyone in your community to dish, to speculate, and to completely nerd out over a property; and if someone cries foul, even you as the administrator can point to the channel name and add "Moose out front shoulda told ya."

Selfies

Whether it is a self-portrait of you at le Tour de Eiffel (the world's most popular spot for selfies) or a photo taken with you and your best furry friend or an impromptu group shot at a convention, the selfie provides instant common ground between you and your community. Everyone enjoys a moment captured in pixels, and there are a variety of channels you can create in order to connect with your Discord. I have on my server a #pet-selfie channel, and as seen in Figure 9-9, I tend to get a lot of traffic there. Not to mention a lot of terrific shots of beautiful doggos, kittehs, and other fun critters.

REMEMBER

If the photo is taken at arms-length, it's a selfie. If you are using a selfie stick and the self-portrait is taken from either a distance or a high angle, it's a selfie. If someone else is taking a full body photo of you, it's not a selfie. It's a photo. So please, influencers, be it on Discord or elsewhere — stop abusing the freakin' selfie tag. (There, I said it and now it's in print. So let it be written. So shall it be done.)

Think about what selfies you'd like to use as a bridge with your community. Do you want to have a showcase of household pets, create a travel log from various parts of the world, or maybe you want a different kind of selfie taken in the kitchen or maybe a hobby selfie if you're wanting photos from the gym or the crafting table.

The idea of your channels is to not only reflect your interests but provide touch points for members of your community. Through these channels is common ground, and it is that common ground where you will strengthen the foundations of your online community.

FIGURE 9-9:
Selfies, whether they are focused on location or furry family members, make for great connection points in your community.

Why Engagement Matters

You can call your community whatever you wish. The Fam. Your Hype Team. The Crew. No matter what you call them or how you address them, they are there in your server, becoming fixtures to your Discord like Cliff and Norm at the *Cheers* pub in Boston. These are the people and the atmosphere you build around your server to let those new to your corner of Discord know exactly what kind of server they have arrived at. Newcomers will pick up from your community what to expect and what's in store for their stay.

Engagement remains the best way to grow your community. Whether you make your engagement happen from the content you create online, in real time at meetups and special events, or just in the various channels you create on your server, connection is essential. Without it, a community cannot evolve. Find the best approach to those who join your server, and work on what best reflects you and best connects with those visiting your server.

Chapter **10**

A Day on Discord

I've thrown a lot at you in this book. Discord may not be a hard application to master, but a lot is happening both in the background and in your various channels. When your community starts to grow, you may find a need to jump from random chapter to random chapter, just to keep up with the fast changes you're managing. You may also forget, with all the different preferences you have learned about, where exactly are the preferences over your account versus where the preferences to your server reside, and if troubleshooting arises, where do you begin to look?

We have talked about ways of making your server your own, strategies of engagement that will spark responses from your community, and how to nurture those frequenting your channels, but all of these chapters are exercises set to teach you how to do a specific skill. I'd like to think these tasks will get you going, but how do these skills actually work in practice?

Let's take a look at a day in Discord. Note I didn't say *typical* day as each day on this platform varies. Some days, you may find your attention divided between Discord, Instagram, and Facebook. Other days, you may need to step away from Discord so that you can tend to other social media outlets. Then there are days you will begin and end your day checking your server. No matter the day, there is a method in approaching Discord. This chapter I'm intending to be a road map for you if you are new to Discord. If you have experience with the platform, but feel as if you might be skipping a step or looking for a new approach to your community, have a look at how a day in Discord could go.

Discord in the Morning

Good morning, sunshine. You're up and out for the day, maybe heading out to the office or en route to your classes. Provided you are not driving a car (because, yes checking Discord while driving is not only dangerous, it is downright stupid — *eyes on the road!*), you have a moment to look at your Discord app.

 You notice that your server, and a few others that you've joined, has a small white dot to the left of it. This means you have unread messages waiting for you to read. If your server or another server has a small red indicator with a number inside it, that means you have unread messages tagged to you. As you are administrator to your own server, the best order of priority for servers would be:

>> Any servers where you are founder/administrator

>> Any server where you serve as moderator

>> Any servers with a tagged message indicator

>> Any servers you are a member of

TIP

Posts that are tagged with @everyone or @here will be regarded as messages tagged to you directly.

The immediate priority here, though, is your server. Let's get to it.

1. **Go to your server by clicking its icon in the left menu.**

   Look at your list of channels. Any that are highlighted with a marker to the left of a channel are channels with new messages.

2. **Click the highlighted channel and review any of the new posts there.**

   Some of these new postings may be open for anyone to answer or random thoughts similar to tweets or Facebook updates. Review them carefully if you are mentioned (but not tagged) or if the post is anything you can reply to directly.

   The channel labeled #destiny has as the most recent post a message from GuardianGaladriel:

   Anyone available to help with the Chasm of Screams (Thorn Quest)? My Fireteam got to the boss but we failed at the knight spawn on last phase. We can do tomorrow too, if need be.

3. **In the text field underneath the post, type the @ symbol and select GuardianGaladriel's name and tag, as seen in Figure 10-1.**

You can also drop an @ and begin the person's screen name, and Discord should offer you either the person you wish to tag or available options for this username.

4. **To the right of GuardianGaladriel's name, type the reply:**

Good luck on the quest. (Next time, though, use #lfg-destiny — thanks.)

TIP

If a message appears in an incorrect channel, politely remind the original poster of other channels more appropriate. If it is a repeat offender, delete the message and then drop a private message to the sender explaining why you deleted the message.

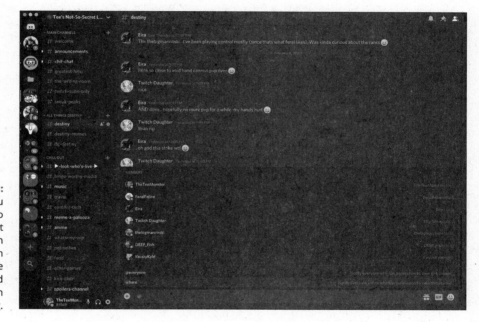

FIGURE 10-1:
Find who you need to reply to by starting out your post with an @ symbol. Then choose from the menu offered who you wish to tag.

5. **Go to your #chit-chat channel, and type the following post:**

Good morning, everyone! It's the start of a new day. What's the plan for you today?

TIP

Kick off a conversation with a simple greeting. It can always lead on to other tangents and discussions.

6. **Under the channel for #entertainment, type the following post:**

Right now on Netflix, I am watching _Kingdom_. This is the most expensive production out of Korea and it shows. It is a lavish, breathtaking period piece set in the Golden Age of Korea, and the writing is just as air tight. _Kingdom_ features at its core a struggle for power. A family has married into the throne and are willing to do anything to keep their hold on it. The Crown Prince is accused of leading a revolt against his own father, and is branded a traitor by the family attempting to seize the throne for themselves. What could make this epic period piece of court intrigue better?

Fast Moving Zombies.

See, to hold on to the throne, the rival family employed an old doctor who possessed knowledge of an immortality herb. It brings the dead emperor back to life, turning him into a terrifying monster. What follows is a chain of events that unleashes an apocalypse.

This show is a combination of _Crouching Tiger, Hidden Dragon_ and _The Walking Dead_. If you've seen _Train to Busan_, another Korean zombie horror offering, then you have an idea of how good this series is. I cannot rave enough over this. And _Sense8_ fans, our ass-kicking corporate badass Doona Bae is in this, and she's awesome!

Settle in and brace yourself for this series.

When you're composing a large post like the review I suggest here, you should either use the Discord app on the laptop or on a tablet. Creating something this detailed on a smartphone could prove challenging.

If you make a post and discover a typo, you can edit the post after it goes live and correct it. You can also use strikethrough and display your corrections if you want to let people know how your post change.

7. **Go to your Google app or a browser, search for an image (either a poster or a scene) from what you are reviewing, and download it on your device.**

8. **Return to your Discord post, tap the Add Media option to the left of the emoji option, and add the image you just downloaded into your post.**

   On the desktop version of the Discord app, the Add Media feature is located to the far left of the Add Post field and is a + symbol.

9. **Post your entry into Discord. It should look something like Figure 10-2.**

   On the mobile versions of the app, the Post icon looks like a paper airplane. On the desktop app, you press the Enter key.

This is a good start to your morning on Discord. You have run down the list for any outstanding mentions on your server, and you have contributed content to your server with open-ended posts that invite interaction. With the door propped open, we can see if there are any responses. Don't feel disappointed if replies don't come rolling in straightaway. Some topics of conversation are slow burns. Just make sure to pop your head into your virtual office and say hi.

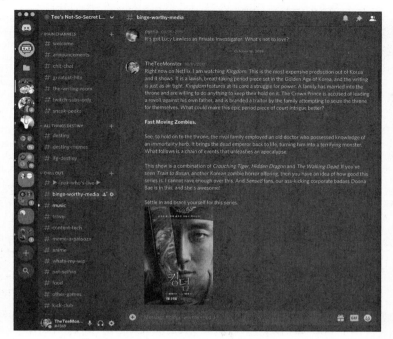

FIGURE 10-2:
It's more than okay to go into detail with a post. Add artwork as well to make your post eye-catching, so long as the artwork is relevant to your post.

Discord in the Afternoon

All right — halfway through the day, and it's been a good day so far. Nothing too alarming at your office or your classes are hitting a solid stride (and the test that you felt a little wary about turned out to be an A so, well done). It's lunch and you're settling down with your tablet or laptop. Now's a good time to check on your server as you had your phone on silent. That distinct Discord chirp was not going to bother anyone.

Your server has been relatively quiet but there has been some activity on other servers you have joined. Chances are good that most of the notifications that are specifically tagging you are messages to @everyone or @here but could be worth taking some time to review. This afternoon, we're going to change up the workflow looking at Discord by this list of priorities:

>> Any servers where you have been tagged

>> Any servers for which you are founder/administrator

>> Any server where you serve as moderator

>> Any other servers you are a member of

1. **In the upper-right corner of your Discord, click the Mentions option to review any outstanding post you are tagged in on other servers.**

   Scrolling down the list of tagged messages, you see this posting from AvgJoe, an admin from a nonprofit podcast and stream called GuardiansMH:

   @everyone

   Hi all! I wanted to take a minute and thank everyone for being here even during the quiet times.

   This year is going to be a great year for promoting mental health awareness and helping others. We are looking at hosting several MH focused streams through 2020 but first I'd love to bring up reviving the Destiny community Podclash!!!

   With returning the Podclash we will use the event to raise money for St. Jude's through one of the destiny community campaigns or whatever charity everyone wants.

   Who would be down to partake in a Podclash event in the community months?

2. **Move your cursor to the top right of the post to see the Jump option, and click to go from your present server to the server where this post appears.**

3. **On arriving at the message you jumped to, go to the text field.**

   At the bottom-right is a GIF option.

4. **Click the GIF option to go into the Tenor.com-powered GIF library.**

   While there can be professionalism in Discord, there is nothing wrong with having a little fun in your replies. GIFs are nice ways of making people in your and other communities smile.

5. **In the Search Tenor field at the top of grouped animated GIF categories, type the search string** you have my attention **and wait for your search results to appear.**

   Depending on the quality of your Internet connection, your search results will either quickly load or take some time. The previews are also animated so the search results may take some time to render.

6. **Find a GIF you like, and post it into your message as your reply.**

   As seen in Figure 10-3, a GIF of actor Leonardo DiCaprio from the film *Django Unchained* saying "You had my curiosity, but now you have my attention" is the reply to AvgJoe's question.

7. **In AvgJoe's post, click his name to access a quick link to his profile and the Direct Message option.**

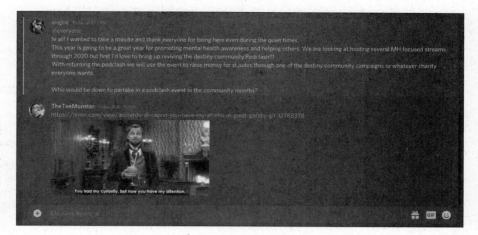

8. **In the field currently marked Message AvgJoe, type the following:**

   Hey, Joe. In all seriousness, I would like to make the _Happy Hour from the Tower_ podcast available for the Podclash. I just have a couple of questions:

   1. Did you have a timeframe in mind of when you wanted to do this?

   2. What exactly **is** a Podclash?

   Officially count us in whatever this project is. We cannot wait to get involved.

   As you are working on a single-line field, remember that you can edit the post after it goes live.

REMEMBER

9. **Click the Mentions option again and then click the Display: everything drop-down menu.**

10. **Turn off Include @everyone and Include @role to only show the Display: direct only function option.**

    The Display drop-down menu allows you a quick shortcut to the type of mentions you will see in this window. You can be as broad or as focused as you like.

11. **Finish reviewing any directly tagged posts.**

    If you want to return your Mentions back to all tagged messages, click Display: direct only and select both Include options.

    You notice one of the @everyone posts is a streamer you follow announces she is heading on a trip to Australia. You click Jump to read the post in detail. It's in her #announcements channel which is in Read-Only mode. You switch to her #general-chat channel and post the following:

I just saw this, and must have missed you talking about it. Is Australia a vacation trip or streaming-related? Will you be heading to New Zealand as well, or will this be an adventure solely in Oz? (Safe travels!)

It comes to mind that a channel you moderate on writing has been a little quiet and needs a bit of inspiration.

12. **Go to the Google app, search for an image using** `writing prompt` **as your search term, find one you like, and download it to your computer.**

Giving credit to an artist matters. If what you find is a piece of original artwork, make sure to cite the source and the artist before posting.

13. **Return to Discord, go to the server where you are moderating the #creative-writing channel, and compose the following post:**

Hey, everyone @here.

I apologize for being so quiet here. I've been working on a deadline and the pace has been fast and furious. The good news is I am closing in on finishing up the current project, so I wanted to celebrate with a writing prompt. If you are new to this channel and don't know the routine, you can write whatever you like — poetry, excerpt short story, flash fiction, or even an idea for a novel — so long as you share it!

Be inspired! Let's go!

Image Credit: (Artwork by [artist, URL])

14. **Go to the Add Media option, and add the image you just downloaded into your post.**

15. **Post your entry into Discord as seen in Figure 10-4.**

This time, you're going to want to let this post ferment for a bit. It's an open-ended post, and it will take some time for people to compose something.

Be a good example for the channels you moderate. If you offer up a challenge like the one depicted above, make sure to have your own entry ready to post ether straightaway or a little later in the day.

Glancing at the clock, it's nearly time to get back to your daily gig, so with a final glance at your laptop or tablet, you close down for the afternoon and get something to eat. After all, you do want to grab something to eat so your brain is firing on all cylinders. In the back of your mind, though, you are thinking about the writing prompt you posted on your friend's server. Those kinds of posts always tend to linger with you because you are hoping to inspire creativity. A couple of writing prompts in the past fell flat, and that always feel like a disappointment. Your friend, SheSnaps, assures you that she appreciates your efforts (she's always one for positivity) but you want to make sure you're meeting expectations.

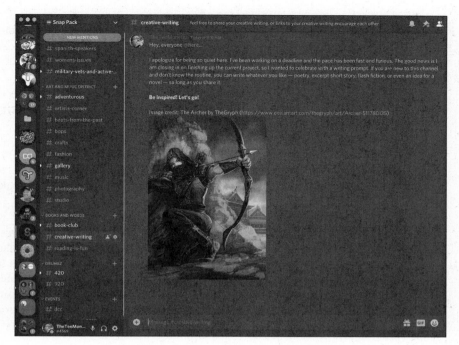

FIGURE 10-4:
During your review, don't forget to check any channels you are moderating. If you are posting artwork, make sure, if you can, to include the author's name and a URL to the artist.

An email arrives on your desktop or your phone alarm goes off, a subtle reminder that you have to get to class. You slip your phone back into your pocket and get back to the day.

The Unexpected Alert

It's later in the day and your eyes are drifting to the clock as you near the end of your stretch. It's either time to relax after class or count down to catching your train home. You're still focused on the task at hand when your phone, as it has been doing on occasion throughout the day, vibrates with an alert. In any other social situation, you might let this go, but you've got a moment, so you flip your phone around.

It's a private message from one of your moderators who is reaching out to you on a back channel:

We might have a problem. Check recent comments on the #esports channel.

Someone you've welcomed into your community last week — RockDudeBro — is getting into a heated conversation on your #esports channel about the members of Team Rogue. He's getting a little testy with several (long-time) members of your server, but then he drops what is currently the most recent comment on there:

Team Rogue are just a lot of hype and not that good. Known cheaters, too. It wouldn't be a sad day if someone just grabbed an AK-47 at their next event and empty a clip on them.

Woah.

You find a break room or somewhere semi-private where you take a deep breath and take care of this now.

WARNING

When situations like this pop up in your feed like this, as discussed in Chapter 8 on our section about trolls, your moderators can be quick and make the final judgment call on the community member. However, if the person is just new to your server, this could just be a lapse in judgment or something said impulsively. If your mods ask for your input on this, you should get involved immediately. Leaving offensive comments or inappropriate material on your Discord could send out the wrong impression to anyone just arriving to your stream.

1. **Find the offensive message, and click the the ••• option to the right of the message, which brings up the More menu.**

As a moderator and administrator, you have the option to do the following:

- Pin Message

- Quote

- Mark Unread

- Delete Message

2. **Select the Delete Message option.**

You can only edit a message when you are the composer of it. Moderators granted permission and administrators are the only ones who should have the ability to delete a message.

3. **In this channel, post the following message:**

@everyone

Please refrain from statements advocating violence, whether it's feigned or not, funny or not. It's not happening here. It's in poor taste, highly inappropriate, and not tolerated on this server.

A statement like this is important for your accountability concerning the content your server is posting. Good, bad, whatever the intention falls back to you as the administrator. Make sure to take responsibility and handle the situation without fault.

4. **Go to your Direct Messages in the Home section of your server menu, located to the left of the app, and click the mod's name, which should be at the top of the list.**

5. **Compose and send the following:**

Good catch. Thanks for bringing it to my attention. Next time, though, feel free to use your own judgement on something like that. I trust you. That's why I made you a mod. :)

Mods sometimes need encouragement in order to grow as moderators. They should always be thanked for doing their jobs because they are volunteers. Remember that. They are in the driver's seat because they want to be, so make sure you appreciate them.

As this is a direct message, you do not need to tag anyone. This is a one-on-one communication line between you and the other person.

And since you're in Discord . . .

6. **Click the Mentions option to see if there are any new tagged posts needing your attention.**

You find that the streamer heading to Australia responded to you:

@TheTeeMonster LOL I'll DM you :) But it's a vacation. No NZ trip.

7. **Click Jump to see the post in detail.**

You notice she added after the tagged post:

Sadly not going to live with the hobbits.

You notice there were a good amount of postings between her reply and now so you will want to make sure you tag her in your reply.

8. **In the field at the bottom of Discord, compose and post:**

@FemmeFatale Very cool! Travel safe, and I'll keep an eye out for that DM!

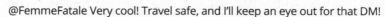

The Mentions option begins with the most recent tagged message. The more you scroll down, the further back you go in the Timeline.

9. **Return to the Mentions option and review any additional posts either tagged to you, @everyone, or @here.**

10. **When you are caught up, go to your server to review any new posts.**

You've managed what could have been a very nasty, slightly awkward post in your server. Hopefully, the fire is put out and there will be no additional fallout. (Yes, that's foreshadowing for anyone playing along at home.) Sometimes, when you get those unexpected alerts, your Discord jumps to the front of the line in your priorities, and it is up to you to make sure your server is the place you want it to be online. Remember: At the end of the day it is your server, your rules. Be responsible and be responsive.

Discord in the Evening

Feels good to be home, doesn't it? We've had dinner, we're unwinding a bit — maybe catching up on something recorded on your DVR or curling up with a book, just a chapter or two. . .or three, if it's Chuck Wendig's *Wanderers* — and now you're wanting to get into Discord one more time today. This is something closer to the Discord routine you started your day with, but here is where you try to wrap things up for the day. There should be something of a *Goodnight, Moon* vibe in your postings, and there is nothing wrong with a simple *Goodnight, Discord* post to wrap up your day.

At the end of the day, if you have any @everyone or @here messages needing to go out, now would be a good time to post them. The workflow suggested for Discord in the evening should go

>> Any servers for which you are founder/administrator

>> Any server where you serve as moderator

>> Any servers with a tagged message indicator

>> Any servers you are a member of

>> One more return visit to any servers you are founder/administrator

It's been both a productive and an eventful day on Discord for us. Let's see if we can end this day on a high note, and then either get some sleep or find a pic-up game to end our day with.

1. **Return to Discord and see if your server has any new messages.**

2. **If so, access your server by clicking its icon.**

3. **Look at your list of channels for any that are highlighted, and click the highlighted channel to review any of the new posts there.**

    Your #lfg-destiny channel has a new post in it:

@here Good evening, Guardians. We're planning an Eater of Worlds and Scourge of the Past this evening. Helping out a friend who needs both clears. We've got two slots open at the time of this post. We're on PC. Any takers?

You check the timestamp of the post. The invite is an hour old. There is already one affirmative response.

4. **In the text field underneath the post, post the following:**

If the spot is still open, I'd love to join your Fireteam. I can be on in 30 minutes.

You then notice the #entertainment channel is highlighted.

5. **Click the channel.**

You find a reply to your Kingdom review waiting for you from SkyeDancer:

So on a scale of *The Walking Dead* to *Warm Bodies*, how is the graphic content of Kingdom? I figure it's zombie lore so there will be some violence and gore, but how intense are we talking here?

6. **Post a reply:**

@SkyeDancer It's got a few gross moments. (Not to give them away, but it's not overtly gross.) If you've seen *Train to Busan* or if you've played The Last of Us, then you have an idea of what Kingdom will be like. It relies less on the gore you see in some zombie films, and ramps up the tension and creepiness factor. If you can handle the tension, you'll love this!

7. **Return to the #creative-writing channel you moderate where you posted a writing prompt.**

During the day, one person actually shared a short story across four posts, each post a paragraph in this short story.

8. **Where you see the Reaction option (the smiley face icon), click it to access the Reactions menu.**

9. **Select an appropriate reaction — preferably a positive one — and post it.**

Reactions are collections of emojis and stream emotes that you can use in your posts. If your post is just a reaction, the reaction is posted at a larger-than usual size, as seen in Figure 10-5. When used with text, reactions appear as small icons roughly the same size of the post's font.

REMEMBER

Reactions come in two varieties. As seen in Figure 10-5, you can use the Reaction option either as part of your post, or use the reaction as the post itself. The other variety is the reaction you see at the far right of any post you roll your mouse over. That reaction appears underneath its associated post with a counter. Other members of the server can click these reactions, similar to likes you see in other social media platforms.

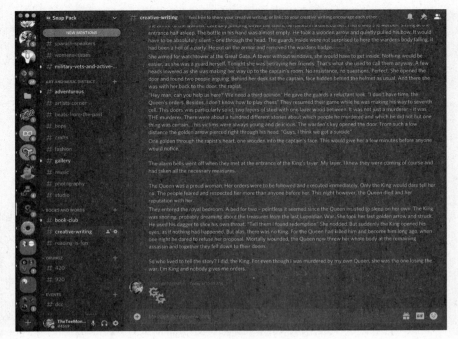

FIGURE 10-5:
Your writing
prompt earned
you a short story.
A really good one.
Show your
appreciation by
dropping a
reaction as a
post.

10. **Look over any other servers you are a member of, and casually pop into channels to see what people are discussing.**

You see in the #music channel of one server, the topic is *Songs you shouldn't love but do*. People have posted a few novelty songs.

11. **You decide to go all in and post this:**

I have no doubt that I'm going to receive hate mail on this one, but no matter how miserable I may feel, if I play this particular rendition of "My Heart Will Go On" from *Titanic*, my face will hurt from laughing so hard.

```
https://youtu.be/G44xTr8D_bw
```

The preview for this YouTube link will be for My Heart Will Go On (terrible recorder meme) which is, without a doubt, an Internet classic. Your post will also get reactions. Guaranteed.

You are about to go and look at another server when you notice the icon of RockDudeBro at the top left of your Discord with an indicator that two direct messages are waiting for you.

12. **Click the icon and read.**

My comment got deleted? Is your server too sensitive for jokes?

What's the problem?

The time stamps say both these posts went live roughly five minutes ago.

13. **You take a deep breath and reply.**

What you posted was not only highly inappropriate, it could get the server shut down. You can't post things like that. And you won't post anything like that on this server.

RockDudeBro responds:

You might want to look up the First and Second Amendments, and I am well within my rights. You might want to relax and respect freedom of expression.

14. **Take another deep breath, and then post your reply:**

So you don't care about Terms of Service or wish to respect the rules of this Server?

RockDudeBro responds:

Bruh, chill.

15. **Post your reply:**

Thank you for your time.

16. **Go to the far-right column of Users, right-click the offender's username (in this scenario, RockDudeBro), and select Block RockDudeBro to permanently remove RockDudeBro from your server.**

The Users featured on the right column of your Discord are those online, active, or offline. Users are organized by assigned roles which vary from server to server. In this scenario of a problematic user, two options are available:

- Kick [Member]

- Block [Member]

Kicking a member only removes the offender from a server until they are invited back. Blocking a member removes the offender from a server and makes that user unable to rejoin.

17. **Return to your server, go to #lfg-destiny, and post this:**

Meet you all online. Booting up and logging in.

A few seconds later, a reply arrives:

See you soon, Guardian.

It is very safe to assume that this day on Discord outlined for you above is not typical, nor is it a step-by-step template for how a day will unfold for you on this platform. No two servers are alike. No individual's experiences are identical to each other. However, what you have in this chapter is a day on Discord based on true events. What I depicted here all happened on my server over many days (even months) but these are possible scenarios you will face — good and bad — on launching a server.

This chapter is less of a template and more of a strategy for approaching Discord. While we talk about strategy throughout the book, our Day in Discord chapter is the strategy applied, offering you different reactions for the actions encountered online. You can take a look at your morning, afternoon, and evening, and find when and where it's time to give your Discord some attention. You could be like my daughter, a power user in my eyes, and check your Discord throughout the day. Her dedicated times are in the morning with her breakfast, in transit to school, and extended pockets of time at night. She doesn't really watch television. Her entertainment is Discord.

But remember, outside of Discord, a world awaits.

I'm all for connections coast-to-coast and around the world. Discord is what I use to get in my weekly *Dungeons & Dragons* fix, after all. I love this platform so much I wrote this book to help people understand it. But Discord is a conduit to the real world and the people in it. My technical editor, for example, I grew to know through this platform and Twitch, but amidst the Raids, the Nightfalls, and all the fun times across Destiny, across streams, and across channels, nothing was as fun as meeting Dan in Indianapolis, hopping from brewery to brewery, enjoying haunts from Dan's past. *That,* to me, sums up the whole reason I go on to these various social platforms: real, human connections.

Although the Old Style Dan did test the limits of our friendship. I can't lie there.

Yes, Discord is a place where you can build a community but a community is not about the platform you use to bring people together. The community is about the people within it. Make sure to make time for the world outside of Discord, and find ways of bringing that community together in the real world. You hear all the time of people describing the world as a scary place, but when you bring your community together, you find out that the world is less scary because your community, your tribe, your fam, or whatever you refer to those circle of friends as, is together. And not only is that community strong, it's got some pretty nice people in it.

This platform is more than game comms, a chat board, or refurbished forum. It is a foundation for a community, and how that community grows and what it accomplishes together all starts with you and the server you create. It is a place where creativity is encouraged, friendships are forged, and people from all backgrounds find common ground.

Welcome to Discord.

4
The Part of Tens

Chapter **11**

Top Ten Essentials for Discord

When starting off with a platform as robust, as multi-layered, and as versatile as Discord, you quickly realize that just downloading Discord is the first step. It's a bit like saying "You want to get started on Facebook? Just sign up and you're ready to go!" or "You're setting yourself up on Twitch? Easy. If you've got a webcam on your camera, you are all set!" But you might notice other Discord servers have a better sound, sharper video, and a better handle on the capabilities beyond text communication. That's because those servers have made investments in ways other than time and attention. The individuals and teams behind those servers invest in hardware that improves the Discord experience they offer.

Don't get me wrong, though. The basics work. Tempting as it is to want to launch a server all tricked out, we all start somewhere. I'll admit — I'm thinking about this as, at the time of writing this book, I am celebrating 15 years of podcasting. I started simply: a microphone, a small mixer board, an audio capture card, and GarageBand. Even as basic setups go, my beginner setup went beyond the laptop mic and a copy of Audacity; but even in those early days, I knew that there were other accessories out there I would eventually be looking at with a very serious eye and some money budgeted.

If you want to take a look at making your Discord experience a step or two beyond the basics, these are some suggestions from items featured in the book, but this time I'll be going a bit deeper into the details behind the items itself and even showcase a few accessories that I may have not gotten a chance to shine a spotlight on. Let's see what small steps we can take into a larger world with accessories that can improve your Discord experience.

Corsair's Void Pro Headset

Maybe it is the podcaster in me, or maybe it's dating even further back to when I was a burgeoning band geek in my youth, but quality audio matters. Whether you are using Discord to record interviews for podcasts, working with a team to coordinate a special event, or simply organizing a fireteam for a raid in *Destiny 2,* quality audio is something that can really make a difference in your experience. It can be incredibly jarring when you are trying to talk to people online and there is that one person who is struggling to hear you or you are struggling to hear them.

This is why, when it comes to audio quality, earbuds of any make and model only offers so much.

Closed-ear headphones are a worthwhile investment, and while there are many headphones on the market, I recommend the *Corsair Void Pro Headset* at $80, pictured in Figure 11-1. The price may sound steep, but for this price the Void Pros offer impressive features:

>> Microfiber mesh fabric and memory foam on the earpads

>> Dolby Headphone 7.1 surround sound delivering immersive multi-channel audio

>> Custom-tuned 50mm neodymium speakers offering wide range and accuracy

>> Optimized unidirectional microphone that reduces ambient noise for enhanced voice quality

The Corsair Void Pro Headset offers quality sound, quality recording, and comfort. If you are looking for the first major investment into your Discord loadout, the Void Pro is an excellent first step. Venture out to your local electronic stores that carry Corsair products and see if they offer a sound bar that allows you to preview a set before purchasing. It's a great way to get an idea of not only how headphones sound, but also how they feel.

Blue Microphone Yeti X

I first saw the *Blue Microphone Yeti X* ($150, with full specs and demo videos available at https://www.bluedesigns.com/products/yeti-x) at TwitchCon 2019. I forced myself to walk away from it. As you can see in Figure 11-2, that was not easy. I honestly didn't need a new microphone for my studio, but after getting a personal demo of it, I *really wanted* this one.

>> High-res, 11-segment LED meter built into the side of the microphone

>> Multifunction smart knob offering mic gain, headphone volume, muting, and balance control between your microphone input and the audio coming from the computer

>> Customizable LED lighting allowing you to personalize the Yeti X. (Hey, it's all in the details.)

>> Four pickup patterns: Stereo, omnidirectional, cardioid, bidirectional

The reviewers at Sound Guys (https://www.soundguys.com) described the Yeti X as "a rather frustration-free experience while giving you the control you need to squeeze as much quality as you can out of a USB microphone. Streamers will find a good ally in the Yeti X." Instead of the limitations of the above featured headset, the Yeti X with its different pickup patterns can be used in studio settings, picking up other hosts or background noise (if desired) when live at an event or mobile setting.

FIGURE 11-2:
Blue
Microphones,
known for
their work in
developing USB
microphones,
released in 2019
the Yeti X, a
microphone that
can function like
four different
microphones.

Blue Microphones have always known what they are doing when it comes to USB microphones. The Yeti X (and its little brother, the Yeti Nano) is another incredible innovation that can improve your Discord signal. If you are looking to expand your studio, this is another worthwhile investment.

MXL 990 XLR Microphone

We have been touting the USB microphone throughout the opening chapters of the book, and for good reason. USB mics have come a long way in the 15 years I've clocked in as a content creator. When you look at the variety of mics on the market, their features, and (more importantly) the high quality of audio they capture, it would be wrong to dismiss how good USB mics perform.

But there is a good reason why XLR microphones are still an industry standard.

Yes, XLR microphones do start on the higher end of the economic structure, but one reason of many they remain so much in demand with content creators is their versatility. Instead of one USB mic taking up a port and serving as the sole input signal, multiple XLR microphones can be plugged into a preamp or a mixer board, offering multiple audio input sources for your studio. So when you have multiple people in studio and Discord is working as your base for a podcast or some other kind of group-oriented stream (outside of gaming), XLR microphones make sense.

And when it comes to XLR microphones and the many I have used in my years, the *MXL 990* remains a favorite.

The MXL 990 has been called groundbreaking by audio professionals on account of the 990 being a high-quality condenser microphone that is considered affordable by the mass market. A couple of reasons the 990 is able to capture sound so well has to do with a field effect transistor (FET) preamp and a large diaphragm within the microphone. That is super audio nerd-speak for the inner-workings of the 990 creates a robust signal that results in a brighter, balanced output, retains high, low, and midrange audio reproduction.

This was my first microphone when I got into content creation, and the fact it comes with a shockmount specific for the 990, a mic stand adapter, and a carrying case is something of a bonus. This mic comes in at $65 but you might find other variations of the 990 with higher price tags, like the Blaze model seen in Figure 11-3. Take a look at the specs and look for any add-ons or packages it is part of, as that can affect the price.

FIGURE 11-3: Regarded as the best of first-time microphones, the MXL 990 is an affordable solution for content creators of all backgrounds. The Blaze, pictured here, is a variation of the 990 that comes with built-in LEDs for a nice aesthetic.

Shure X2u XLR-to-USB Microphone Adapter

If you are looking ahead to expand in the future, investing in an XLR microphone makes sense. This way, you don't feel like you have a USB mic gathering dust while you have your new XLR taking the lead. Before you upgrade your studio, though, how do you get a mic connected? Either purchase a USB mic only to retire on upgrade, or pick up an XLR but have no microphone for your Discord.

Or you can make the most of your XLR microphone and pick up an XLR-to-USB microphone adapter.

The Shure X2U XLR-to-USB adapter serves as a bridge between your XLR microphone and your computer. (See Figure 11-4.) The device has a female XLR connection on one end and a male USB connection. XLR-to-USB adapters provide phantom power, making it something like a handheld preamp. Remember, if the mic cannot work with phantom power, the mic won't work at all. With this bridge, you and your XLR are ready to go.

FIGURE 11-4:
Turn any XLR microphone into a USB mic and control the strength of your mic signal with the Shure X2U XLR-to-USB adapter.

Other features of the Shure X2U include a small ¼-inch jack for headphones or hardwired earbuds, both monitor and volume control if you are using the headphones feature, and finally, gain control in case your mic needs a little kick to pick up your input. The best part of using an adapter is you can still use it with a laptop computer once you take your Discord studio to the next level with a mixer board.

REMEMBER

When working with USB mics, there is usually one source. You cannot plug multiple USB mics into a hub and record all signals coming in. Each mic Discord will recognize as an independent, dedicated audio source.

Røde Boom Mic Stand

Why is a mic stand such a big deal?

True, many USB mic either come with their own mic stands or are part of the headset you have for your gaming. If, however, you are looking for something more out of your Discord and your studio altogether, or if you are upgrading to XLR microphones that do not come with mic stands (but they do come with attachments for mic stands so riddle me that, Batman), then you are going to need a mic stand.

Are boom mic stands expensive? Yes. Are they fantastic to work with? Oh absolutely.

The nice thing about boom mic stands, like the Røde Boom Mic Stand, pictured in Figure 11-5, is that these mic stands lift the microphone off the desk and closer to you. By doing this, they free up desk space so you do not have to carefully position your keyboard, mouse, or any other peripherals around the microphone itself. A hidden, underappreciated bonus with boom mic stands is they help you keep a better posture when at the desk. It is not unusual for people to slouch around a desktop mic stand, which is one reason why boom mics are so commonplace in recording studios. Instead of hunched over, you are eyes up and straight-backed, making your breathing and posture that more confident. All this comes out in your presence when on comms, as well. Boom mic stands can also free up desk space for you to have your thoughts organized if you are hosting on Discord an interview or an event organization.

FIGURE 11-5:
The Røde Boom Mic Stand frees up desk space for where you are chatting from, and also promotes better posture.

Boom mic stands can either be secured to a desk or table, or can be standing independently off to one side of your setup. They range in price based on the kind of mic stand you purchase. No, you may not have the budget to start out on Discord with a boom mic stand, but it is something to keep on your studio improvements list for future upgrades.

Logitech C922 Pro HD Stream Webcam

Looking up *webcams*, USB-powered cameras specifically geared for streaming video, yields a lot of various makes and models ranging from just under $20 to nearly $200. That's a pretty big jump as far as accessories go, so exactly what are you paying for with these various models.

Perhaps the two biggest differences between webcams, including the ones built into laptops, are their video resolution and maximum video frame rates. The video resolutions of camera will tell you exactly how good your image will look when you are streaming video. A $20 camera will come with 1280×720 pixels while the built-in camera for a MacBook Pro has a resolution of 2880×1800. At the top of the heap, a 4K camera will shoot as high as 4096×2160. Video frame rates also play into the clarity of your video signal. While the $20 camera and MacBook Pro have different screen resolutions, both capture at 30 frames per second. The more frames per second, the sharper the image. This is why some higher quality cameras can capture at 60 frames per second.

If I suggest a webcam that can offer you great results without breaking your budget, the Logitech C922 Pro HD Stream Webcam offers a lot of top-shelf features at $80, pictured in Figure 11-6. Coming with either an optional tripod or attachments for the top of a monitor, the C922 captures at a high definition rate of 1920×1080 at 30 frames per second, or at a lower resolution at 60 frames per second. Other features include automatic low light correction, and the utility Personify, which can replace a bland, bare background with something more dynamic.

Video may not be a big deal for you on Discord, but if the streaming feature continues to evolve and your own need for videoconferencing begins to rise, consider the C922 and its capabilities and what it can offer your server.

FIGURE 11-6:
The Logitech
C922 Pro HD
Stream Webcam
adjust to the
needs and
abilities of your
server, capturing
at either
1920 × 1080 at
30 frames
per second for
advanced servers,
or at a lower
resolution at
60 frames per
second.

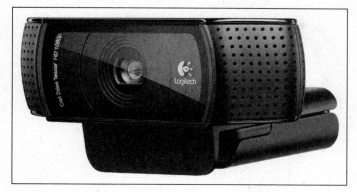

ZOMEi 16-Inch LED Ring Light

Ring lights are all the rage for influencers, streamers, and photographers. These accessories are used with SLR cameras, webcams, and smartphones as an economic solution to full-on professional lighting kits, and as they are LED lights, there is low heat output. Ring lights have become a solution for streamers struggling against poor or dim lighting, and can offer hosts of webinars and videoconferences a way to avoid what I call the "Witness Protection Program" effect where a subject is backlit. You hear them. You just don't *see* them. If you are having issues with your Discord video and being seen, a light ring may be what you need.

The ZOMEi 16-inch LED Ring Light Kit, pictured in Figure 11-7, is full of features and accessories that can help you light yourself before going live. In the light ring itself, two-toned LEDs can adjust color temperature and brightness, which is especially helpful when working with green screens (if green screens are something you want to work with). The ZOMEi provides plenty of fill light while still allowing for continuous natural light to help out.

Along with the ring light himself, the ZOMEi kit comes with an adjustable 18- to 670-inch light stand and can rotate 180 degrees, perfect for live streaming, or videoconferencing. The kit rounds off with a phone holder, power adapter, and a tote bag for this kit to make all this portable.

You may not need the kit if you are not interested in the videoconferencing aspects of Discord. However, if you want to make sure your lighting is on point, the ZOMEi option can do a lot for improving the quality of your video.

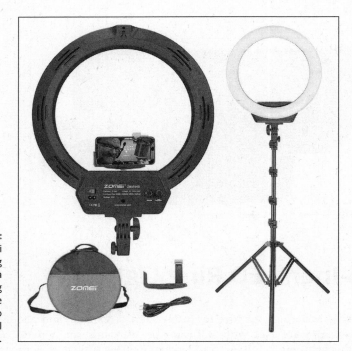

FIGURE 11-7:
The ZOMEi
16-inch LED Ring
Light Kit is a
complete lighting
solution for those
not ready to
invest in a full
lighting kit.

TIP

Some models of webcams come with light ring attachments of their own. These webcams' built-in solutions may have limitations; but if you are looking for quick and dirty solutions to inadequate lighting, take a look at UNZANO PC Streaming Webcam with Ring Light or the Razer Kiyo Streaming Webcam, both models equipped with modest lighting.

Mee6

Bots, first introduced back in Chapter 2, are usually not welcome on social media platforms. If you are dealing with bots, you're dealing with automated messages spamming malicious links or suddenly following you on Discord, Twitter, Twitch, and other platforms. Rarely are these unwelcomed, unwanted guests on social media doing anything good, but there are exceptions to the rule. Not all bots are jerks, and I've got three here that are worth your attention with Discord.

Mee6 (`https://mee6.xyz`), pictured in action in Figure 11-8, wants to actually help you make your Discord server a better place to be. (Yeah, the reference is subtle, but it's there.) The bot is quick and easy to install (as we saw in Chapter 7) and performs tasks that help you be more productive. Some of the things Mee6 does for you include:

>> Customized welcome messages that truly make an arrival to your server memorable

>> Gamification of things people do (make posts, share media, and so on), encouraging activity from your server members

>> Additional security from spammers and trolls

>> Automated alerts for when you go live with a stream, post a new video on YouTube, or begin a new thread on Reddit

FIGURE 11-8:
Mee6 offers Discord servers a little help in completing redundant tasks and helps in making your server run more efficiently.

If you are a programmer, you can also use Mee6 to create custom commands assigned to roles in your server. You have a lot to do when you are managing a Discord server, especially if it is a busy, bustling server. Mee6 is that friend in your corner that happily says "Can do!" and undertakes redundant tasks that need to get done. So feel free to lean a little on this blue bot. Mee6 is there to help.

Carl-bot

Another bot getting attention in Chapter 7 and worth mentioning as an essential for Discord is *Carl-bot* (https://carl.gg), featured in Figure 11-9. For our #welcome page, we used Carl-bot to create what was called a *reaction role*, a role created once the appropriate reaction is made to a post in a designated channel. Reaction roles are only one feature available from Carl-bot.

Along with creating reaction roles, you can also create:

>> Log for just about every activity from generation of invite links to message management to server updates

>> Advanced moderation over your server including bulk management of roles and additional mod commands from the default Discord commands

>> A suggestion box for your server that you can manage easily

>> Advanced permission systems that allow both you and Carl-bot to moderate your server without interfering with conversations that matter to you

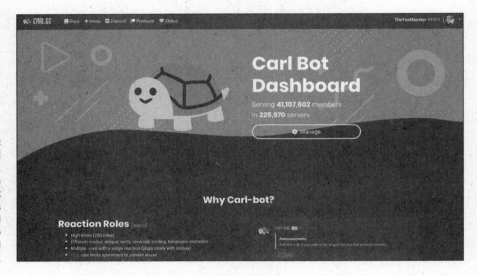

FIGURE 11-9:
First introduced in Chapter 7, Carl-bot is a virtual assistant that offers expanded capabilities to your Discord server.

Carl-bot can do a lot for you and your server. Similar to when connections are made to applications, Carl-bot create roles and commands suited to your exact needs and wants for your server. You were given a hands-on introduction to this virtual assistant back in Chapter 7. When you can, take a closer look at what you can achieve with Carl-bot as part of your server.

WARNING

Exclusive content shared on your Members Only channels should remain there. If you have members of exclusive channels sharing your content on open channels, have your mods remove the content as soon as possible and then ask the server member to refrain from sharing exclusive content on open channels. If the same server member shares such exclusive content again, consider a timeout or (if it's really an issue) ban. Moderation isn't easy, and sometimes hard choices need to be made. Exclusive content should remain exclusive.

Nightbot

We finish up our essentials of Discord with Nightbot (`https://nightbot.tv`), the first bot you were introduced to back in Chapter 2. Nightbot is a virtual assistant, similar to Mee6 and Carl-bot, and is managed by you and mods to help a stream run smoothly and efficiently. When triggered, commands type into Twitch's Chat window different kinds of messages. They can be visual (like an emotes cheer as seen in Figure 11-10), links to your Discord server, or just simple text messages.

FIGURE 11-10: Nightbot's Custom Command feature allows you to create frequent messages by dropping in a quick keyword into your chat.

With an integration of Nightbot into your own server, you can bring over from your stream a variety of quick shortcuts:

» **Greetings/Icebreakers:** A command reading "Good morning, Twitch Monsters! Make sure you say 'Hi' and @TheTeeMonster will give you a shout on stream!" welcomes newcomers and regulars to your stream to start talking.

» **Shout-outs:** If you're talking about a content creator you met at a meetup or online somewhere, dropping a shout-out is a good thing to do.

>> **Relevant links:** If you have a product or service you want to promote with a quick command (the command itself being a quick description of what the product/service is and a URL point to more information, contracting details, and so on), you can create a quick promo to share with your Chat.

Nightbot also offers spam protection from trolls and offers Blacklists of various terms and phrases that, when triggered, immediately timeout offenders. It also gives your mods an opportunity to look over these potential trolls (sometimes, people just make mistakes) and see if it was an honest mistake or not.

Connecting this virtual assistant to your Discord server brings all the perks of Nightbot streamers enjoy to your Discord. Spam protection. Custom commands. The things that Nightbot helps streamers everywhere take care of is now accessible with Discord servers.

WARNING

While custom commands that are text based and using URLs work fine in Discord, the *emotes* — small pieces of artwork used for expression in Twitch, Mixer, and other streaming platforms — do not necessarily carry over as they are formatted differently in Discord.

As you can see, these essentials can be easily integrated, and sometimes with no cost to you. Others may not be necessary if you are not taking full advantage of the video capabilities, but what is listed here is a look at where to expand your Discord studio from its bare bones beginnings with the download of the app. This is where you open your Discord — and yourself — into exciting new directions. If you decide to take your Discord server to the next level, consider this chapter as a wish list or some suggestions.

TIP

Podcasting is a possibility. So is streaming. Discord can serve as a springboard for a number of avenues for content creations. If you have been enjoying my approach to Discord, and you know that podcasting or streaming (specifically on Twitch) is something you want to explore, take a look at my other titles, *Podcasting For Dummies* and *Twitch For Dummies*.

Chapter **12**

Top Ten Ideas for Channel Topics

Y ou may have jumped to this chapter as you are drawing a complete and utter blank on what you want to do with your Discord server.

Join the club.

When you are starting off, the blank canvas that is your server can be daunting, and while I throw out a few ideas, I don't really go into details on how to make these channels work. Channels are one reason why people decide to join a server and why they stick around. You want to connect with people who arrive to your server, and it will be the channels that you make an introduction. People will see a reflection of the server's host based on the channels listed to the left.

And now you find yourself here. You need ideas. No worries here. I got your back, fam.

Five Topics for the Fun of It

Let's say you really don't feel as if you have a good idea of where to start with your server. You want to make your Discord server stand out, but you also want to make sure anyone swinging by your server feels like they have a channel relevant to their interests. It's something of a conundrum. You want to stand out from the Discord crowd with unique and original topics, but you also want to appeal to your community with popular subjects.

Common ground is always the best starting point for a new community. You want to have shared interest to best get to know the frequent visitors to your server. So let's consider five ideas that make for good icebreakers on your Discord.

Games

This is the best place to start for Discord as this is why Discord was initially built: gaming. If you are not a gamer, don't worry. There will be other topics, from the personal to the professional, all worth your consideration.

When I say *games* as a topic, I need to express that just making a channel called Games would be opening a floodgate of tangents. It would be like going to your state senate and saying "I would like to debate politics."

So here's a method to the madness.

If you are kicking off your Discord and you want to have a Games channel, approach the channel(s) this way:

>> **What are you playing?** Are you into *Destiny*? What about *Fortnite*? Or maybe *Overwatch*? You want to set up channels specific to those games. Have channels dedicated to individual games you are frequenting in your gaming schedule.

>> **Looking for folks to play with?** Grouped with your dedicated game channels, create channels labeled *lfg* (looking for game). So you would have underneath your #destiny channel the #lfg-destiny channel where members of your server will go there specifically to put together a fireteam. Repeat this for each of your dedicated game channels.

>> **What other games are you playing?** This would be a channel like #other-games, where if people are playing games on a rare occasion or just finished a single, indie game, this would be a place to mention it. So let's say you're trying out *Borderlands 3* or *Sole*; drop a mention or a quick review here.

>> **Are you playing board games?** If you are a multi-platform gamer and you enjoy a good board game or two, then why not have a channel about #board-games, or maybe you are into *Dungeons & Dragons* or *Traveller*? Then #rpg-games would be a good channel to offer.

The topic of games is synonymous with Discord, but one channel cannot completely cover what your gaming community has on its mind. As you can see, the topic of games can cover a lot of ground.

So, how far do you want to travel?

Movies and television

Depending on your passion, you might be making quite a few channels dedicated to whatever it is you are watching. Much like with games, you may want to consider multiple channels that cover a lot of ground.

>> **Dedicated channels:** If you are tracking with specific shows like #the-witcher, #lost-in-space, or #the-boys, then dedicated channels would be great places for you to talk shop about your favorite shows currently dropping episodes or all completed for a season. This would be a great channel to talk and go deep into what's coming next.

>> **Recent movies:** The topic of motion pictures covers a lot of ground, much like a games channel could. With a channel called #movies or #box-office, films currently out in theaters can be discussed (spoiler-free) through opinions, reviews, and maybe even a few articles about the films and their creators.

>> **Bingeworthy television:** Depending on the show you watch, some streaming services will drop an entire season on their premiere. If you're the kind of person who has a tough time not stopping after one more episodes, then maybe a #binge-worthy channel would be worth developing. After the final episodes of *Carnival Row, Altered Carbon,* or *The Expanse*, you may want to share your review with your community. Keep your thoughts brief, and see if you can turn new viewers on to what caught your attention.

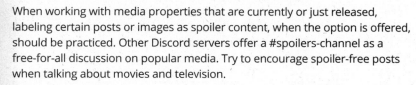
When working with media properties that are currently or just released, labeling certain posts or images as spoiler content, when the option is offered, should be practiced. Other Discord servers offer a #spoilers-channel as a free-for-all discussion on popular media. Try to encourage spoiler-free posts when talking about movies and television.

>> **Classic films:** Offering a channel for #classic-films invites film buffs of all kinds to offer up some of the favorites from the past. Here, the discussion would be less about the recent *Pearl Harbor* film but more about the genius of *Tora! Tora! Tora!* When it comes to historical epics, are you all about

Lawrence of Arabia or more about *Apollo 13*? How would you compare the modern *Man of Steel* against the 1978 classic *Superman: The Movie*? While #movies covers what's playing, #classic-movies go back to those films we watch again and again.

>> **Movie trailers:** It is always exciting to look ahead and speculate on what's coming soon to theatres. So you can expect a #coming-soon channel to be many YouTube links along with speculation, hype, and — depending on the preview — trepidation about what's currently in production.

You will see movies and television across many servers, all of them very different in their tone and content. These channels are great places to find new things to watch or fandoms to discover. It is also fun to surf from channel to channel across your servers, just to see what people are watching and either raving about or advising caution before viewing.

Music

If music be the food of love, play on. Give me excess of it.
— WILLIAM SHAKESPEARE

Bill knows what he's talking about. I bet he was a band nerd, too.

You don't necessarily need to be a band nerd (like me — trombones rule!) to appreciate good music, and your #music channel can be the ultimate guide to the most eclectic Spotify playlist ever. If you want to treat your music channel dedicated to specific artists or to specific genres, that's your call but it can also be open to interpretation.

Content might vary from open Spotify playlists to YouTube music videos to links to concert venues. There can also be articles to musicians in the news. The conversation can also cross genres, the music selections jumping from country to heavy metal to electronic Gregorian chant bluegrass. (Oh you might laugh, but I guarantee you it's a thing!) If you're keeping the discussion open to all genres, then you can expect the unexpected with what your community brings to the channel. The idea of hosting a music channel is not to necessarily make it a competition of what genre is better but more about a celebration of what is out there for curious ears to consume.

Pets

Kittehs.

Doggos.

Domesticated danger noodles.

The Internet belongs to your pets. Let's just admit that. And people love to take selfies with their pets or just pull themselves out of the equation (and the photo) and feature their fur babies in their smartphone snapshots.

So why not give household pets their own channel?

Whether you call it #pets or #selfies-with-pets, it's a parade of pictures in this channel. You can also expect fun stories about what trouble these pets are up to, and it's always fun when — among the photos of dogs and cats — you see snapshots of pet snakes, ferrets, rats, or tarantulas. Pets say a lot about a person, and here your community rallies around those four-legged members of their family. Reach out to your community members by giving them a place to share personal shots of their pets.

Food

We all love to eat, and if there is anything we know about social media, platforms are ruled by our pets and by today's menu. Especially if it's you being the chef, the satisfaction of making something that might make Antoni Porowski nod in approval is only equaled by that of people in your Discord replying *"I'll be right over!"* after you post pictures. Under a #food channel, each picture or video you post chronicles a step forward to the final dish you'll be enjoying that night.

Your food channel can also take on several other avenues and even inspire channels of their own:

>> **Recipes:** Discord can give you a place to not only post photos of your dish-in-progress, but add an accompanying step to each photo, creating a step-by-step instruction of what it is you're making. If a particular step is best told by video, post 15 to 30 seconds worth, showing what the step calls for.

>> **Healthy eating:** When my wife and I started eating healthier, we started posting some of the dishes (and products) we were working with. Plant butter. Protein shakes. Impossible beef ragu. Even posting healthier recipes from cookbooks like *Cook This, Not That* could inspire your community to give some of your favorites a shot.

>> **Out and about:** While healthy lifestyles are great for the body and the mind, there is nothing wrong with enjoying an evening of fine dining on occasion. When you are taking pictures of your meal for Instagram, make sure to share the love on Discord as well. It is just as *#instaworthy* on your server.

Food is a great equalizer with people, and as someone overlooking the development and growth of a server, you want to find that common ground I mention at the beginning of this chapter. This also hinges, of course, on whether or not you enjoy culinary arts. If yes, then take a page from Shakespeare and see what a food channel can do for your community.

Five Topics for the Professional

The five topics above are all solid for moderators starting off their first-ever Discord server. The suggested channels should serve as something of a catalyst for other channels you may want to launch in your Discord.

You have been hearing me say, though, that Discord is more than just games and gamers. As my buddy Danfinity (https://twitch.tv/danfinity) told me, *"Discord is Facebook for gamers."* Its capabilities and potential reach well beyond video games.

These channel ideas are for you, the power user of Discord, looking to take your server into areas that do not involve video games unless it includes video game development. This is where the conversation leans more towards the servers that want to encourage productivity, rally the community, and maybe make the world a better place.

Travel

The world is a pretty beautiful place. There are far corners of it that, when captured by smartphones and digital SLRs, can inspire you to pack a bag and go somewhere. Then you discover that your own corner of the world is a pretty cool place, too, with its own hidden treasures. Travel blogs, be they WordPress-powered or a lively Instagram account, catalog getaways and suggest destinations for wayfarers of all backgrounds and interests. Now, Discord offers a new platform that allows for photos, video clips, and (if your bandwidth can offer it) live streams.

Establishing a #travel channel can encompass many kinds of travelogues:

>> **Weekend getaways:** Heading off on a road trip? What's within driving distance of you? The Smoky Mountains? The Shenandoah Valley? The Outer Banks? Share your thoughts (and your media) about where you are recharging your batteries, not sparing on the details of where you are staying, especially if it's a rental property.

>> **Grand tours:** For my 50th birthday, I went somewhere I have always wanted to visit but never got an opportunity to do so before: Germany. In my own travel channel, I shared the sights, the food, and the amazing history I was experiencing over there. I even delved into the details of where I was visiting, so that if others were heading overseas, these places could serve as potential must-see points. Grand tours make for great talking points on Discord.

>> **Special appearances:** Being a writer means I get to travel to some pretty cool places. I have been a guest at conventions in San Francisco, San Diego, Los Angeles, Richmond, Baltimore, and Washington, DC. When I head out to these events, I make sure I have plenty of room on my camera for photos and video. Discord reminds my community that I may be signing books in their part of the world, and a visit would be welcome. If you are a traveling artist of any background — music, art, theatre — you can let fans know where you are when on the road.

Tech support

Along with gamers, game developers are online, running verified accounts as their game titles. *Destiny* is on Discord. So is *Cyberpunk 2077*. You can also find other software developers like Streamlabs (https://streamlabs.com), an all-in-one streaming solution. What these developers have in common with one another when it comes to Discord is how the platform is an extension of the tech support.

On visiting these servers, you find several channels dedicated to

>> Known technical issues

>> Server outages

>> Hot fixes

>> Guides and tutorials

Other channels you might find at developers' Discord servers may include

>> Twitter feeds

>> Blog updates

>> Announcements

Tech support is becoming more and more a trend on Discord as it is another platform for devs of any and all backgrounds to reach their audiences. While social media offers a multitude of platforms, regardless of what statistics may tell you, not everyone is on Facebook. Same can also be said for Twitter. You can be on both of those platforms, along with blogging, podcasting, streaming, Instagram, LinkedIn, and heck — let's throw in Untappd (https://untappd.com) for giggles — make one single post, and still not reach everyone in your audience. This is why boosting your own signal is important, and Discord helps you do just that.

Works in progress

Writers of all backgrounds refer to current projects as works in progress, but if you are an actor working on a production, an artist working on a commission, or a musician in rehearsal, you have your own works-in-progress. The idea of a #works-in-progress channel is that you are inviting your community to a behind-the-scenes look at your creative process. It can be really exciting for fans as they get an exclusive look at what you do when it comes to your outlet, be it creative writing, music, art, film, or theater.

WARNING

If you are sharing your work-in-progress, make sure you have permission to do so. Some commissions and contract work have rules on keeping their work off social media platforms. If you do want to share any work in development, find out if you have permission.

Keep in mind:

>> For writers, the character limit is 2,000 characters.

>> For images, on the standard Discord app, the image size cannot exceed 8MB.

>> For video, unless you are using their streaming feature, clips cannot exceed 8MB.

A concern some creatives may have with sharing works-in-progress is unintentionally workshopping their projects with their community. You may think the work is so raw it is not ready for exposure, or perhaps you just want to give fans a taste of what is coming only to have fans begin a round of critiques. If your intent is to not open up your work (or your community's work as the idea is the channel is a place for everyone to share their creativity), make sure to lay down a few rules before anyone (even you) shares a work in progress.

The joy of a channel like this, though? Sharing the final work. Fans then get online bragging rights to say Yeah, I was there before it ever saw the light of day. That is pretty freaking cool.

Event planning

Part of building a community around your cause, brand, or your own works is building a network of people you can rely on to get things done. This is essential when planning a special event.

Event planning is where creative minds collaborate and set up for themselves a list of "honey do" items. The end goal can be anything from a meetup of local community members, all coming together to enjoy some actual interaction in the waking world outside of Discord, to a charity event you're hosting on your Twitch or YouTube stream. Discord has been instrumental for streamers like Aura (https://twitch.tv/aura), who yearly hosts Gaming4Pits, a charity stream benefitting the Villalobos Animal Rescue Shelter (the same shelter featured in Animal Planet's *Pitbulls and Parolees*). GuardiansMH (https://twitch.tv/guardiansmh) use Discord to offer participants in their yearly GuardiansMH Mental Health Awareness and Charity Stream, a place to provide any resources needed for the 24-hour stream, including suicide prevention hotline numbers, graphics and widgets pointing people to the 401c's website, and promotional graphics showcasing the roster of streams appearing. The DC Twitch Community MeetUp group (https://twitter.com/TwitchWDC) brings streamers of all levels, of all gaming, creative, and outreach backgrounds, together on Discord, then goes one step further in using the platform to arrange special meetups throughout DC as well as Virginia and Maryland. A #meetups or #charity-event channel would clearly designate for your community a planning location for special events.

Keep in mind, though, if your event grows beyond a handful of channels in their own section of a server menu, it may be time to consider launching an entirely new server dedicated to the event itself. Aura did just this with the launch of a Gaming4Pits server, making a server specific to the event's participants, its channels offering both information and resources needed to effectively raise money for Villalobos.

Resources

Since we are talking about Aura and his charity event server, let's look a little deeper at the channels featured there. The Important section features

>> **#announcements:** Any specific news or last-minute developments pertaining to the weekend-long event.

>> **#welcome:** An official welcome from Aura and Layla, the two hosts behind the Gaming4Pits weekend stream.

>> **#about-the-charity:** This channel goes into the origins of the Gaming4Pits charity event as well as features basic information about the Villalobos Rescue Center.

- » **#rules:** Even charity events have guidelines participants need to follow. After all, you are not just representing Aura and his beautiful doggo, Layla, you are representing Villalobos Rescue Center.

- » **#stream-related-links:** These URLs point to the Streamlabs URL where Villalobos collects donations. Another URL is a progress bar and alert bar so you get notifications for when people are donating for locations other than yours.

- » **#graphics:** For your own publicity and hype machine, a selection of graphics for your social media and your stream.

- » **#commands:** These commands are being used by all the various streamers involved, so Aura has taken care of the phrasing so you don't have to.

- » **#vrc-faq:** Still want to know more about Villalobos Rescue Center? Participants can bone up on the background of the Center here.

- » **#raffle-prizes-for-donations:** In other channels here, Aura and participants have brainstormed on bigger prizes in order to bring in bigger donations. Participants can look here for the top tier prizes.

- » **#other-ways to help:** There are other ways besides donations where your viewers can participate, and in this channel, Aura has written up a few suggestions.

And this is only the first of three sections in the Gaming4Pits server.

Resources are another great way to convey a sense of dedication and professionalism on your server. You see this not only in the resources offered by Aura's Gaming4Pits server but all across Discord. GuardiansMH, taking a page from Aura's playbook, created the GuardiansMH Events channel, offering to their members a variety of references and assets necessary to host their own charity and awareness streams. Those assets range from logos and stream elements needed to brand a stream during one of their events to mental health resources both online and in the waking world if a streamer has to reach out quickly to anyone visiting their stream.

Servers do not necessarily have to be dedicated to a cause or a corporation to offer resources to their community. Phil Rossi (https://philrossimedia.com) goes beyond talking about the media he's consuming; he makes it a point to suggest it to people, giving mini-reviews and endorsements on what's on his bookcase or in his headphone with an entire section of his Discord dedicated to recommendations. SheSnaps, mentioned in Chapter 4, offers in her Affinity Groups section resources for people with disabilities, for those who are LBGTQIA+, for people of color, and other specific societal groups all looking for online leads to assistance in matters that are either challenging or overwhelming. Even on my own server,

I offer #the-writing-room where I offer to my community an open workshop for their creative works. Also here, I feature writing and research tools that help authors get their daily word count met, and their next title one step closer to publication.

Discord is known for providing better game comms and a social space for hardcore gamers, for casual gamers, and for those gamers in-between; but Discord can do more than help build you and your friends the finest fireteams. This platform offers people of all backgrounds and all cultures a place to hang out and make friends. Channels open up to allow you to network with artists, developers, and professionals of all kinds, making connections that will help you find your next freelance job, offer terrific resources to help broaden your skill set, or even plan an event that will bring your community closer. Maybe Discord was initially built for gamers; but like social media platforms that have come before, Discord is evolving into something more. With new features continuously being developed and current features improved upon, it should be something to watch Discord grow. Like the community you are starting to build. It all starts with that first set of channels, those first few posts, and something to say.

So, what's on your mind? Make a posting. Talk to me. I'm listening.

Index

Symbols

A

About the Author

Tee Morris began his writing career with the 2002 historical epic fantasy *MOREVI: The Chronicles of Rafe & Askana*; and it was in 2005 when the idea of podcasting a novel not only promoted *MOREVI's* sequel but established him as a pioneer in the social media movement, the first author to podcast a book in its entirety. That experience led to him to write with Evo Terra *Podcasting For Dummies* (later editions with Chuck Tomasi). He has penned and contributed to other titles covering social media, including *All a Twitter, Social Media for Writers, Making YouTube Videos,* and *Twitch For Dummies.*

Along with writing books on technology and communication, Tee still finds time for his first love — writing science fiction and fantasy — collaborating with his wife, Pip Ballantine, with *Phoenix Rising: A Ministry of Peculiar Occurrences Novel.* This title went on to win the 2011 Airship Award for Best Steampunk Literature and was a finalist (the only steampunk title to make the final round in any category) for Goodreads' Choice Awards under Best Science Fiction of 2011. The six-book series won the Steampunk Chronicle's Readers' Choice of 2012 for Best Steampunk Literature and RT's 2015 Best Steampunk of the Year; and its companion podcast *Tales from the Archives* received the 2013 Parsec Award for Best Podcast Anthology.

In between titles, Tee plays a variety of video games, including *Destiny, Detroit: Become Human,* the *Tomb Raider* series, the *BioShock* series, and *The Last of Us.* He established a regular Twitch schedule on September 6, 2017 (his Discord server launching shortly thereafter) and continues to develop his stream to include live podcast recordings, charity streams, and special in-studio guests. Tee can also be heard podcasting with *The Shared Desk, Tales from the Archives,* and *Happy Hour from the Tower: A Destiny Podcast.*

Discord For Dummies is his fifth title with John Wiley & Sons, Inc.

Find out more about Tee Morris at www.teemorris.com.

Author's Acknowledgments

Discord For Dummies truly was a title I never pictured myself writing. The inspiration for this title came from friends I've known for years and from friends I know through various servers and channels, each wishing there was a good beginner's guide for this multifaceted program.

This is me, digging deep, and hopefully helping you all out.

Turns out *Discord For Dummies* was the toughest *For Dummies* title I have ever undertaken. There's a lot to this application, and a lot into laying down foundations for a community and building upon it. Much like it was with *Twitch For Dummies* and *Podcasting For Dummies*, the server administrators, community members, and dear friends I have made through Discord have all left their impression on this book. A part of you is within these pages, and has kept me going all the way to the end. I cannot begin to thank you all for the inspiration you've provided me throughout this light-speed project.

But there are some people who were crucial to this project. Without them, you wouldn't be holding this book in your hands. . .

Serena Aeryn Morris, mentioned a few times in this book under her "Sonny" and "Twitch Daughter" aliases, has been an oracle of information and knowledge (just without the baking cookies part) on Discord. If I had a direct line to the people at Discord, I'd tell them to hire her or at least allow her to intern there. (No bias, even though she's my daughter.) Serena, I have always been proud of you in so many ways, but this project taught me that parents can not only love and be proud of their kids, but they also can respect them as skilled experts and voices of authority. It has been a real pleasure and a real education working with you.

Dan Snodgrass, otherwise known as Danfinity (https://twitch.tv/danfinity), helped me get over my (first) Discord hump with a simple sum-up of what this platform was all about. From there, his Bearded Legion server and the beloved "Beirdos" that contribute content to it helped me develop "TheTeeMonster's Not-So-Secret Lair" to the server it is today. This was only a small part of why I reached out to Dan to take on the role of Technical Editor for this title. I found on your stream a gamer that insisted on fun first, triumphs later. With time, I made a friend who inspired me to push forward through darker times. Today, I know a guy far wiser than his years let on. Of course, Dan, this was the project for you. No question.

Finally, a very special thank you to Steve Hayes, Christopher Morris (no relation this time), and Wiley Publishing. With the time frame given this title, we pulled off a little wonder , but what I find humbling — and yes, inspiring — is the belief and the faith you all have in me. It's one thing to have the trust of an editor, but to have earned the trust of a publishing house like Wiley was something I would have never foreseen in my writing career. Guess I must have done something right. Thank you, all, for the incredible opportunities you all have provided over these 15 years.

Publisher's Acknowledgments

Executive Editor: Steven Hayes

Project Editor: Christopher Morris

Copy Editor: Kathy Simpson

Technical Editor: Daniel Snodgrass

Proofreader: Debbye Butler

Production Editor: Mohammed Zafar Ali

Cover Image: © RyanKing999/Getty Images

Take dummies with you everywhere you go!

Whether you are excited about e-books, want more from the web, must have your mobile apps, or are swept up in social media, dummies makes everything easier.

Find us online!

dummies.com

Leverage the power

Dummies is the global leader in the reference category and one of the most trusted and highly regarded brands in the world. No longer just focused on books, customers now have access to the dummies content they need in the format they want. Together we'll craft a solution that engages your customers, stands out from the competition, and helps you meet your goals.

Advertising & Sponsorships

Connect with an engaged audience on a powerful multimedia site, and position your message alongside expert how-to content. Dummies.com is a one-stop shop for free, online information and know-how curated by a team of experts.

- Targeted ads
- Video
- Email Marketing

- Microsites
- Sweepstakes sponsorship

20 MILLION PAGE VIEWS EVERY SINGLE MONTH

15 MILLION UNIQUE VISITORS PER MONTH

43% OF ALL VISITORS ACCESS THE SITE VIA THEIR MOBILE DEVICES

700,000 NEWSLETTER SUBSCRIPTIONS TO THE INBOXES OF

300,000 UNIQUE INDIVIDUALS EVERY WEEK

Custom Publishing

Reach a global audience in any language by creating a solution that will differentiate you from competitors, amplify your message, and encourage customers to make a buying decision.

- Apps
- Books
- eBooks
- Video
- Audio
- Webinars

Brand Licensing & Content

Leverage the strength of the world's most popular reference brand to reach new audiences and channels of distribution.

For more information, visit dummies.com/biz

PERSONAL ENRICHMENT

Staying Sharp
9781119187790
USA $26.00
CAN $31.99
UK £19.99

Facebook
9781119179030
USA $21.99
CAN $25.99
UK £16.99

Guitar
9781119293354
USA $24.99
CAN $29.99
UK £17.99

Investing
9781119293347
USA $22.99
CAN $27.99
UK £16.99

Beekeeping
9781119310068
USA $22.99
CAN $27.99
UK £16.99

Digital Photography
9781119235606
USA $24.99
CAN $29.99
UK £17.99

Meditation
9781119251163
USA $24.99
CAN $29.99
UK £17.99

Pregnancy
9781119235491
USA $26.99
CAN $31.99
UK £19.99

Samsung Galaxy S7
9781119279952
USA $24.99
CAN $29.99
UK £17.99

iPhone
9781119283133
USA $24.99
CAN $29.99
UK £17.99

Crocheting
9781119287117
USA $24.99
CAN $29.99
UK £16.99

Nutrition
9781119130246
USA $22.99
CAN $27.99
UK £16.99

PROFESSIONAL DEVELOPMENT

Windows 10
9781119311041
USA $24.99
CAN $29.99
UK £17.99

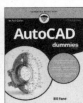
AutoCAD
9781119255796
USA $39.99
CAN $47.99
UK £27.99

Excel 2016
9781119293439
USA $26.99
CAN $31.99
UK £19.99

QuickBooks 2017
9781119281467
USA $26.99
CAN $31.99
UK £19.99

macOS Sierra
9781119280651
USA $29.99
CAN $35.99
UK £21.99

LinkedIn
9781119251132
USA $24.99
CAN $29.99
UK £17.99

Windows 10
9781119310563
USA $34.00
CAN $41.99
UK £24.99

SharePoint 2016
9781119181705
USA $29.99
CAN $35.99
UK £21.99

Fundamental Analysis
9781119263593
USA $26.99
CAN $31.99
UK £19.99

Networking
9781119257769
USA $29.99
CAN $35.99
UK £21.99

Office 2016
9781119293477
USA $26.99
CAN $31.99
UK £19.99

Office 365
9781119265313
USA $24.99
CAN $29.99
UK £17.99

Salesforce.com
9781119239314
USA $29.99
CAN $35.99
UK £21.99

Coding
9781119293323
USA $29.99
CAN $35.99
UK £21.99

dummies.com

dummies
A Wiley Brand

Learning Made Easy

ACADEMIC

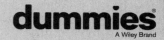

Small books for big imaginations

9781119177173
USA $9.99
CAN $9.99
UK £8.99

9781119177272
USA $9.99
CAN $9.99
UK £8.99

9781119177241
USA $9.99
CAN $9.99
UK £8.99

9781119177210
USA $9.99
CAN $9.99
UK £8.99

9781119262657
USA $9.99
CAN $9.99
UK £6.99

9781119291336
USA $9.99
CAN $9.99
UK £6.99

9781119233527
USA $9.99
CAN $9.99
UK £6.99

9781119291220
USA $9.99
CAN $9.99
UK £6.99

9781119177302
USA $9.99
CAN $9.99
UK £8.99

Unleash Their Creativity

dummies.com

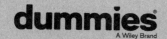